RULE OF POWER OR RULE OF LAW?

AN ASSESSMENT OF U.S. POLICIES AND ACTIONS REGARDING SECURITY-RELATED TREATIES

EDITORS
Nicole Deller, Arjun Makhijani, and John Burroughs

CONTRIBUTING AUTHORS
John Burroughs
Merav Datan
Nicole Deller
Mark Hiznay
Arjun Makhijani
Elizabeth Shafer
Pam Spees

**Institute for Energy and Environmental Research
and
Lawyers' Committee on Nuclear Policy**

The Apex Press
New York

Cover Design: Ken Shields
Interior Design: Mary Ellen McCourt

Published by The Apex Press, an imprint of the Council on International and Public Affairs,
located at 777 United Nations Plaza, Suite 3C, New York, NY 10017. Its publications office may
be reached at (800) 316-2739 or (914) 271-6500, P.O. Box 337, Croton-on-Hudson, NY 10520.
Web site: www.cipa-apex.org.

Library of Congress Cataloging-in-Publication Data

Rule of power or rule of law? : an assessment of U.S. policies and actions regarding
security-related treaties / edited by Nicole Deller, Arjun Makhijani, and John Burroughs ;
contributing authors, John Burroughs ... [et al.].
     p. cm.
Includes bibliographical references and index.
ISBN 1-891843-17-6 (pbk.)
     1. International law--United States. 2. United States--Foreign relations. 3. National
security--United States. I. Deller, Nicole. II. Makhijani, Arjun. III. Burroughs, John,
1953-

KF4581 .R85 2002
341'.0973--dc21

                                                                    2002027969

Printed in the United States of America by Thomson-Shore, Inc., an employee owned company.

CONTENTS

ACKNOWLEDGMENTS

Chapters concerning specific treaties were reviewed by a number of people who are specialists in the relevant treaty regimes. Most of the reviewers and the chapters they reviewed are named below. The reviewers who are not named wished to remain anonymous.

GEORGE BUNN, consulting professor at the Institute of International Studies, Stanford University, and first general counsel of the U.S. Arms Control and Disarmament Agency, chapter on the Nuclear Nonproliferation Treaty

KEVIN GURNEY, atmospheric scientist, Colorado State University, chapter on the UN Framework Convention on Climate Control and the Kyoto Protocol

EDWARD HAMMOND, The Sunshine Project, chapter on the Biological Weapons Convention

CLAUDINE MCCARTHY, researcher, Henry L. Stimson Institute, chapters on the Chemical Weapons Convention and the Biological Weapons Convention

JOHN PIKE, Director, GlobalSecurity.org, chapter on the Anti-Ballistic Missile Treaty

PROFESSOR BARBARA HATCH ROSENBERG, Federation of American Scientists, Director of Project on Biological Weapons Verification, chapter on the Biological Weapons Convention

JAYA TIWARI, Physicians for Social Responsibility, chapters on the Chemical Weapons Convention and the Biological Weapons Convention

JONATHAN TUCKER, Director of the Chemical and Biological Nonproliferation Program, Center for Nonproliferation Studies, Monterey Institute of International Studies, chapters on the Chemical Weapons Convention and the Biological Weapons Convention

JOHN WASHBURN, Convenor, American NGO Coalition for the International Criminal Court, chapter on the Statute of the International Criminal Court

We deeply appreciate the time and expertise that the reviewers have given this work. The book is much better for it. But the contents of the book, its findings, and its recommendations are the responsibility of the authors, who are, of course, also responsible for any omissions and errors that might remain. The reviewers named here do not necessarily endorse the content, findings, or recommendations of the book.

We would also like to thank Matthew Bliwise, Susan Philipose, and Jessica Catlow for proofreading; Elizabeth Outes for research and proof-reading; IEER librarian Lois Chalmers and staff scientist Sriram Gopal for providing library research, preparing the reference list, and formatting the original report.

This book is a part of the global outreach project of the Institute for Energy and Environmental Research, which is funded by grants from the W. Alton Jones Foundation, the John D. and Catherine T. MacArthur Foundation, and by general support grants for IEER's work on nuclear issues from the Ford Foundation, the HKH Foundation, the Turner Foundation, Rockefeller Financial Services, the New Land Foundation, and the Colombe Foundation. Outreach in the United States for this work will be carried out as part of IEER's U.S. program, which, in addition to general support grants, is funded by the Public Welfare Foundation, the John Merck Fund, the Ploughshares Fund, the Town Creek Foundation, and the Stewart R. Mott Charitable Trust.

The Lawyers' Committee on Nuclear Policy is funded by the Boehm Foundation, Ploughshares Fund, Rockefeller Financial Services, the Samuel Rubin Foundation, the Simons Foundation, and individual donors. We thank them all.

PREFACE

This book has its origins in a dialogue over the last two years among several non-governmental organizations about the trend of powerful states to erode existing international legal regimes and to resist the development of new ones, to the detriment of security, disarmament, international justice, human rights, and protection of the environment. The United States is foremost among those states, despite its widely admired and emulated commitment to the rule of law within its society.

Two of the concerned organizations, the Institute for Energy and Environmental Research and the Lawyers' Committee on Nuclear Policy, undertook this study to focus on U.S. policies toward security-related treaties. It assesses the compliance record of the United States with respect to treaties that it has ratified, the Chemical Weapons Convention (CWC), the Biological Weapons Convention (BWC), the Nuclear Nonproliferation Treaty (NPT), and the United Nations Framework Convention on Climate Change (UNFCCC); the U.S. record of refusing to enter into other treaties, the Comprehensive Test Ban Treaty (CTBT), the Treaty Banning Anti-Personnel Mines, the Statute of the International Criminal Court (ICC), and the Kyoto Protocol; and the U.S. decision to withdraw from the Anti-Ballistic Missile (ABM) Treaty. We believe that global problems should be solved through a rule-of-law approach that employs treaties as valuable instruments for safeguarding the long-term collective interests of societies and humanity, promoting peaceful resolution of conflicts, implementing disarmament, protecting human rights and securing justice, and preserving the environment. It is crucial to the very idea of the rule of law that the most powerful should comply with law even when it is difficult or costly or when a superiority of economic, military and diplomatic power makes it seem unnecessary. For that reason we have chosen first to focus on U.S. policies.

A trend of U.S. disengagement from or hostility toward international legal instruments, evidenced during the Clinton administration by the refusal to sign the Treaty Banning Anti-Personnel Mines, the Senate's rejection of the CTBT, and the attempt to obstruct completion of the Rome Statute creating the ICC, has accelerated under the Bush administration. In the months leading up to September 11, the administration indicated its intention to abandon the ABM Treaty; withdrew its support for the Kyoto Protocol on global warming, though the United States played an integral role in its creation; opposed completion of negotiations on an international agreement to promote compliance with the BWC; and refused to seek ratification of the ICC Statute, which the United States had signed in the last days of the Clinton administration.

After September 11, when the United States appealed for international cooperation in the fight against terrorism, many hoped that law-governed multilateralism would return to favor. Instead, the United States continued its policy of relying first of all on its national military and intelligence capabilities rather than on international agreements. The Bush administration withdrew from the ABM Treaty; in an unprecedented step, formally notified the United Nations of its intention not to ratify the ICC Statute despite the U.S. signature; sought to terminate the multilateral process established to strengthen the BWC; and suggested inadequate unilateral measures to replace the proposed binding obligations of the Kyoto Protocol.

The United States not only refuses to participate in newly created international legal mechanisms, it fails to live up to obligations undertaken in treaties that it has ratified. The NPT obligates the United States to "pursue negotiations in good faith on effective measures relating to cessation of the nuclear arms race at an early date and to nuclear disarmament," but the United States has not integrated this obligation into its national nuclear policy. Instead, the January 2002 Nuclear Posture Review plans for the maintenance of large and modernized nuclear forces for the indefinite future. As a party to the UNFCCC, the United States is obligated to take "precautionary measures to anticipate, prevent or minimize the causes of climate change." However, the Bush administration's call for slow decreases in greenhouse gas "intensity" rather than the total level of emissions is essentially a continuation of past modest increases in energy efficiency that have not prevented an ongoing increase in greenhouse gas emissions. As a party to the CWC, the United States is obligated to meet reporting and inspection requirements, but Congress passed legislation that restricts U.S. compliance. The BWC prohibits the United States from manufacturing bio-weapons, but the United States in the late 1990s built a test bomb and weaponized anthrax and carried out these activities in secret, making it impossible for other states to assess U.S. compliance with the prohibition.

Treaties by their very nature involve some sacrifice of sovereignty. In exchange, treaty regimes contribute to national and global security in important ways, including by:

- articulating global norms;
- promoting and recognizing compliance with norms;
- building monitoring and enforcement mechanisms;
- increasing the likelihood of detecting violations and effectively addressing them;
- providing a benchmark for measurement of progress;
- establishing a foundation of confidence, trust, experience, and expertise for further progress;
- providing criteria to guide states' activities and legislation, and focal points for discussion of policy issues.

Over the long term, treaty regimes are a far more reliable basis for achieving global policy objectives and compliance with norms than "do as we say, not as we do" directives from an overwhelmingly powerful state.

The concept of the rule of law was integral to the founding of the United States, which has been one of its staunchest advocates. The rule of law in international affairs is still emerging, evolving quickly as global forces drive countries closer together. Its development is largely a response to the demands of states and individuals living within a global society with a deeply integrated world economy. In this global society, the repercussions of the actions of states, non-state actors and individuals are not confined within borders, whether we look to greenhouse gas accumulations, nuclear testing, the danger of accidental nuclear war, or the vast massacres of civilians that have taken place over the course of the last hundred years and still continue. The people of the United States are part of this global society, and failures at the global level will affect their security and well-being adversely, along with that of people elsewhere. The importance and weight of the United States makes a U.S. withdrawal from the global legal process, except when its gets its own way, a dangerous course for security as well as the environment.

In this study, we define "security" broadly, to include legal instruments relating to international justice, protection of the global environment, notably with respect to the buildup of greenhouse gases, and non-proliferation and disarmament of weapons of mass destruction. Developments in all these areas can affect the likelihood of conflict and degrees of its destructiveness. First we review the process of how treaties are entered into by the United States, and the historical tension in the U.S. government between those favoring and those opposing international treaty regimes. We then examine recent U.S. policies and actions with respect to the treaties mentioned above. We conclude with reflections about the value of international law in promoting national and global security. An annex is attached which shows the participation of states in major security and human rights treaties. We also include an Executive Summary of our findings.

This book is an updated version of a report released by the Institute for Energy and Environmental Research and the Lawyers' Committee on Nuclear Policy in April 2002.

Nicole Deller
Arjun Makhijani
John Burroughs
September 5, 2002

EXECUTIVE SUMMARY

U.S. AMBIVALENCE TOWARD INTERNATIONAL LEGAL REGIMES

While the United States currently resists a range of global security treaties, it is also the principal architect of the post-World War II international legal system. We begin by tracing the roots of the ambivalent U.S. approach to international law and institutions, setting the stage for examination of specific treaty regimes.

International law can take the form of written agreements between or among states, treaties, or generally accepted norms based on states' practices, known as customary law. This study, while recognizing the importance of customary law as a foundation for and outgrowth of treaties, focuses primarily on treaties.

Methods by which states accept treaties as law vary according to states' legal systems. In the United States, for a treaty to become law, two-thirds of the Senate must give its "advice and consent" to ratification. Ratification occurs when the President gives formal notice of U.S. acceptance of a treaty to other signatories. Pursuant to Article VI of the U.S. Constitution, treaties are part of the "supreme law of the land," along with federal statutes and the Constitution itself. Regardless of whether a treaty is enforced within the United States, courts recognize that it is a legal obligation of the United States on the international plane.

The United States can be credited as one of the founders of the modern system of international law. Its own founding as a country was based on the idea that a system of constitutional law is superior to rule by a king. Nevertheless, the history of the past century reveals that the U.S. desire to contribute to the creation of a global framework of law that builds national and global security has been counteracted by fears that international obligations will injure U.S. interests and sovereignty.

An early example is the League of Nations, a body of global governance whose principal architect and advocate was U.S. President Woodrow Wilson. There was formidable opposition to the League, due to its perceived encroachment on U.S. sovereignty, and the Senate declined to approve ratification of the treaty establishing the League. Twenty-five years later, the United States played a leading role in the creation of the United Nations, but only agreed to participate on condition of a veto in the UN's highest political body, the Security Council. Despite the U.S. role as host to the UN, and the general support that the U.S. public has expressed for the UN, a vocal faction of the U.S. government expresses wariness, and oftentimes hostility, toward the UN. In the 1980s and 1990s, the United States withheld dues from the UN, citing a need to reduce bureaucracy and ensure preservation of U.S. sovereignty. After the September 2001 terrorist attacks, Congress approved payment of a large sum of back dues on the basis that international cooperation through the UN is needed to fight terrorism.

U.S. policy toward international criminal justice has been similarly conflicted. Following World War II, the United States took the central role in convening the Nuremberg trials of major Nazi war criminals. In the 1990s, the United States supported the Security Council's establishment of *ad hoc* tribunals to try persons accused of war crimes, crimes against humanity, and genocide in the former Yugoslavia and Rwanda. However, the United States now opposes the International Criminal Court, largely due to its objection to the fact that U.S. nationals, along with those of other states, will be subject to the Court's jurisdiction.

With respect to international human rights law, the United States was a key participant in the elaboration of international human rights instruments following World War II. Acceptance within the U.S. political system has been slow to follow. The United States did not ratify the 1948 Genocide Convention until 1988. The Senate imposed significant reservations and conditions when it approved ratification of the Covenant on Civil and Political Rights and the Convention Against Torture. The United States has not yet ratified the Convention on Discrimination against Women, the Covenant on Economic, Social and Cultural Rights, and the Convention on the Rights of the Child (Somalia is the only other state not to have ratified the last treaty).

Another international legal body to have wavering support from the United States is the International Court of Justice, the UN judicial branch that adjudicates disputes among countries. In 1946, when the United States accepted the general jurisdiction of the International Court of Justice, it sought to exempt matters "within [U.S.] domestic jurisdiction as determined by the United States." In the 1980s, after the Court ruled that it had jurisdiction to decide a case brought by Nicaragua charging that the United States violated international law by supporting the contras in their effort to overthrow the Nicaragua government, the United States withdrew from the case and also withdrew its acceptance of the Court's general jurisdiction.

Since the fall 2001 terrorist attacks, the United States has invoked various international laws to help prosecute its war on terrorism. Under U.S. leadership, the UN Security Council adopted a resolution requiring all states to suppress financing of terrorist operations and to deny haven to terrorists. The Bush administration submitted two anti-terrorism treaties, on bombings and finance, to the Senate, the Senate approved ratification, and the United States became a party to the treaties in June 2002. The United States is now a party to all 12 global treaties on terrorism, which in large measure require states either to prosecute or extradite persons accused of various specific acts of violence. On the other hand, the United States declined *a priori* to treat captured members of Taliban forces as prisoners of war under the Third Geneva Convention, though it requires that, in case of doubt, a competent tribunal determination detainees' status. The United States also essentially sidelined the Security Council with respect to military operations in Afghanistan.

The heated debate over U.S. involvement in the international legal system, now nearly a century old, continues with an influential segment of opinion now contending strongly that the United States must rely on its own capabilities rather than treaties to protect its interests and sovereignty. As this study documents, resistance to law-governed multilateralism is manifested both by disregard of obligations imposed by treaties to which the United States is a party, and by a pattern of shaping treaties during negotiations only later to reject them.

Present U.S. Policies Regarding Security-Related Treaties

Nuclear Nonproliferation Treaty

The 1970 Nuclear Nonproliferation Treaty (NPT) bars almost all states in the world from acquiring nuclear weapons, and commits states parties that do possess nuclear weapons (Britain, China, France, Russia, and the United States) to negotiate their elimination. Only four states are outside the regime, Cuba and three nuclear-armed countries, India, Pakistan, and Israel. In return for agreeing not to acquire nuclear weapons and to accept safeguards to ensure that nuclear materials are not diverted to weapons from non-military programs, non-nuclear weapon states insisted that the NPT include a promise of assistance with peaceful nuclear energy, set forth in Article IV, and a promise of good-faith negotiation of cessation of the nuclear arms race "at an early date" and of nuclear disarmament, set forth in Article VI. Also part of the bargain are declarations by the NPT nuclear weapon states that they will not use nuclear weapons against non-nuclear weapon states parties. In 1995, in connection with indefinite extension of the treaty, a commitment was made to complete negotiations on the Comprehensive Test Ban Treaty (CTBT) by 1996. In 1996, the International Court of Justice unanimously held that Article VI obligates states to "bring to a conclusion negotiations leading to nuclear disarmament in all its aspects." In the 2000 NPT Review Conference, all states agreed upon a menu of 13 disarmament steps, including an "unequivocal undertaking" to "accomplish the total elimination" of nuclear arsenals pursuant to Article VI, ratification of the CTBT, U.S.-Russian reductions of strategic arms, application of the principle of irreversibility to disarmament measures, further reduction of the operational status of nuclear weapons, and a diminishing role for nuclear weapons in security policies.

Since 1970, the record of compliance with the non-acquisition obligation and safeguards agreements is reasonably good, with the exception of Iraq and North Korea. In contrast, the nuclear weapon states, including the United States, are now clearly are out of compliance with the Article VI disarmament obligation as specified in 1995, 1996, and 2000.

The U.S. Senate rejected the CTBT in 1999. As set forth in the U.S. 2002 Nuclear Posture Review (NPR), reductions of deployed strategic arms will be *reversible*, not irreversible, because they will be accompanied by the maintenance of a large "responsive force" of warheads capable of being redeployed in days, weeks, or months. The May 2002 U.S.-Russian agreement limiting "strategic nuclear warheads" on each side to no more than 2200 by the year 2012 does not provide for destruction or dismantlement of reduced delivery systems and warheads. It is therefore consistent with the U.S. plan for a "responsive force" and contrary to the NPT principle of irreversible disarmament. There are no announced plans to employ dealerting measures to reduce the operational status of the large deployed strategic forces that will remain after reductions. The NPR expands options for use of nuclear weapons against non-nuclear weapon states, including preemptive attacks against biological or chemical weapon capabilities and in response to "surprising military developments," and to this end, provides for development of warheads including earth penetrators. This widening of use options is contrary to the pledge of a diminishing role for nuclear weapons in security policies, the declaration of non-use of nuclear weapons against non-nuclear weapon states parties, and the obligation to negotiate cessation of the arms race at an early date. The NPR also contains plans for the maintenance and modernization of nuclear warheads and missiles and bombers for the next half-century. Above all, the lack of compliance with Article VI lies in the manifest failure to make disarmament the driving force in national planning and policy with respect to nuclear weapons.

Recommendations

In order to preserve and strengthen the NPT, the United States must demonstrate good-faith compliance with its Article VI obligations. The United States and Russia should drastically reduce strategic nuclear arms in a verifiable way codified by treaty, account for and destroy or dismantle reduced delivery systems and warheads, and engage other nuclear-armed states in a process of reductions leading to verified elimination of nuclear forces. The United States, Russia, and other nuclear-armed states should verifiably dealert their nuclear forces by such means as separating warheads from delivery systems, to achieve a condition of "global zero alert." The United States should reject the expansion of nuclear weapons use options set forth in the 2002 Nuclear Posture Review, and together with other nuclear-armed states adopt a policy of no first use of nuclear weapons. The United States and other nuclear-armed states should make achievement of total elimination of nuclear arsenals the centerpiece of their national planning and policy with respect to nuclear weapons.

Comprehensive Test Ban Treaty

After four decades of discussions and partial test ban agreements, negotiations on the Comprehensive Test Ban Treaty were completed in 1996. The achievement of a CTBT in 1996 was an explicit commitment made by the nuclear weapons states to all parties to the NPT, in connection with the indefinite extension of the NPT in 1995. The CTBT bans all nuclear explosions, for any purpose, warlike or peaceful. Though it contains no explicit definition of a nuclear explosion, the public negotiating history makes it clear that any nuclear explosive yield must be much less than four pounds of TNT equivalent and that the achievement of a nuclear criticality in explosive experiments involving fissile materials is prohibited.

In order to enter into force, the CTBT must be signed and ratified by 44 listed countries that have some form of nuclear technological capability, including commercial or research nuclear reactors. The CTBT still requires the ratification of 13 out of 44 nuclear capable states, including the United States, for entry into force. Of these, India, Pakistan, and North Korea have not signed the treaty. Of the five NPT nuclear weapon states, Russia, Britain, and France have ratified the treaty. The United States and China have signed but not ratified it.

India was included on the list of 44 countries, though it had explicitly rejected the CTBT during the negotiations. India claimed that while the treaty was originally intended to contribute to both nonproliferation and disarmament, it became a discriminatory instrument designed to promote nonproliferation but enable existing nuclear weapons states to maintain their nuclear arsenals. A similar problem in the 1960s led to India's refusal to sign the NPT. During the negotiations, India pointed to the stockpile stewardship program of the United States and similar, if less extensive, programs in other nuclear weapons states, that have the explicit purpose of maintaining nuclear design capability and existing nuclear arsenals over the long run. India tested nuclear weapons on May 11 and 13, 1998, and Pakistan followed with its own tests less than three weeks later.

Despite appeals from allies and large sections of U.S. opinion, the U.S. Senate voted in October 1999 to reject ratification of the CTBT. The Bush administration opposes the CTBT, and does not plan to ask the Senate to re-consider ratification. However, the United States has not made a formal notification of intent not to ratify the treaty and is maintaining the test moratorium, as are the other nuclear weapons states.

The merits of the CTBT as an instrument of nonproliferation and to a modest extent as an instrument of disarmament are reasonably clear. While the design of rudimentary nuclear weapons can be done without testing, it is essentially impossible to build an arsenal of the type that might be delivered accurately by intercontinental ballistic missiles without testing. Hence, in this regard, countries that have tested extensively, notably the five nuclear weapons states that are parties to the NPT, have an advantage in having previously tested nuclear weapons designs that can be put on intercontinental missiles.

The issues at stake in the arguments against the CTBT are not technical ones, but an assertion by the United States of the right to continue over the long haul not only to possess but to further develop an already extensive nuclear weapons capability despite its commitments for disarmament under the NPT. This approach was most recently codified in the Bush administration's Nuclear Posture Review (see above).

In our analysis, the United States and France are preparing to violate Article I, para. 1 of the CTBT because they are building large laser fusion facilities (the National Ignition Facility, NIF, and Laser Mégajoule, LMJ, respectively) with the intent of carrying out laboratory thermonuclear explosions of up to ten pounds of TNT equivalent. They also appear to be currently violating Article I, para. 2 of the CTBT because by building these facilities they are engaged in the process of causing nuclear explosions. Britain appears to be violating the CTBT because it is providing funds to the NIF program. Japan and Germany also appear to be in violation because they are the home countries of corporations whose subsidiaries are providing glass for the NIF and LMJ lasers.

Nothing in the public negotiating record or in the language of the CTBT provides for exceptions allowing laboratory thermonuclear explosions. Yet the United States has claimed, based on the NPT record, that they are permitted. That explanation does not withstand close scrutiny. There appears to be a secret negotiating record of the CTBT. It is possible that not all countries that have signed the CTBT are aware of the entire record.

Recommendations

A ban on testing is integrally related to the obligations of the NPT and therefore adds to the strength of that regime. It also directly contributes to prevention of further development and spread of nuclear weapons. The United State's interest should be in maintaining that ban by submitting itself to the same standards it seeks for other states. In that regard, the United States, and all countries should maintain the nuclear test moratorium until such time as the CTBT enters into force. The United States and all countries should *unconditionally* ratify the CTBT. This would be in the spirit the achievement of both nonproliferation and disarmament that animated the decades-long, worldwide demand for a comprehensive nuclear test ban. The United States, France, Britain, Japan and Germany should stop all preparations for carrying out laboratory thermonuclear explosions. The matter of laboratory thermonuclear explosions should be taken up explicitly by the parties to the CTBT, so as to reaffirm the complete ban on all nuclear explosions. Finally, the entire negotiating record of the CTBT should be published. In particular, the record of any confidential discussions and any confidential agreements (if they exist) between or among sub-groups of countries regarding inertial confinement fusion explosions should be made public.

Anti-Ballistic Missile Treaty

The Anti-Ballistic Missile (ABM) Treaty was created by the United States and the Soviet Union in 1972 in the context of their growing armories of missiles that had several warheads, each of which could be independently targeted. These weapons raised the theoretical possibility of a surprise first strike by one of the Cold War antagonists that might wipe out most of the strategic nuclear forces of the other side. An extensive defense system could then prevent the remaining nuclear warheads of the adversary's retaliatory strike from harming its territory.

The ABM treaty was supposed to maintain the credibility of retaliatory deterrence based on the threat of a successful second strike, also known as the policy of Mutually Assured Destruction (MAD). The ABM Treaty was unusual in also putting limits on future technological development in the interest of preserving the "strategic balance" between the United States and the Soviet Union.

During the 1990s, sentiment in the United States grew that the policy of mutually assured destruction should be replaced by a more flexible nuclear doctrine that included missile defenses at a variety of levels, including defenses against strategic missiles far beyond the very limited defenses permitted by the ABM Treaty.

For some years, the United States pursued a policy of attempting to negotiate changes in the ABM Treaty while researching missile defense technology. The Bush administration was less favorably inclined toward maintaining the treaty at all. In December 2001 the United States notified Russia of its intent to withdraw from the treaty in six months pursuant to a treaty provision permitting withdrawal based upon extraordinary events jeopardizing the withdrawing state's supreme interests. The unilateral U.S. decision to withdraw came despite the fact that many planned missile defense tests could have been implemented within the constraints of the treaty.

The U.S. withdrawal from the ABM Treaty is the first formal unilateral withdrawal of a major power from a nuclear arms control treaty after it has been put into in effect. The U.S. action is especially troubling in the context of its decision to make a list of countries that may be targeted with nuclear weapons in its Nuclear Posture Review. One of the rationales in the targeting strategy is the possession of weapons of mass destruction by countries contrary to their treaty commitments. But what if North Korea, following the U.S. example, gave three months notice of withdrawal from the NPT and then proceeded to build a nuclear arsenal because it felt its national survival was threatened by U.S. policy?

The problem of preventing the deliberate or accidental use of weapons of mass destruction is a complex one. The risks of the use of weapons of mass destruction by terrorist groups or by states that do not now possess them are real. But so are the risks that nuclear weapons states would use them. The risks of nuclear war by accident or miscalculation because the United States and Russia maintain large numbers of nuclear weapons on hair-trigger alert are also significant. Moreover, the nuclear posture of the United States includes possible first use of nuclear weapons in a variety of circumstances and does not rule out a first strike. U.S. development and deployment of missile defenses will impede further U.S.-Russian arms reductions and may stimulate an arms race in Asia. Russia has already announced a withdrawal from its commitments under the START II arms reduction treaty (not yet in force) in the wake of the U.S. withdrawal from the ABM Treaty. In this overall context, the U.S. withdrawal from the treaty also jeopardizes the most important treaty preventing the spread of nuclear weapons and nuclear materials – the NPT.

In a different context that included complete, verified dealerting of nuclear weapons and a commitment to complete disarmament, including missile control, it is possible to imagine missile defenses, globally applied, as theoretically positive, though it is not clear whether that would be a worthwhile priority even then. At the present time, justifying a unilateral withdrawal from the ABM Treaty as an act of defense stretches credibility beyond the limit, especially when taken in combination with the U.S. record on other treaties detailed in this report, as well as the technical reality that a functioning missile defense system would enhance the ability of the United States to carry out a first strike with reduced damage to itself.

Recommendations

The United States should commit itself to the goal of strategic stability and to reducing the threat of a first strike by nuclear states, instead of increasing it as the present policy tends to do. Missile defenses should be ruled out unless there is universal and verified dealerting of nuclear weapons. In this context, a global missile defense system could be created to prevent nuclear attacks by non-state parties or nuclear weapons states. A global system should protect all populations, not just the populations of one country or an exclusive alliance. Protection of all populations can only succeed in a context of demonstrated commitment to universal nuclear disarmament. An aggressive first use and first strike policy cannot be a foundation for missile defense. To achieve global nuclear cooperation and therefore to prevent non-state groups and non-nuclear states from acquiring or using nuclear weapons, the United States must take the essential first step of pursuing verified dealerting of all nuclear weapons bilaterally with Russia as well as multilaterally with other nuclear weapons states, thus demonstrating its commitment to complete nuclear disarmament.

Chemical Weapons Convention

The Chemical Weapons Convention bans the development, possession, transfer and use of chemical weapons and creates a regime to monitor the destruction of chemical weapons and to verify that chemicals being used for non-prohibited purposes are not diverted for use in weapons.

The CWC contains three basic obligations:

(1) Prohibition of Weapons. States parties agree to never develop, acquire or use chemical weapons or transfer them to anyone;

(2) Destruction of Weapons. States parties agree to destroy all of their existing chemical weapons production facilities and stockpiles;

(3) Declarations and Inspections. Each state party must declare any chemical weapons facilities or stockpiles. States parties are not restricted in the use of chemicals and facilities for purposes other than the manufacture/use of chemical weapons, but must allow routine inspections of declared "dual-use" chemicals and production facilities that could be used in a manner prohibited by the convention. The annexes of the Convention set forth the list of such chemicals and facilities.

In addition to the routine inspections, the treaty also gives states parties the right to request a challenge inspection of any facility, declared or undeclared, on the territory of another state party that it suspects of possible non-compliance.

The United States played a significant role in negotiating the CWC, advocating a treaty broad in scope and with a thorough verification and inspection regime. The CWC was supported by three presidential administrations, Democratic and Republican. The treaty enjoyed public support, and endorsement from the intelligence community, the Department of Defense and the chemical industry. Despite the widespread support, several influential Senators, including Jesse Helms, then Chair of the Senate Foreign Relations Committee, threatened to prevent ratification of the CWC unless U.S. commercial and national security interests were better safeguarded. After lengthy negotiations, the treaty was ratified, but Congress imposed limitations on how the United States implements its terms.

Several of the restrictions imposed by Congress amount to a refusal to comply with terms of the treaty relating to inspections. Under CWC Article VI, states parties are required to subject specified toxic chemicals and facilities to verification measures (inspections and declarations) as provided by the Verification Annex. Pursuant to the implementing legislation, however, the President has the right to refuse inspection of any U.S. facility upon determining that the inspection may "pose a threat to the national security interests." Another restriction narrows the number of facilities that are subject to the inspection and declaration provisions. Also, the United States refuses to allow samples to be "transferred for analysis to any laboratory outside the territory of the United States," though the Verification Annex permits, if necessary, "transfer [of] samples for analysis off-site at laboratories."

These limitations may prevent accurate inspection results. Also, it is in the interest of the United States to foster thorough inspections of other states parties, but they may seek to apply the U.S. limitations to their own inspections. For example, in its implementing legislation, India prohibits samples from being taken out of the country, and Russia proposed similar legislation.

In April 2002, the United States led a mid-term vote to remove the Director-General of the Organization for the Prohibition of Chemical Weapons, the treaty-created body charged with overseeing the implementation of the treaty. The United States explained that the decision was based on the Director-General's financial mismanagement, and threatened to withhold paying its dues if the official was not removed. Critics charged that the dissatisfaction was due to the Director-General's independence from U.S. influence. The OPCW is expected to undergo further U.S.-led changes as a result of the Director-General's removal.

The CWC has not yet been used to its fullest potential. No state party has used the challenge inspection provision of the CWC to address alleged treaty violations by other states parties. The United States has alleged that states parties, including Iran, have violated the prohibitions of the CWC, but has not addressed the matter using the CWC. Use of the challenge inspection mechanism would bolster the treaty as a tool for gathering information and deterring the spread of chemical weapons. On the other hand, the longer the challenge inspection goes unused, the less credible the treaty will appear as a protection for the international community.

Recommendations

In order to maintain the CWC as a tool for preventing the development and spread of chemical weapons, the United States should commit to full inspections of the subject chemicals and facilities according to the terms of the Verification Annex. The United States should also avail itself of the challenge inspections to investigate allegations of violations by other states parties.

Biological and Toxin Weapons Convention and Draft Protocol

The BWC was signed in 1972 and came into force on March 26, 1975. Article I states that:

> Each State Party to this Convention undertakes never in any circumstances to develop, produce, stockpile or otherwise acquire or retain:
>
> (1) Microbial or other biological agents, or toxins whatever their origin or method of production, of types and in quantities that have no justification for prophylactic, protective or other peaceful purposes;
>
> (2) Weapons, equipment or means of delivery designed to use such agents or toxins for hostile purposes or in armed conflict.

Assessing compliance with the prohibitions is complicated by the fact that the BWC permits possession of biological weapon materials in small amounts needed for defensive purposes, such as development of vaccines. However, the BWC contains no mechanisms for verifying compliance. The need for such measures has long been evident.

Over a period of seven years, a committee open to all BWC states parties (the Ad Hoc Group) has worked toward the creation of a legally binding agreement to strengthen the BWC, known as the "BWC Protocol." The parties agreed that the Protocol would include declarations of national bio-defense programs, facilities with high biological containment, plant pathogen facilities and facilities working with certain toxic agents; on-site visits to encourage the accuracy of declarations; and rapid investigations into allegations of noncompliance. Although difficult issues remained, the Ad Hoc Group had hoped to present a draft of the Protocol to the conference of BWC States Parties in November 2001.

The United States had initially endorsed the general approach contained in the Protocol, but neither the Clinton nor Bush administrations took a leading role in negotiations. Many national security officials opposed a verification protocol because it required information relating to bio-defense work. In addition, biotechnology firms raised concerns about the protection of their propriety information. In May 2001, the Bush administration performed a policy review regarding the BWC Protocol, and in July 2001 announced that it could no longer endorse the Protocol, even if it were revised. The justification for rejecting the Protocol was that it did not adequately protect bio-defense and industrial information, and also that the verification measures would not be effective in detecting cheating. As an alternative to the Protocol, the United States proposed voluntary undertakings that would only minimally improve the existing biological weapons control regime.

The stated reasons for the U.S. opposition to the Protocol are suspect at best and do not stand up to serious scrutiny. They are contrary to the very positions taken by the U.S. government over a considerable period while the Protocol was being negotiated. Negotiators from the United States and other countries fully recognized that the treaty could not detect all instances of cheating; the very nature of biological weapons makes their detection exceptionally difficult. No treaty is foolproof, but through its provisions for declarations and clarifications, the Protocol would promote transparency of a state's biological activity and would help to deter proliferation. Moreover, during negotiations, the United States advocated weaker verification procedures in the interest of protecting industrial and biodefense information. If the United States were genuinely interested in creating a technically feasible Protocol that would also safeguard its information, it could have conducted extensive trials of the possible monitoring regime. Indeed, the U.S. was called upon to do so in a 1999 U.S. law.

The United States not only rejected the specific text of the Protocol under consideration, but also, in November 2001, at the end of the BWC Review Conference, called for the termination of the Ad Hoc Group, meaning complete abandonment of the process that had been created seven years ago to strengthen the BWC through a legally binding instrument. The fate of the Ad Hoc Group, and thus the ability of the states parties to create a legally binding verification regime, is now up in the air.

The United States does not endorse a mandatory regime of openness with regard to biological agents and equipment. The policy might be explained by the U.S. commitment to biodefense work, much of which has been carried out in secret, that the U.S. fears may be exposed by a verification regime. As part of its biodefense program, the United States has already constructed a model bio-bomb, weaponized anthrax, built a model agent-producing laboratory and begun developing a genetically enhanced super-strain of anthrax. All of this was done in secret and without notification to other BWC states parties. At least the first two of these activities may be seen as violating the BWC, because, although the stated purpose for all the activities is defensive, the BWC does not permit the production of weapons. The U.S. program may prove to be a dangerous model, as states parties may undertake similar covert biodefense programs, citing the U.S. example. Any party could then easily divert such programs for offensive purposes.

Recommendations

The United States should strengthen the laws against biological weapons in two ways. It should commit to the earliest possible completion of a protocol establishing a verification regime including declarations, on-site visits and challenge inspections. To that end, the United States should conduct trials to ensure that any monitoring regime in place will be capable of producing accurate results. Also, the United States should ensure that it is adhering to its existing commitments by immediately terminating all biodefense programs to construct biological weapons.

Mine Ban Treaty

In 1996, a group of like-minded countries working with non-governmental and humanitarian relief organizations commenced a process for the creation of a treaty banning anti-personnel landmines. This process resulted in the creation of the Convention on the Prohibition of the Use, Stockpiling, Production and Transfer of Anti-Personnel Mines and On Their Destruction (the Mine Ban Treaty).

The Mine Ban Treaty bans all anti-personnel landmines without exception. It entered into force in March 1999. States parties are required to make implementation reports to the UN Secretary-General within 180 days, destroy stockpiled mines within four years, and destroy mines in the ground in territory within their jurisdiction or control within 10 years. The Mine Ban Treaty also requires states parties to take appropriate domestic implementation measures, including imposition of penal sanctions for violation of its provisions.

Although President Clinton was the first world leader to call for the "eventual elimination" of landmines, during negotiations on the Mine Ban Treaty, the Clinton administration demanded that certain types of antipersonnel mines be permitted, that U.S. mines in South Korea be exempted from the ban, and that an optional nine-year deferral period for compliance be established. The U.S. demands were rejected, and the United States declined to sign the treaty.

The U.S. landmines policy was refined in 1998 when President Clinton committed the United States to cease using antipersonnel mines, except those contained in "mixed systems" with antitank mines, everywhere in the world except in Korea by the year 2003. By the year 2006, if alternatives have been identified and fielded, the United States will cease use of all antipersonnel mines, including those in mixed systems, and join the Mine Ban Treaty.

Current U.S. policy hinders efforts to universalize the core prohibitions of the Mine Ban Treaty on the production, use, stockpiling, and transfer of antipersonnel mines. Many military experts have argued that antipersonnel mines have little to no utility in the war fighting principles currently being developed and adopted by the U.S. military for the 21st century. The unique exceptions that United States claims as critical are also reflected in the justifications used by other non-parties. Moreover, the multi-year $820 million program to identify and field alternatives to antipersonnel mines may not meet the 2006 objective and may result in munitions that would, in any case, be banned under the Mine Ban Treaty. Significantly, compliance with the Mine Ban Treaty is not a criterion for any of the alternatives programs. In 1999, as a condition of ratification of a separate treaty which regulates but does not prohibit landmines, Protocol II to the Convention on Conventional Weapons, President Clinton agreed that the search for alternatives to antipersonnel landmines would not be limited by whether they complied with the Mine Ban Treaty. The contradiction between the policy objectives established under President Clinton and the subsequent interpretation of his instructions jeopardizes the overall success of the alternatives program and threatens the 2006 target date.

The fate of the alternatives program and the 2006 target date is now in question because the Bush administration is currently conducting a review of U.S. mine policy. As the U.S. policy currently stands, the United States keeps company with Russia, China, India, Pakistan, Iran, Iraq, Libya, North Korea, Burma, Syria, and Cuba by refusing to join the Mine Ban Treaty. The United States joins Turkey as the only members of NATO not to have signed the treaty, though Turkey has pledged to accede to the accord. The United States is one of just fourteen countries that have not forsworn production of mines. It possesses the third largest stockpile of antipersonnel mines in the world, totaling more than 11 million, including 1.2 million of the long-lasting "dumb" mines. The United States stockpiles at least 1.7 million antipersonnel mines in twelve foreign countries, five of which are party to the Mine Ban Treaty. The United States exported over 5.6 million antipersonnel mines to thirty-eight countries between 1969 and 1992. The United States manufactured antipersonnel mines that have been found in twenty-eight mine-affected countries or regions.

Recommendations

President Bush should submit the Mine Ban Treaty to the Senate for its advice and consent to accession (essentially one-step signing and ratification, done after the period for signature has ended), and should through executive actions begin immediate implementation of the treaty's provisions. Short of joining the treaty, there are other important steps that the Bush administration could take, including setting a definitive deadline for joining the Mine Ban Treaty, not a conditional objective; declaring a ban or an indefinite moratorium on the production of antipersonnel mines; immediately committing the United States to a policy of no use of antipersonnel mines in joint operations (NATO and otherwise) with states that have signed the Mine Ban Treaty; committing the United States to a policy of no transiting of antipersonnel mines across the territory, air space, or waters of Mine Ban Treaty signatory states; immediately withdrawing all stockpiles of antipersonnel mines from countries that have signed the Mine Ban Treaty; and taking steps necessary to ensure that any systems resulting from the Pentagon's landmine alternative programs are compliant with the Mine Ban Treaty.

UN Framework Convention on Climate Control and
the Kyoto Protocol

The 1992 United Nations Framework Convention on Climate Change
(UNFCCC) and the 1997 Kyoto Protocol are linked treaties relating to climate change. The former is the fundamental treaty on climate change,
since it sets forth a framework of basic obligations. The Kyoto Protocol
was signed pursuant to those obligations. A chapter on the Kyoto Protocol
is included in this report on security-related treaties because climate
change could have vast security implications. For instance, it could cause
millions or even tens of millions of people to become refugees because of
flooding or changing food production patterns.

The United States ratified the UNFCCC in 1992; it entered into force in
1994. The UNFCCC recognizes that "the largest share of historical and
current global emissions of greenhouse gases has originated in developed
countries, that per capita emissions in developing countries are still relatively low." The treaty therefore puts the burden of taking "the lead" in
reducing those emissions on the developed countries. Such action was to
be taken despite uncertainties relating to climate change. Over the past
decade, evidence has accumulated that the global climate is changing due
to human activities. The possibility of very rapid change and consequences far more catastrophic than were commonly discussed only a
decade ago now seem within the range of possibility.

The 1997 Kyoto Protocol was designed to be the first step to give speci-
ficity to commitment made in the UNFCCC. It is generally recognized
that the emissions reductions the Kyoto Protocol mandates are moderate,
that further reductions to protect the climate will be required, and that
developing countries will need to be brought into the framework in subsequent steps. Under the Kyoto Protocol, the developed countries agreed
to reduce their greenhouse gas emissions relative to 1990 by at least five
percent by the period 2008 to 2012. The Clinton administration signed the
treaty but did not seek ratification since it was likely to be defeated. The
Bush administration has rejected the Kyoto Protocol altogether. The other
developed country parties completed their negotiations on specific targets
in 2001 and have announced their determination to achieve them.

Regardless of whether it accepts the Kyoto Protocol, the United States, as
a party to the UNFCCC and as the producer of one quarter of the world's
greenhouse gases, is obligated to take "precautionary measures to antici-

pate, prevent or minimize the causes of climate change." The Bush administration, in a recent UNFCCC report, conceded the impact of climate change, yet its policies focus more on the "challenge of adaptation" than on mitigation. The administration endorses largely voluntary measures, and the climate change plan in place is aimed only at reducing greenhouse gas "intensity" of the U.S. economy. This plan would reduce emissions per unit of economic output, but the target for the reduction in intensity is so low that total emissions would still continue to grow. Indeed, the announced target is in line with historical trends in decreased emissions per unit economic output and increased total emissions. In other words, the plan maintains the status quo of modestly increasing energy efficiency and rising greenhouse gas emissions.

The U.S. rejection of the Kyoto Protocol coupled with its publication of a plan that will actually result in increased greenhouse gas emissions over the next decade puts the United States in violation of its commitments under the UNFCCC.

Recommendations

The United States should create policies and targets for actually reducing total greenhouse gas emissions. This will require reductions in greenhouse gas intensity at a rate faster than the anticipated rate of economic growth. The United States should announce a process by which it will re-engage with the world community to find ways to reduce greenhouse gas emissions globally over the next three to four decades by far larger absolute amounts than now envisioned in the Kyoto Protocol over the next decade.

Rome Statute of the International Criminal Court

The Rome Statute of the International Criminal Court (ICC) creates the world's first permanent criminal court to try individuals for genocide, war crimes, crimes against humanity, and aggression once that crime is defined. It recognizes no immunities; therefore even heads of state, traditionally insulated from prosecution, can be brought to justice for committing atrocities when their countries are unable or unwilling to address the crimes at the national level. The ICC also includes as crimes violent acts against women that had long been overlooked as war crimes. Together with associated improvement of capabilities in national legal systems, the ICC will bolster global security by deterring and prosecuting serious international crimes. It will "end the culture of impunity," the assumption that atrocities can be committed without fear of legal consequences. A functioning ICC will also strongly reinforce the existing taboo against use of weapons of mass destruction.

One of two conditions must be met for the Court to exercise jurisdiction in most cases: (1) the state where the crimes occurred ("territorial state") is party to the Rome Statute or consent to the jurisdiction of the Court *or* (2) the state of nationality of the accused is party to the Statute or consents to the jurisdiction of the Court. These "pre-conditions" do not apply when the Security Council refers a case to the ICC acting under Chapter VII of the UN Charter. There are three ways cases may come before the Court: (1) when a state party has referred a situation to the Prosecutor; (2) when the Prosecutor initiates an investigation; and (3) when the Security Council, acting under Chapter VII of the UN Charter, refers a case. The Rome Statute addresses in several ways concerns that individuals will be the subjects of politically motivated prosecutions, including by requiring Court approval of investigations initiated by the Prosecutor. Nor will the Court infringe upon a state's interest in prosecuting crimes; the ICC is a court of last resort, and has jurisdiction only when the corresponding country is unable or unwilling to prosecute.

The ICC is an independent institution and not an arm of the United Nations. In contrast to the *ad hoc* international criminal tribunals for the Former Yugoslavia and Rwanda, the ICC will also be largely independent of the Security Council. The United States had argued for a court that would be made dependent on the UN Security Council for the cases that could come before it. However, the role of the Security Council was greatly circumscribed in the final text of the Rome Statute. It is this aspect – the degree of independence of the Security Council – that caused the United States to oppose the permanent Court at the same time that it fully supported the creation and maintenance of the *ad hoc* tribunals.

Even before formal negotiations commenced on the draft statute in 1996, the United States attempted to thwart altogether the process toward a permanent and independent court. During the negotiations, the United States unsuccessfully sought amendments to limit the Court's jurisdiction over nationals of non-states parties and to require consent of the state in question prior to exercising jurisdiction over officials and military personnel. When the Statute was adopted by a conference of states in July 1998, the United States voted against it.

The United States engaged in intensive diplomatic pressure tactics and other efforts to alter the statute long after it had been adopted.

Nevertheless, President Clinton opted to sign the Rome Statute hours before the period for signature expired on December 31, 2000. In international law, signature of a treaty signifies intent to ratify and not to engage in activities or enact laws contrary to the treaty's object and purpose. Yet Clinton simultaneously backtracked from the prospect of U.S. ratification at the same time that he signed the Statute: "I will not, and do not recommend that my successor submit the Treaty to the Senate for advice and consent until our fundamental concerns are satisfied." U.S. opposition boils down to one problem: U.S. nationals would be subject, like those of other states, to the jurisdiction of an international court.

When the Bush administration entered office, it undertook a high-level policy review of the Statute and concluded that the United States should not be party to the Statute. By letter dated May 6, 2002, the Bush administration notified UN Secretary-General Kofi Annan that the United States does not intend to ratify the treaty and therefore has "no legal obligations arising from its signature of December 31, 2000." Under the laws governing treaty making, now that the United States has expressed its intention not to be bound by its signature, it is no longer required to refrain from any actions that would defeat the object and purpose of the treaty and the Court.

Since the signing of the Rome Statute in 1998, the United States has followed several avenues to limit the jurisdiction and power of the ICC. The United States began introducing provisions prohibiting the extradition to the ICC of U.S. personnel in the negotiations of Status of Forces Agreements (agreements providing for the placement of U.S. military personnel in other countries). In the absence of existing or renegotiated SOFAs, the United States is now seeking separate agreements which deal solely and specifically with the issue of extradition to the ICC. The United States has also been pursuing similar clauses in Security Council resolutions authorizing peacekeeping forces. When its demand for a blanket exemption for peacekeeping troops from states not party to the ICC was rejected by the Security Council, the United States vetoed the continuation of the UN peacekeeping operation in Bosnia. The move was vociferously opposed by some of the United States' closest allies, including Mexico, Canada and members of the European Union, who resented the cynical strategy of pitting peacekeeping against justice. Intensive negotiations resulted in a Security Council resolution allowing a one-year *deferral* of prosecutions for peacekeepers from non-ICC countries for all peacekeeping operations – not just that in Bosnia – in exchange for the renewal of the Bosnian mission.

Members of the U.S. government are also working domestically to undermine the ICC. On August 2, 2002, President Bush signed into law the American Servicemembers' Protection Act (ASPA), which prohibits military assistance to most countries that ratify the Statute; bars U.S. participation in UN peacekeeping missions; and authorizes the President to use "all means necessary and appropriate" to free individuals held by or on behalf of the ICC (generally interpreted to mean military force).

The current direction of U.S. policy is therefore not only to keep U.S. citizens out of the Court's jurisdiction but also to make it as difficult as possible for participating countries to cooperate with the Court. U.S. policy seems to be aimed at making such cooperation especially difficult for developing countries, which need U.S. support in other arenas such as the World Bank and the IMF. Regardless of U.S. opposition, the International Criminal Court is a reality. The Rome Statute entered into force on July 1, 2002, and the ICC's jurisdiction took effect that day. The Court is expected to be operational in 2003.

Recommendations

The United States should ratify the Rome Statute and fully participate in the International Criminal Court. Short of total participation, the United States should end the pursuit of bilateral agreements to prohibit the extradition of U.S. nationals to the ICC; repeal legislation prohibiting support for the ICC; and refrain from enacting legislation which conditions military or financial support on a state's non-participation in the ICC. The United States should also end attempts to use the Security Council to undermine the jurisdiction and development or practices of the Court.

TREATIES AND GLOBAL SECURITY

The evolution of international law since World War II is largely a response to the demands of states and individuals living within a global society with a deeply integrated world economy. In this global society, the repercussions of the actions of states, non-state actors, and individuals are not confined within borders, whether we look to greenhouse gas accumulations, nuclear testing, the danger of accidental nuclear war, or the vast massacres of civilians that have taken place over the course of the last hundred years and still continue. Multilateral agreements increasingly have been a primary instrument employed by states to meet extremely serious challenges of this kind, for several reasons. They clearly and publicly embody a set of universally applicable expectations, including prohibited and required practices and policies. In other words, they articulate global norms, such as the protection of human rights and the prohibitions of genocide and use of weapons of mass destruction. They establish predictability and accountability in addressing a given issue. States are able to accumulate expertise and confidence by participating in the structured system established by a treaty.

However, influential U.S. policymakers are resistant to the idea of a treaty-based international legal system because they fear infringement on U.S. sovereignty and they claim to lack confidence in compliance and enforcement mechanisms. This approach has dangerous practical implications for international cooperation and compliance with norms. U.S. treaty partners do not enter into treaties expecting that they are only political commitments that can be overridden based on U.S. interests. When a powerful and influential state like the United States is seen to treat its legal obligations as a matter of convenience or of national interest alone, other states will see this as a justification to relax or withdraw from their own commitments. When the United States wants to require another state to live up to its treaty obligations, it may find that the state has followed the U.S. example and opted out of compliance.

Undermining the international system of treaties is likely to have particularly significant consequences in the area of peace and security. Even though the United States is uniquely positioned as the economic and military sole superpower, unilateral actions are insufficient to protect the people of the United States. For example, since September 11, prevention of proliferation of weapons of mass destruction is an increasing priority. The United States requires cooperation from other countries to prevent and detect proliferation, including through the multilateral disarmament and nonproliferation treaties.

No legal system is foolproof, domestically or internationally. While violations do occur, "the dictum that most nations obey international law most of the time holds true today with greater force than at any time during the last century." And legal systems should not be abandoned because some of the actors do not comply.

In the international as in the domestic sphere, enforcement requires machinery for deciding when there has been a violation, namely verification and transparency arrangements. Such arrangements also provide an incentive for compliance under ordinary circumstances. Yet for several of the treaties discussed in this report, including the BWC, CWC, and CTBT, one general characteristic of the U.S. approach has been to try to exempt itself from transparency and verification arrangements. It bespeaks a lack of good faith if the United States wants near-perfect knowledge of others' compliance so as to be able to detect all possible violations, while also wanting all too often to shield itself from scrutiny.

While many treaties lack internal explicit provisions for sanctions, there are means of enforcement. Far more than is generally understood, states are very concerned about formal international condemnation of their actions. A range of sanctions is also available, including withdrawal of privileges under treaty regimes, arms and commodity embargoes, travel bans, reductions in international financial assistance or loans, and freezing of state or individual leader assets. Institutional mechanisms are available to reinforce compliance with treaty regimes, including the U.N. Security Council and the International Court of Justice. Regarding the latter, however, the United States has withdrawn from its general jurisdiction.

One explanation for increasing U.S. opposition to the treaty system is that the United States is an "honorable country" that does not need treaty limits to do the right thing. This view relies on U.S. military strength above all and assumes that the U.S. actions are intrinsically right, recalling the ideology of "Manifest Destiny." This is at odds with the very notion that the rule of law is possible in global affairs. If the rule of power rather than the rule of law becomes the norm, especially in the context of the present inequalities and injustices around the world, security is likely to be a casualty.

International security can best be achieved through coordinated local, national, regional and global actions and cooperation. Treaties, like all other tools in this toolbox, are imperfect instruments. Like a national law, a treaty may be unjust or unwise, in whole or in part. If so, it can and should be amended. But without a framework of multilateral agreements, the alternative is for states to decide for themselves when action is warranted in their own interests, and to proceed to act unilaterally against others when they feel aggrieved. This is a recipe for the powerful to be police, prosecutor, judge, jury, and executioner all rolled into one. It is a path that cannot but lead to the arbitrary application and enforcement of law. For the United States, a hallmark of whose history is its role as a progenitor of the rule of law, to embark on a path of disregard of its international legal obligations is to abandon the best that its history has to offer the world. To reject the system of treaty-based international law rather than build on its many strengths is not only unwise, it is extremely dangerous. It is urgent that the United States join with other countries in implementing existing global security treaties to meet the security challenges of the twenty-first century and to achieve the ends of peace and justice to which the United States is committed under the United Nations Charter.

1

AN OVERVIEW OF U.S. POLICIES TOWARD THE INTERNATIONAL LEGAL SYSTEM

While the United States currently resists a range of global security treaties, it is also the principal architect of the post-World War II international legal system. This chapter traces the roots of the ambivalent U.S. approach to international law and institutions, setting the stage for examination of specific treaty regimes in following chapters. We begin with some basics about the role of treaties in international and U.S. law.

MAKING INTERNATIONAL LAW

WHAT IS INTERNATIONAL LAW?

International laws are created in two main ways. One is by making written agreements between or among countries, known as treaties, which may be bilateral or multilateral. The second is the derivation of customary law from states' practices. Customary law is universally binding law based on a general and consistent practice of states followed out of a sense of legal obligation (*opinio juris*).

These two methods often overlap. Many customary obligations are later codified in treaties. For example, diplomatic immunity was "a widely accepted customary legal obligation before it was codified by treaty in 1972."[1] Many human rights, such as the right to be free from torture and the right to life, are rights conferred under customary law and are also codified in treaties.[2] Customary laws may also grow out of terms of an existing treaty. When a provision of a treaty is the basis for a customary rule, or when a customary rule is later codified in a treaty, states that are not parties to the treaties are still bound by the customary rule. For example, the prohibitions on use of chemical and biological weapons set forth in the Geneva Protocol of 1925 are also considered customary law, and thus are binding on states not party to the Protocol.

One difference between customary law and treaty law is the manner in which a state may refuse to be bound by the law. If a state does not wish to be bound by treaty laws, it abstains from joining the treaty. But to be free from application of a customary law, a state must consistently object to the existence of the rule. Also, certain customary laws are not subject to objection. These laws, the rules of *jus cogens*, are peremptory norms, that is, they are laws that are accepted by the international community as a whole as binding without exceptions. Genocide is one such example; no state may enter into an international agreement or adopt domestic laws superseding the prohibition of genocide.

While this study focuses primarily on international law as codified in treaties, it is important to recognize the role and influence of customary law in shaping the international legal system.[3] International law is based on both treaty and custom; it builds both on states' obligations set forth in agreements and on their actions and practices.

THE PROCESS OF TREATY MAKING

Article VI of the Constitution makes treaties part of the "supreme law of the land," along with federal statutes and the Constitution itself. Enforcement of treaties *within the United States* is conditioned by several rules.[4] They include the "last-in-time" rule, which provides that when there is a conflict between a treaty and a federal statute, the most recently adopted prevails. Another important rule is that a "non-self-executing" treaty will not be applied absent implementing legislation. Importantly, though, courts recognize that regardless of its status within the United States, a treaty obligation remains a legal obligation of the United States on the international plane.

Article II of the Constitution governs the procedure by which the United States enters into treaties: the President "shall have Power, by and with the Advice and Consent of the Senate, to make Treaties, provided two-thirds of the Senators present concur." Generally, the Senate does not advise on detailed treaty questions prior to completed negotiations, though there have been important exceptions. Rather, the Senate's role is "primarily to pass judgment on whether completed treaties should be ratified by the United States."[5]

The process of treaty making begins with the President initiating negotiations, appointing negotiators (these appointments may require advice and consent of the Senate), and negotiating with other states on the form and substance of the agreement. Members of Congress are sometimes involved in this phase through consultations, or as delegates or observers. After the negotiators have reached an agreement, the treaty is adopted; signature by the President or his or her representative follows.[6]

Next, the President submits the treaty to the Senate, and it is referred to the Senate Foreign Relations Committee, which holds hearings and prepares a written report. If the Foreign Relations Committee supports the treaty, it releases or "reports" it, usually with a proposed resolution of ratification. The Foreign Relations Committee sometimes recommends that approval should be subject to certain conditions.

After the treaty is reported out of the Foreign Relations Committee, the Senate may choose to put it to a vote. If the treaty is approved by a 2/3 majority, the Senate sends the treaty to the President. If the treaty fails to receive the 2/3 majority vote, it may be returned to the Committee or to the President, and the treaty does not proceed unless it is re-considered or re-submitted.[7]

Once the Senate approves the treaty, the President may then ratify the treaty by exchanging the instrument of ratification (for bilateral treaties) or submitting the instrument of ratification to the "depository" for the treaty, often the UN Secretary-General (for multilateral treaties). A multilateral treaty generally enters into force after a designated number of parties deposit their instruments of ratification. Once the treaty is in effect, Congress still may be required to pass laws to make the treaty obligations binding within the United States, called the "implementing legislation."[8]

The security treaties that are the subject of this book were negotiated and/or ratified through the above-described constitutional process. An increasing number of international agreements, however, are approved by a simple majority of both houses, not the process of 2/3 majority vote by Senate. These "executive agreements" are considered to have the same binding effect under international law as treaties. Executive agreements occur when the President seeks Congressional authorization by joint resolution or act of Congress or by relying on existing legislation as the legal basis for ratification of the agreement.[9] Some executive agreements are concluded by the President alone.

Most executive agreements are authorized in advance by Congress or submitted to Congress for approval. Congress has authorized the conclusion of international agreements for postal conventions, foreign trade, foreign military assistance, foreign economic assistance, atomic energy cooperation and international fishery rights.[10] The use of executive agreements in lieu of the treaty process challenges the primary role that the Senate is given under the Constitution to legislate international agreements. Critics are particularly concerned that the executive agreement process is used to end-run the constitutionally required 2/3 approval by the Senate. For example, anti-World Trade Organization (WTO) advocates argue that the Senate would have lacked the votes to approve membership into the WTO as a treaty, but because it was presented as an executive agreement, it only required a simple majority of both houses and was approved.

While the use of executive agreements as a means to enter into international agreements has grown steadily in recent years, the Senate has insisted that arms control agreements be adopted through the traditional treaty process. Beginning with the INF Treaty in 1988, the Senate, when consenting to arms control treaties, has added a declaration that future arms control agreements should be concluded as treaties.[11]

The requirement of Senate approval has often worked as a restriction on Presidents seeking broad participation in international regimes. Presidents, often visionaries of global engagement, have characteristically been tempered by Senators concerned that treaties restrict U.S. interests. Increasingly, however, resistance to multilateral treaties has come from the executive branch as well. The following discussion explores both the traditional and emerging trends of U.S. behavior toward the international legal system.

U.S. AMBIVALENCE TOWARD INTERNATIONAL LEGAL REGIMES

The United States can be credited as one of the founders of the modern system of international law. Moreover, its own founding as a country was based on the idea that a system of constitutional law, that is the rule of law, was superior to and more just than rule by a king. Nevertheless, the history of the past century reveals that in the United States the desire to create international laws in support of national and global security is counteracted by fears that international legal obligations will injure U.S. interests and sovereignty.

The struggle between these two views of U.S. involvement in international law, which could be identified as pro-engagement and pro-sovereignty,[12] has restrained U.S. global leadership and has weakened the international regimes themselves. Oftentimes, the result of the tension between these two views is that the United States supports the application of international legal instruments to other countries, but seeks to exempt its behavior from their provisions.

One scholar of U.S. policies toward the UN described this state of affairs as "seeming intractable contradictions in American perspective [that] have resulted in an almost perpetual crisis in U.S. relations with the very bodies it has worked to establish."[13] Before addressing the subject of the costs associated with the U.S. approach, we explore how U.S. ambivalence has shaped its participation in various international legal regimes in the past century.

THE UNITED NATIONS AND THE LEAGUE OF NATIONS

The United States took its largest step into the global legal framework with the creation of and entrance into the United Nations in 1945.[14] Twenty-five years prior to the adoption of the UN Charter, however, the United States declined to join the League of Nations, the first international body organized to govern global peace and security. Although the League was a product of the vision of U.S. President Woodrow Wilson, opposition within the Senate blocked ratification of the treaty to enter into the League (the Treaty of Versailles).

Senator Henry Cabot Lodge, Chair of the Senate Foreign Relations Committee, led the campaign against the League of Nations. He evoked a theme that recurs in debate on multilateral treaties to this date, that is, the risk to sovereignty posed by multinational institutions:

> I want to keep America as she has been — not isolated, not prevent her from joining other nations for these great purposes — but I wish her to be the master of her fate. ...I want her left in a position to do that work and not submit her to a vote of other nations with no recourse except to break a treaty she wishes to maintain.[15]

The League of Nations went forward without the participation of the United States, but collapsed when it was unable to prevent the aggressions that led to World War II.

After the bombing of Pearl Harbor, the isolationist impulses in the United States gave way to military engagement, and the United States took the lead in the creation of the United Nations. But the United States agreed to be a part of the UN only on condition of having a veto in the Security Council – a prerogative also granted the other victors in World War II. At U.S. insistence, China's seat in the United Nations and in the Security Council was held by Taiwan until 1972.

Despite the U.S. role as host to the UN, and the general support that the U.S. public has expressed in favor of the UN,[16] a vocal faction of the U.S. government expresses wariness, and often times hostility, toward the UN. Jesse Helms, onetime Chair of the Senate Foreign Relations Committee, acts as one of the most vociferous critics of the UN and views the UN as a U.S.-funded threat to sovereignty:

> [T]he United Nations has moved from facilitating diplomacy among nation-states to supplanting them altogether. The international elites running the United Nations look at the idea of the nation-state with disdain; they consider it a discredited notion of the past that has been superseded by the idea of the United Nations. . . . Nation-states, they believe, should recognize the primacy of these global interests and accede to the United Nations' sovereignty to pursue them.[17]

In addition to the perceived threat to U.S. sovereignty, critics objected to the inefficiencies of the UN bureaucracy and other states' use of the UN to press agendas unfavorable to the U.S. These criticisms of the UN within Congress resulted in U.S. refusal to pay its allotted UN dues.

In 1985, President Reagan became the first President to approve a Congressional effort to withhold dues, citing the need for reforms.[18] Withholding of funds continued until 1999, and by that time the United States owed the UN over one billion U.S. dollars in unpaid dues. The withholding of dues was based in large part on U.S. legislation that unilaterally capped the U.S. contribution to costs of UN peacekeeping efforts and on the desire to reform the UN (including reducing bureaucracy and ensuring preservation of sovereignty).[19] The issue of payment of UN dues became a bargaining chip to force concessions on highly contentious political issues. For example, Congress conditioned payment of arrears on a restriction of funding for international family planning organizations that perform abortions using their own funds.[20] Congressmen also attempted to condition payment on passage of legislation to prohibit cooperation with the International Criminal Court.[21]

The legality of the U.S. decision to unilaterally withhold its dues was the subject of much debate within the U.S. government. The UN Charter states, "The expenses of the Organization shall be borne by the Members as apportioned by the General Assembly."[22] John Bolton, presently U.S. Under Secretary of State for Arms Control and International Security and a prominent advocate of the sovereigntist viewpoint, argued that withholding the dues was not illegal and that "the U.S. shall meet its commitments when it is in its interests to do so and when others are meeting their obligations as well."[23] Critics countered that the withholding was a Congressional maneuver around a binding treaty obligation: "If we want to get out of the United Nations, then let us vote to do that. If we want to say we will never spend another cent in the United Nations, let us vote to do that. But to first give our word that we will pay what we contractually owe and then . . . to say we break our word, we can't do that."[24] Moreover, aside from the question of the legality of the U.S. action, the lack of funding left the UN in "financial crisis" and many feared its imminent collapse.[25]

In 1999, Congress passed legislation for the United States to pay $926 million in back dues "if the United Nations reformed its huge bureaucracy and cut the U.S. share of its financial burden."[26] Prior to September 11, only $100 million of the money allocated for payment to the UN had been sent. After the September 11 terrorist attacks, the House of Representatives unanimously approved legislation for payment to the UN of $582 million in back dues.[27] The concern that the UN threatened U.S. sovereignty yielded to the understanding that cooperative efforts are needed to combat threats to national and global security. Representative Tom Lantos of California, a senior member in the House International Relations Committee, argued to House members that "we cannot ask the United Nations to bring freedom to difficulties-possessed people, battle terrorism, resolve international conflicts and conduct extensive peacekeeping operations, and yet fail to pay our dues..."[28]

The House members concluded that funding the UN will not only facilitate cooperative efforts, but will also ensure that the UN is attentive to the U.S. agenda: "Meeting our financial obligations to the United Nations will help to ensure that our policymakers can keep the focus on broad policies that unite the members of the Security Council in the fight against global terrorism."[29]

For the United States, paying its dues has been at least as much about whether the United Nations will follow the U.S. agenda, as whether it should comply with its treaty obligations.

THE INTERNATIONAL HUMAN RIGHTS LEGAL SYSTEM

Along with the end of World War II and the creation of the UN came the development of the international legal system of human rights. The United States, a principal founder of the system, has rejected significant human rights treaties, in several instances because it does not want to be held to the same standards as other states.

International Criminal Justice

At the end of World War II, the United States led the cause of international criminal law in bringing the perpetrators of the holocaust to justice. In the Nuremberg trials, the United States "took the lead in establishing a system of law by which certain categories of international criminals would be brought to justice through a fair trial where the defendants' rights were respected."[30] U.S. Supreme Court Justice Robert H. Jackson, Chief Prosecutor for the United States at the Nuremberg trials, believed the trials were developing binding laws not only for the prosecution of the Nazis but to govern the conduct of all of humanity:

> In untroubled times, progress toward an effective rule of law in the international community is slow indeed. Inertia rests more heavily upon the society of nations than upon any other society. Now we stand at one of those rare moments when the thought and institutions and habits of the world have been shaken by the impact of world war on the lives of countless millions. Such occasions rarely come and quickly pass. We are put under a heavy responsibility to see that our behavior during this unsettled period will direct the world's thought toward a firmer enforcement of the laws of international conduct, so as to make war less attractive to those who have governments and the destinies of peoples in their power.[31]

The role of the United States in the Nuremberg trials signaled the endorsement of and adherence to international law as a means of protecting U.S. interests and safeguarding the rights of all individuals. The legacy of the Nuremberg trials includes the war crimes tribunals for the Former

Yugoslavia and Rwanda, and the International Criminal Court (ICC). "[T]he international community has embraced the key concepts Jackson and the tribunals stood for: the universal unacceptability of certain crimes and accountability of both individuals and heads of state for the commission of such crimes."[32] But as we discuss in Chapter 9, the United States refuses to participate in the ICC, largely because of its objection to the fact that U.S. nationals would be subject – along with nationals of other states – to the jurisdiction of an international court. In addition to refusing to ratify the statute establishing the International Criminal Court, the United States has actively worked to limit its authority. The United States, once the leader of international criminal justice, now opposes its most significant application.

The Human Rights Treaty System

Corresponding with the development of international criminal law, human rights protections were incorporated into the UN Charter and the 1948 Universal Declaration of Human Rights. Although a nonbinding UN General Assembly resolution, the Universal Declaration aimed to be a "common standard of achievement for all peoples and all nations."[33] The UN Commission on Human Rights was established in 1946, and the Convention on the Prevention and Punishment of the Crime of Genocide was adopted in 1948 and entered into force in 1951. Americans, including Eleanor Roosevelt, played a key role in the drafting and development of key human rights instruments.

Yet, there has been strong political opposition within mainstream U.S. politics to the idea that the United States should be judged by the standards of human rights treaties. In addition to the general concerns about sovereignty, opponents viewed the laws as too vague, believed that with their concentration on social issues they might infringe on states rights, and feared they would confer rights on U.S. citizens to sue their government.[34] For example, opponents feared that the Convention on Genocide, signed by the United States in 1948 but not ratified until 1988, would be used as the basis for a legal claim that U.S. polices toward African-Americans or Native Americans constituted genocide.[35]

In the 1950s, Senator John Bricker led a movement to halt U.S. entrance into human rights treaties. Bricker and his followers, supporters of states' rights and opponents of civil rights, sought an amendment to the Constitution to make it "impossible for the United States to adhere to human rights treaties."[36] Bricker explained that his purpose was to "bury the so-called Covenant on Human Rights so deep that no one holding high public office will ever dare to attempt its resurrection."[37]

According to the proposed amendment, treaties would only be effective "through legislation which would be valid in the absence of treaty."[38] The amendment would thus ensure that treaties could no longer be self-exe-cuting (made effective without passage of implementing legislation) and would "make clear that treaties would not override the reserved powers of the states."[39]

The amendment was defeated, but, in exchange, the Eisenhower adminis-tration promised that the United States would not enter into any more human rights treaties.[40] Not until the Carter administration did the United States re-commit to entering into human rights treaties. Since then, the human rights treaties that have been ratified, the International Covenant on Civil and Political Rights, and the Convention Against Torture and Other Cruel, Inhuman or Degrading Treatment or Punishment, have been made subject to considerable reservations and conditions, which critics argue prevent the United States from adhering domestically to its treaty commitments.[41] Essentially, the United States has ratified these treaties in a manner that will not make any changes to existing laws.[42] Moreover, the United States has not yet ratified the Convention on Discrimination against Women (CEDAW),[43] the Covenant on Economic, Social and Cultural Rights (CESCR) and the Convention on the Rights of the Child (CRC). The failure to ratify the CRC is a distinction that the United States shares with only one other country – Somalia.

Certainly, the United States stands as a leader in the defense and protec-tion of human rights, but it refuses to do so as a full participant within the treaty-based human rights regime. One result of this policy may be that as global norms evolve, the protections guaranteed by the United States will fall short of those developing in the international legal system.

THE INTERNATIONAL COURT OF JUSTICE

U.S. participation in the International Court of Justice (ICJ or World Court) offers another example of U.S. insistence on exceptional treatment under international law. The World Court, founded in 1945, was estab-lished by the UN Charter as "the principal judicial organ of the United Nations."[44] It replaced the Permanent Court of International Justice, which had been operating since 1922. As with other international institutions set up at the time, the United States had a leading role in its formation. The two main responsibilities of the ICJ are to settle disputes submitted by states (contentious cases) and to give advisory opinions on legal questions referred to it by authorized UN bodies.

States must consent to having their cases heard by the ICJ, and under Article 36.2, a state party is permitted to accept compulsory jurisdiction over any contentious case where other involved states have also given such an acceptance. The United States accepted compulsory jurisdiction in 1946, but in so doing, the Senate attached a condition that exempted the World Court's jurisdiction from "disputes with regard to matters which are essentially within the domestic jurisdiction of the United States *as determined by the United States*"[45] (emphasis added). This provision, known as the Connally Amendment (after Tom Connally, chair of the Senate Foreign Relations Committee), violated the provision of the ICJ Statute establishing that "in the event of a dispute as to whether the Court has jurisdiction, the matter shall be settled by the decision of the Court."[46] The Connally Amendment also ignored the fundamental principle of law "that no one can judge his own case."[47] In the words of Ernest A. Gross, U.S. Ambassador to the United Nations in the early 1950s, "[i]nsistence upon keeping the key to the courthouse in our pocket is strangely out of keeping with the traditional American respect for the judicial process as prime guarantor of the rule of law."[48] Thus, from the beginning of the World Court, the United States reserved the option to refuse equal application of the law to its actions.

Then, in 1984, Nicaragua brought a case against the United States in the World Court for laying mines in Nicaragua's harbor and funding and training a rebel group (the contras) to overthrow the existing government. Nicaragua claimed that "the United States of America is using military force against Nicaragua and intervening in Nicaragua's internal affairs, in violation of Nicaragua's sovereignty, territorial integrity and political independence and of the most fundamental and universally-accepted principles of international law."[49] The United States strenuously objected that the ICJ did not have jurisdiction over the case. The conflict in Central America was a political issue and not a legal one, the United States argued, and the ICJ "was never intended to resolve issues of collective security and self-defense and is patently unsuited for such a role."[50]

The ICJ rejected the U.S. argument, ruling that it was authorized to adjudicate questions of collective security and self-defense. In response, the United States withdrew from the proceedings and also withdrew from the compulsory jurisdiction of the Court. In defense of the U.S. withdrawal, Jeane Kirkpatrick, then U.S. ambassador to the United Nations, explained that "[t]he court, quite frankly, is not what its name suggests, an international court of justice. It's a semi-legal, semi-juridical, semi-political body which nations sometimes accept and sometimes don't."[51] A minority of Senators voiced outrage over the U.S. handling of the Nicaragua case, and proposed an unsuccessful amendment to bar funding to international organizations unless the United States rejoined and accepted the compulsory jurisdiction of the ICJ:

> We have praised the Court when it has ruled in favor of the United States, but international law became an inconvenience that stood between the United States and the forceful overthrow of the Sandinista regime in Nicaragua. The only appropriate national posture given the current world situation is to advance the rule of international law. The other option is the jungle. And terrorism is the great weapon of the jungle. By our actions we have only enhanced the ability of the Pol Pots, the Khomeinis, and the Qadhafis to work their will in the world of lawlessness. We are denying an institution which, however imperfect, holds out some promise of a future system by which nations can resolve their differences peacefully.[52]

The ICJ ultimately ruled in favor of Nicaragua without the participation of the United States, and ordered, among other things, U.S. payment of reparations to Nicaragua. An effort to enforce the judgment in the UN Security Council was vetoed by the United States. The United States refused to pay the reparations; after elections brought a new government in Nicaragua, the countries settled the matter. The United States has not reinstated its acceptance of the compulsory jurisdiction of the Court.[53]

U.S. RESPONSE TO TERRORISM AFTER 9/11

The U.S. response to the September 2001 terrorist attacks includes elements of engagement and protection of sovereignty, but has more of a multilateral character than U.S. actions in other areas examined in this study.

The United States led military operations in Afghanistan in concert with selected other countries. The Security Council was essentially sidelined, though it is charged by the UN Charter with the maintenance of international peace and security. On September 12, 2001, the Security Council adopted resolution 1368 condemning the attacks. While the preamble referred to "the inherent right of individual or collective self-defence in accordance with the [UN] Charter," the resolution did not expressly authorize military action and referred to the Security Council's *"readiness to take all necessary steps"* (emphasis added), indicating that the Security Council might later take some role with respect to military action, at least to authorize it clearly. No such role was assumed, however, and the United States and its allies interpreted the reference to self-defense as approval of the military operations. There has been no openly voiced dissent to this interpretation by UN member states. Subsequently, with U.S. support, the Security Council and the UN secretariat have played a central part in forming and securing a post-Taliban regime in Afghanistan.

Regarding apprehension, detention and prosecution of suspected terrorists, the United States has hewed to a unilateralist path. The United States has ignored calls for the establishment of an *ad hoc* international tribunal to try suspects on the model of the tribunals for Rwanda and the former Yugoslavia. The United States also has declined *a priori* to treat captured members of Taliban forces as prisoners of war under the Third Geneva Convention, although the convention requires that determination of status in case of doubt be done by a competent tribunal (Geneva Conventions 1949, Art. 5, Third Geneva Convention). Further, there is a good case that such persons do qualify as prisoners of war, and giving them prisoner of war status would promote reciprocity in treatment of U.S. soldiers .

In responding to the general threat of terrorism post-September 11, the United States has adopted a strategy of engagement relying on the United Nations and multilateral treaties, taking full advantage, however, of its powerful position within the UN system. As noted earlier, Congress finally approved payment of back dues to the United Nations. In another highly significant move, the United States led the Security Council in the adoption of Resolution 1373 on September 28, 2001. The resolution made instant global law,[54] *requiring* all states to implement measures to suppress financing of terrorist operations; deny safe haven to terrorists; eliminate the supply of weapons to terrorists; bring persons who finance, plan, or perpetrate terrorist acts to justice, and cooperate with other states in doing so; and employ effective border controls to prevent the movement of terrorists. Among other things, it also "notes with concern the close connection between international terrorism and transnational organized crime, illicit drugs, money-laundering, illegal arms-trafficking, and illegal movement of nuclear, chemical, biological and other potentially deadly materials…," and calls for a global response through national, sub-regional, regional and international cooperation.

As an indication of the seriousness with which the mandate to take these measures is regarded, the resolution establishes a committee to monitor implementation consisting of all Security Council members, the "Counter-Terrorism Committee," chaired by Britain. The committee has been considering and responding to reports on compliance with the resolution which all states were required to submit by the end of 2001. So far, the level of participation by states has been very high, likely both a signal of the importance that they attach to accomplishing the objectives of the resolution and a recognition of the priority given the resolution by the Security Council and the United States.

The Security Council was able to require all states to take the identified measures because the resolution was adopted pursuant to its powers under Chapter VII of the UN Charter. Under that chapter, once the Security Council determines that there is a threat to international peace and security, it has the authority to obligate states to comply with the measures it determines are appropriate to meet the threat. Such measures have included in the past economic sanctions, the use of military force, and establishment of international tribunals. Resolution 1373 marks the first time, however, that the Security Council has made such a far-reaching intervention into how states are to organize their national legal systems.

Such global law-making is ordinarily done through multilateral treaties like those analyzed in this study. In fact, there is one treaty that sought to accomplish a key objective of Resolution 1373: the suppression of financing for terrorist operations. Like the resolution, the International Convention on the Suppression of Financing of Terrorism requires states parties to criminalize collecting and providing funds for terrorists and to freeze funds used to support terrorism. The treaty also requires states to direct financial institutions to take steps, *e.g.* to identify the real owners of accounts, to ensure that funds the institutions handle are not being used to support terrorist operations. This requirement is paralleled by the more general requirement of the resolution that states prohibit their nationals from making funds and services available to persons engaged in or financially supporting terrorist operations. Negotiation of the treaty was concluded in 1999, and it entered into force in April 2002. But it will only apply to states parties, and it may be years before a large number of states are parties. Resolution 1373 applies to all states, and was law the moment it was adopted. Moreover, the resolution is more demanding, for example requiring states to "freeze without delay" funds for the support of terrorist operations, while the treaty requires states to freeze such funds by "appropriate measures, in accordance with its domestic legal principles."

Thus the United States, with the support or acquiescence of other states on the Security Council, employed the Council's vast powers under the UN Charter to circumvent the cumbersome and time-consuming processes of treaty negotiation and then ratification pursuant to each state's constitutional procedure. Resolution 1373 in effect was an order from on high to the world's states, as opposed to a political process in which they participated. This has its obvious advantages: speed and avoidance of the necessity of gaining the consent of parliaments in countries whose ratification procedure requires legislative approval. One such country, of course, is the United States, whose Senate has been notoriously slow and recalcitrant in giving advice and consent to treaty ratification. The Senate certainly would have taken this attitude with respect to the convention on suppression of financing of terrorism prior to the September 2001 attacks because of its intrusion into the workings of financial institutions.

Disadvantages are not as obvious but are potentially consequential. One is the foregoing of the deliberate consideration of issues that would accompany negotiation of a treaty, in this case, for example, privacy issues relating to transparency of financial transactions, and refugee rights in relation to border controls. Another is the lack of in-depth consent from each country's political institutions, which may result in a lack of commitment to implementation. A third is the lack of democracy in international policy-making, bolstering the already pervasive resentment of the Security Council and the United States and other powerful countries, resentment which in turn can impede international cooperation in achieving worthwhile goals across a range of issues.

The use of the Security Council as a law-making institution demands careful scrutiny. The five permanent members of the Security Council hold veto power over all Security Council decisions. When the UN Charter was written, China, France, the Soviet Union, the United Kingdom and the United States were named as the permanent members, and in more than five decades, despite insistent demands for reform, the veto power has not been modified, nor have any other states been given comparable status.

That means that major countries are frozen out of decision making on matters of international peace and security, notably India, the world's second largest country, but also many others from both the developed and developing world. Because the Security Council fails to adequately represent the worlds' states and people, its use to create global law is problematic. The Council's lack of representativeness may make law it enacts less efficacious than law created through a widely subscribed to multilateral treaty.

It may be that Resolution 1373 will turn out to be an exceptional case. With respect to terrorism, post-September 11, the United States has shown itself to be ready to make use of the more traditional law-making technique of multilateral treaties. After the attacks, the Bush administration submitted the treaty on suppression of terrorist financing to the Senate for its advice and consent to ratification, along with a treaty on terrorist bombing. The Senate approved both treaties, and President Bush ratified them on June 26, 2002. The United States is now party to all 12 existing global treaties relating to terrorism. For the most part, these treaties concern specific proscribed acts like hijacking of aircraft, violent acts in airports, violent acts on ships, taking of hostages, and attacks on diplomats. They require states to enact legislation enabling prosecution of persons committing the acts, and to either prosecute suspects or extradite them to states with jurisdiction who so request. Additionally, the United States has participated in negotiations for the creation of a convention on nuclear terrorism and, in the most recent round of negotiations, on a comprehensive convention on terrorism that would apply to all terrorist acts.

RECURRENT THEMES OF U.S. TREATY POLICY

Looking from the history of the past century to the current state of U.S. behavior, it is clear that "[e]ight decades after the great debate of the League [of Nations], Americans still have not resolved their differences over the effect on national sovereignty of participation in international arrangements."[55] The original ideas of isolationists have evolved with the recognition that the United States must be a global leader. However, the fear of entrance into multilateral legal institutions whenever they might actually limit the United States in any significant way has not subsided. There is a strong and influential segment of U.S. policymakers that believes that the United States should rely mainly on its own strength rather than treaties to protect its interests and its sovereignty. This trend has been more pronounced since the Bush administration came to office. One supporter of this view, Charles Krauthammer, proclaimed: "This decade-long folly—a foreign policy of norms rather than of national interest—is over."[56]

U.S. resistance to a law-governed multilateralism is manifested in its disregard of obligations imposed by treaties it has ratified, and also by a pattern of shaping treaties during negotiations only to later reject them. These trends are described briefly below; then the following chapters examine U.S. policies with respect to specific security-related treaties.

DISREGARD OF OBLIGATIONS AFTER RATIFICATION

The United States has adopted a comply-when-expedient policy in dealing with many of its treaty obligations. For instance, the Nuclear Nonproliferation Treaty obligates the United States to "pursue negotiations in good faith on effective measures relating to cessation of the nuclear arms race at an early date and to nuclear disarmament," but the United States has not integrated this disarmament obligation into its national nuclear policy. Instead the January 2002 Nuclear Posture Review plans for the maintenance of large and modernized nuclear forces for the indefinite future. Despite its own disregard of its disarmament obligations under the NPT, the United States has taken on the role of confronting certain countries that are or may be in violation of their NPT obligations.

As a party to the Chemical Weapons Convention, the United States is obligated to meet reporting and inspection requirements, but Congress passed legislation that restricts U.S. compliance. The Biological Weapons Convention prohibits the United States from manufacturing bio-weapons, but in the late 1990s, the United States built a test bomb and weaponized anthrax. These activities, which would certainly be viewed as non-compliant if done by a different country, were performed in secret. As a party to the United Nations Framework Convention on Climate Change, the United States is obligated to take "precautionary measures to anticipate, prevent or minimize the causes of climate change." However, the Bush administration's policy on decreasing emissions is largely unenforceable and will not likely reduce emissions below predicted levels. And in a swift departure from a thirty-year security regime with Russia, the United States withdrew from the Russian-U.S. Anti-Ballistic Missile Treaty. The majority of world opinion, including that among U.S. allies, was that this was an ill-considered step that would, on balance, harm global security.

U.S. ROLE IN SHAPING THE TERMS OF AGREEMENTS ONLY TO REJECT THEM

Another recent trend in U.S. treaty policy is its participation in the negotiations and shaping of multilateral treaties only to refuse to sign or ratify them when they are completed. In recent years, the United States negotiated but did not join a number of significant and widely popular security-related treaties.

In negotiations for the ICC, the U.S. vigorously pushed for a variety of proposals. Some were successful, like those regarding due process protections, and some were not, like the attempt to secure a larger role for the Security Council. President Clinton signed the ICC Statute, but Clinton did not recommend its ratification until states parties further compromised on issues of "concern" to the U.S. The Bush administration notified the UN that it will not seek ratification of the treaty. The U.S. negotiated and signed the CTBT and the Kyoto Protocol, and played a central role in shaping their provisions. Yet, first the Senate and now the Bush Administration oppose their ratification. As for the BWC Protocol, which was intended to strengthen the Biological Weapons Convention, the United States endorsed the Protocol's framework, negotiated and achieved compromises to protect its perceived interests, and then rejected the draft before it was even finalized, killing the chances of its completion.

2

THE NUCLEAR NONPROLIFERATION TREATY

The Nuclear Nonproliferation Treaty (NPT) is second only to the United Nations Charter in the number of states parties. One hundred and eighty-seven states are parties; the only non-parties are India, Pakistan, Israel, and Cuba. It is also the only security agreement that permits two classes of members: states acknowledged to possess nuclear weapons and committed to negotiate their elimination, and states barred from acquiring them. The NPT was signed in 1968 and entered into force in 1970. Its initial duration was 25 years. In 1995 it was extended indefinitely.

ORIGINS

In 1961, the UN General Assembly unanimously adopted an Ireland-sponsored resolution which stated that "an increase in the number of States possessing nuclear weapons is growing more imminent" and called on all states to "secure the conclusion of an international agreement" to prevent that development.[57] In the summer of 1965, the United States and the Soviet Union introduced draft treaties in the Eighteen Nation Disarmament Committee (ENDC) in Geneva, the predecessor to today's Conference on Disarmament. The drafts simply prohibited the acquisition of nuclear weapons by and transfer of such weapons to non-possessing states. That fall, going far beyond the United States and Soviet proposals, a resolution adopted by the General Assembly formulated the principles on which the treaty should be based.[58] Sponsored by Brazil, Burma, Ethiopia, India, Mexico, Nigeria, Sweden, and the United Arab Republic (Egypt), it was adopted by a vote of 93 to zero, with five abstentions.[59] The resolution called upon the ENDC to negotiate a treaty "based on the following main principles:"

    a. The treaty should be void of any loop-holes which might permit nuclear or non-nuclear Powers to proliferate, directly or indirectly, nuclear weapons in any form;

    b. The treaty should embody an acceptable balance of mutual responsibilities and obligations of the nuclear and non-nuclear Powers;

    c. The treaty should be a step toward the achievement of general and complete disarmament and, more particularly, nuclear disarmament;

    d. There should be acceptable and workable provisions to ensure the effectiveness of the treaty;

    e. Nothing in the treaty should adversely affect the right of any group of States to conclude regional treaties in order to ensure the total absence of nuclear weapons in their respective territories (GA Res. 1965).

As negotiations proceeded, in accordance with these principles, two fundamental provisions were added to the non-acquisition and non-transfer provisions proposed by the United States and the Soviet Union. Reflecting principles (b) and (c), one was a pledge to negotiate nuclear disarmament set forth in Article VI. It requires each NPT state party to "pursue negotiations in good faith on effective measures relating to cessation of the nuclear arms race at an early date and to nuclear disarmament, and on a treaty on general and complete disarmament under strict and effective international control." Reflecting principle (b), the second provision, contained in Article IV, was a promise of assistance to non-nuclear weapon states with research, production and use of nuclear energy for peaceful purposes. The prohibitions on acquisition and transfer of nuclear weapons are set forth in Articles I and II. In Article III, non-nuclear weapon states also agreed to accept "safeguards" against the diversion of nuclear materials to weapons under the auspices of the International Atomic Energy Agency (IAEA). The safeguards do not apply to the nuclear weapon states. Article IX defines a nuclear weapon state as one which had manufactured and exploded a nuclear weapon or other nuclear explosive device prior to January 1, 1967, that is, the United States, the Soviet Union (and its successor state, Russia), the United Kingdom, France and China. The first three were parties to the NPT at its inception; France and China did not join the regime until two decades later. When they did, the set of five nuclear weapon states parties to the NPT became the same as the set of permanent members of the Security Council, the victors in World War II.

Article X allows states to withdraw from the treaty upon three months notice to states parties and the Security Council of "extraordinary events" related to the treaty that the withdrawing state decides have jeopardized its "supreme interests."

For non-nuclear weapon states, there were three main perceived benefits to entering into the NPT. One was to enhance security by preventing the further spread of nuclear weapons, including in the region of concern to a given state. This has remained fundamental to most states, and accounts for the continuing strong support for the NPT by countries bitterly disappointed by the lack of compliance with the disarmament obligation. A second benefit for many was the promise of assistance with the development of nuclear power. The third was the nuclear weapon states' promise to engage in good faith negotiations on nuclear disarmament.

At the time the treaty was negotiated, the second advantage relating to nuclear power loomed large. Non-nuclear weapon states wanted to prevent the obligation of non-acquisition of nuclear weapons and accompanying IAEA safeguards from impeding development of nuclear power. They also saw the Article IV promise as balancing their non-acquisition obligation. As Mohamed I. Shaker explains in his three-volume study of the NPT:

> Fears were expressed by the [non-nuclear weapon] States that the NPT, by instituting such a control on their peaceful nuclear activities in order to prevent the proliferation of nuclear weapons, would hamper their full access to the knowledge and technology of the peaceful atom most needed for their future progress and prosperity; that international inspection might turn into industrial espionage; and that the Treaty would place them at the mercy of the nuclear-weapon States which would continue to enjoy their privileged position as the major suppliers of nuclear fuel and necessary equipment.
>
> Freedom to exploit the atom for peaceful purposes to the benefit of the non-nuclear-weapon States was considered by the latter as the most tangible counterparts to their renunciation to acquire nuclear weapons.[60]

Extravagant rhetoric prevailed, reflected in Article IV itself, which refers to an "inalienable right" to develop nuclear energy for peaceful uses. One analyst writing from the perspective of the developing world claimed that "the problem of human dignity is increasingly becoming one of maximizing participation in the nuclear age."[61] This view was not restricted to developing countries. The Italian representative to the ENDC saw Article

IV as codifying a new human right,[62] and Willy Brandt, foreign minister for West Germany, stated that West Germany would not accept anything that hindered the peaceful use of nuclear energy, as its future as an industrial state depended on this principle.[63] Continuing the U.S. "Atoms for Peace" initiative of the 1950s that had led to the formation of the IAEA, a paradox was built into the NPT at its inception: It promotes nuclear power programs which in turn provide a foundation of nuclear materials and expertise for any state wishing to acquire nuclear weapons.

The disarmament obligation has been the primary focus of NPT review conferences held every five years. This chapter is mostly devoted to explaining how understanding of the nature and content of that obligation has evolved and to assessing the current state of compliance. The negotiating history of Article VI is illuminating. The United States and the Soviet Union preferred to make no linkages to nuclear disarmament other than in the treaty's preambular provisions. Non-nuclear weapon possessing countries, on the other hand, sought such linkages. In 1965, Sweden and India advocated a "package" solution linking an agreement on non-proliferation with a variety of measures, including security assurances against the use of nuclear weapons, a freeze on the production of nuclear weapons, a comprehensive test ban and a cutoff of production of fissile materials for nuclear weapons.[64] Later, India proposed an article prohibiting the manufacture of nuclear weapons, and also suggested an article affirming that nuclear weapon states would "undertake" nuclear disarmament measures.[65] Many countries sought a guarantee of non-use of nuclear weapons against states that had agreed not to acquire such weapons based on the need for balance in treaty obligations.[66] The United States opposed this proposal due to military resistance to limiting U.S. options.[67] As a compromise approach, Mexico proposed an obligation "to pursue negotiations in good faith" on agreements on a test ban, cessation of manufacture of nuclear weapons, and elimination of nuclear weapons and the means of their delivery.[68] Brazil made a similar proposal.[69] In the end, the United States and the Soviet Union would accept only an obligation of good-faith negotiation on cessation of the nuclear arms race and nuclear disarmament without reference to any specific measures.

The history makes clear, as Shaker remarks, that it "was generally felt that negotiating was not an aim in itself but a means to achieve concrete results at the earliest possible date."[70] The insistence upon the disarmament obligation was tied to the perception of the need for balance in treaty obligations, as stated in principle (b) of the 1965 General Assembly resolution. Shaker elaborates that the Article VI responsibility of the nuclear weapon states "was looked upon by the non-nuclear-weapon States not only in the context of achieving a more secure world but as a quid pro quo for the latter's renunciation of nuclear weapons."[71] A statement by Brazil's representative is illustrative: "It seems to us imperative that the obligations imposed on the non-nuclear nations should be met on the other side by significant commitments related to the subject matter of the treaty."[72] While particular measures were not included within Article VI, they remained prominent in the international disarmament agenda. The NPT preamble refers to a comprehensive test ban and to "the cessation of the manufacture of nuclear weapons, the liquidation of all their existing stockpiles, and the elimination from national arsenals of nuclear weapons and the means of their delivery." And significantly, at the first session of the ENDC after the NPT was opened for signature on July 1, 1968, the United States and the Soviet Union proposed an agenda under a heading taken from Article VI and including measures that had been proposed for inclusion within Article VI:

> 1. Further effective measures relating to the cessation of the nuclear arms race at an early date and to nuclear disarmament. Under this heading members may wish to discuss measures dealing with the cessation of testing, the non-use of nuclear weapons, the cessation of production of fissionable materials for weapons use, the cessation of manufacture of weapons and reduction and subsequent elimination of nuclear stockpiles, nuclear-free zones, etc.[73]

Also, on June 19, 1968, a week after the General Assembly approved the NPT, the Security Council adopted Resolution 255 setting forth what has come to be known as a positive security assurance. It "recognizes" that in the event of aggressive threat or use of nuclear weapons, the Council and its permanent members "would have to act immediately in accordance with their obligations under the [UN] Charter" - that is, the Council would have to act, possibly through military means, to restore international peace and security. The resolution also welcomed the intention announced by the United States, Britain and the Soviet Union to "provide or support immediate assistance" in such a situation. Subsequently, in 1978, the United States, Britain and the Soviet Union made declarations of negative security assurances, that is, policies of non-use of nuclear weapons against states complying with the NPT non-acquisition obligation, subject to certain exceptions. The U.S. declaration stated:

> The United States will not use nuclear weapons against any non-nuclear-weapons state party to the NPT or any comparable internationally binding commitment not to acquire nuclear explosive devices, except in the case of an attack on the United States, its territories or armed forces, or its allies, by such state allied to a nuclear-weapon state or associated with a nuclear-weapons state in carrying out or sustaining the attack.[74]

In 1995, the United States, Britain, and Russia again made similar declarations, this time joined by France and China.[75] Security Council Resolution 984, adopted April 11, 1995, referred to the declarations and also positive security assurances similar to that made in 1986.

None of this was enough for India, which refused to join the NPT due to the vagueness of the disarmament promise and the lack of legally binding negative security assurances.[76] Ironically, apprehension that India would go nuclear following China's 1964 test was a major reason the United States promoted negotiation of the NPT. The overt nuclearization of India and then Pakistan in the late 1990s, signaled by their nuclear explosive tests in 1998, highlighted the failure of the NPT nuclear weapon states over the decades since the NPT entered into force in 1970 to fulfill their disarmament promise. Indeed, the specific measures highlighted in NPT negotiations and placed on the ENDC agenda have for the most part not been achieved even today. This in turn over the years made it far more difficult to persuade India to make good on its longstanding anti-nuclear rhetoric, which in fact was accompanied by considerable restraint in its weapons program. Another non-NPT state, Israel, also has an operational nuclear arsenal, which has caused great tension about the NPT among other states in the Middle East bound by its non-acquisition obligation. The fourth state outside the NPT, Cuba, is not alleged to be seeking nuclear weapons, and has announced it will join the treaty.

RECENT DEVELOPMENTS

Until the 1995 Review and Extension Conference, the declared nuclear powers steadfastly overlooked the fact that the treaty commits them to eliminate their weapons. Selective reading permitted the focus to remain on proliferation rather than disarmament. In 1995, however, in order to obtain the indefinite extension of the treaty, the nuclear powers, in the "Principles and Objectives for Nuclear Non-Proliferation and Disarmament," committed to negotiation of a Comprehensive Test Ban Treaty by 1996, "immediate commencement and early conclusion of negotiation" of a ban on production of fissile materials for nuclear weapons use, and "the determined pursuit by the nuclear-weapon States of systematic and progressive efforts to reduce nuclear weapons globally, with the ultimate goals of eliminating those weapons, and by all States of general and complete disarmament under strict and effective international control." Article VI remains the bedrock legal obligation, as it is set forth in a treaty accepted through constitutional processes by the states parties. However, the "Principles and Objectives" are political commitments by the nuclear weapon states that have added weight given that they are tied to a binding legal decision to extend the treaty indefinitely pursuant to its terms.

Two major developments marked 1996. Based on a text negotiated in the Conference on Disarmament in Geneva, the General Assembly adopted the Comprehensive Test Ban Treaty, and it was opened for signature. Also, the International Court of Justice, the judicial branch of the United Nations, issued an advisory opinion on the legality of threat or use of nuclear weapons requested by the General Assembly.[77]

The ICJ explained that under humanitarian law, states must "never use weapons that are incapable of distinguishing between civilian and military targets,"[78] and held that the threat or use of nuclear weapons was "generally" contrary to international law.[79] While a divided Court was unable to reach a definitive conclusion regarding threat or use in an extreme circumstance of self-defense in which the very survival of a state is at risk, the overall thrust of the opinion was toward categorical illegality. A National Academy of Sciences study, carried out by persons well-versed in the realities of nuclear weapons and deterrence doctrines, found it "extremely unlikely" that any threat or use would meet criteria of lawfulness set forth by the Court.[80] While the ICJ did not definitively find every conceivable threat or use of nuclear weapons to be unlawful, the opinion strongly implies the illegality of the main doctrines of deterrence.[81]

In addition and unexpectedly, the Court, itself not satisfied with its response to the General Assembly, unanimously provided an interpretation of Article VI of the NPT, holding that it requires states "to pursue in good faith and *bring to a conclusion* negotiations leading to nuclear disarmament *in all its aspects* under strict and effective international control" (emphasis added).[82] While not expressly stated, the Court's reasoning makes it clear that this obligation draws on sources other than the NPT and therefore applies to those few states outside the NPT, including the nuclear weapon possessing states of India, Pakistan, and Israel.[83]

By the April 2000 NPT Review Conference, the disarmament record was bleak aside from the conclusion of CTBT negotiations in 1996 and ongoing implementation of the 1994 START I treaty reducing U.S. and Russian strategic nuclear arms. India and Pakistan had tested in 1998, and the U.S. Senate declined to approve ratification of the CTBT in the fall of 1999. Negotiations on a fissile materials treaty were stalled. A critical sticking point was the insistence of some countries that the negotiations address reduction of existing stocks as well as a cap on new production. Also, China and other countries resisted such negotiations absent commitments on other fronts to pursue nuclear disarmament comprehensively and to prevent an arms race in outer space. The United States eventually conceded that it would permit discussions on the latter two topics, but not negotiations. This was rejected as inadequate. Underlying the stalemate was the U.S. drive for missile defense. It pressured China to retain the option to produce more fissile materials for any arsenal buildup desired to maintain a second-strike option against a combined U.S. preemptive attack and missile shield.

At the 2000 review conference, the New Agenda group of Brazil, Ireland, Mexico, New Zealand, South Africa, and Sweden took the lead in seeking to reverse the negative developments and to press for disarmament commitments.[84] The group was formed in 1998, declaring the "need for a new agenda" for a nuclear-weapon-free world (New Agenda Declaration 1998). In 1998 and 1999 it sponsored General Assembly resolutions laying out disarmament measures and calling for the nuclear powers "to demonstrate an unequivocal commitment to the speedy and total elimination of their respective nuclear weapons and without delay to pursue in good faith and bring to a conclusion negotiations leading to the elimination of these weapons, thereby fulfilling their obligations under Article VI" (GA Res. 1998; GA Res. 1999). The New Agenda group's influence was demonstrated at the outset of the 2000 review conference by a joint statement by the five nuclear powers, a first for the NPT. "We remain unequivocally committed to fulfilling all of our obligations under the treaty," the five wrote, "None of our nuclear weapons are targeted at any state" (Statement of Permanent 5 2000). The word "unequivocally" was a nod to the New Agenda's drive to get the nuclear powers to "make an unequivocal undertaking to accomplish the total elimination of their nuclear arsenals and . . . to engage in an accelerated process of negotiations." (New Agenda Working Paper 2000).

The New Agenda group was not satisfied with the nuclear powers' statement and demanded commitments not only to the elimination of nuclear arsenals but also to a range of disarmament measures. By the end of the conference, the New Agenda group and the nuclear weapon states were engaged in separate negotiations that formed the basis for the outcome. This development was most clearly demonstrated in the central passage of the Final Document on 13 "practical steps for the systematic and progressive efforts" to achieve nuclear disarmament.[85] While many states had their preferred language for these measures, the steps as agreed reflected New Agenda demands. A key element was "an unequivocal undertaking by the nuclear-weapon states to accomplish the total elimination of their nuclear arsenals leading to nuclear disarmament, to which all states parties are committed under Article VI" (step 6). That provision reportedly was a *sine qua non* for the New Agenda group. Other steps restated existing commitments, such as support for a nuclear test ban, and included measures favored by the New Agenda group but framed in language that left some room for maneuvering by the five NPT nuclear weapon states. They include:

- early entry into force of the Comprehensive Test Ban Treaty (CTBT) and a moratorium on nuclear-weapons-test explosions pending its entry into force (steps 1 and 2);

- "the necessity of negotiations" on a treaty banning the production of fissile material for nuclear weapons, and agreement on a program of work in the Conference on Disarmament "which includes the immediate commencement of negotiations on such a treaty with a view to their conclusion within five years" (3);

- "the necessity of establishing in the Conference on Disarmament an appropriate subsidiary body with a mandate to deal with nuclear disarmament" (4);

- "the principle of irreversibility to apply to nuclear disarmament" (5);

- "early entry into force and full implementation of START II and the conclusion of START III as soon as possible while preserving and strengthening the ABM Treaty as a cornerstone of strategic stability and as a basis of further reductions of strategic offensive weapons" (7);

- "further efforts by the nuclear-weapon States to reduce their nuclear arsenals unilaterally"(9a);

- "increased transparency by the nuclear-weapon States with regard to their nuclear weapons capabilities" (9b);

- "further reduction of non-strategic nuclear weapons" (9c);

- "concrete agreed measures to further reduce the operational status of nuclear weapons systems" (9d);

- "a diminishing role for nuclear weapons in security policies to minimize the risk that these weapons ever be used and to facilitate the process of their total elimination" (9e);

- "the engagement as soon as appropriate of all the nuclear-weapon States in the process leading to the total elimination of their nuclear weapons" (9f);

- "arrangements by all nuclear-weapon States to place, as soon as practicable, fissile materials designated by each of them as no longer required for military purposes under IAEA or other relevant international verification and arrangements for the disposition of such material for peaceful purposes" (10);

- and "the further development of the verification capabilities that will be required to provide assurance of compliance with nuclear disarmament agreements for the achievement and maintenance of a nuclear-weapon-free world" (13).

These commitments are widely understood to be "political" rather than "legal" in nature. However, given that the agenda was adopted without objection by the Review Conference, it represents all NPT states' view of what Article VI requires as of the year 2000. Further, the "unequivocal undertaking" to eliminate nuclear arsenals clarifies the meaning of Article VI, adding to and reinforcing the ICJ's authoritative interpretation. New Agenda representatives called the Final Document "a significant landmark" and Canadian Senator Douglas Roche, Chair of the Middle Powers Initiative, an international civil society coalition, wrote that "a new moment in nuclear disarmament has occurred."[86] However, speaking to journalists immediately after the document was adopted, U.S. Ambassador Robert Grey said that the undertaking "will have no more impact than it's had in the past . . . It's more of the same."[87]

The NPT outcome was strongly endorsed in the fall of 2000 by the General Assembly in a New Agenda resolution that incorporated the 13 disarmament steps and went further in "affirm[ing] that a nuclear-weapon-free world will ultimately require the underpinnings of a universal and multilaterally negotiated legally binding instrument or a frame-work encompassing a mutually reinforcing set of instruments."[88] In explaining its vote for the resolution, the United States said that the 2000 NPT Final Document "is our guiding light for nuclear non-proliferation and disarmament efforts."[89]

ASSESSMENT OF COMPLIANCE WITH NPT NONPROLIFERATION AND DISARMAMENT OBLIGATIONS

Since 1970, the record of states' compliance with the NPT obligation not to acquire nuclear weapons is reasonably good. It is widely agreed that virtually all NPT non-nuclear weapon states have met the non-acquisition obligation. Iraq and North Korea are two exceptions. In the case of Iraq, its nuclear weapons program was discovered in the wake of the Gulf War when intensive inspections, backed by harsh sanctions, were instituted under Security Council resolutions.[90] The Security Council mandated that Iraq end its nuclear, chemical, and biological weapons programs and prove such termination to the satisfaction of international inspectors. Inspections by the body (not the IAEA) established by the Security Council were suspended in November 1998; negotiations are currently underway regarding their resumption.[91] Since 1998, the IAEA has verified that safeguards on Iraq's declared nuclear facilities are functioning; how-ever, the IAEA emphasizes that this does not demonstrate compliance with the Security Council mandate.[92] Allegations persist that Iraq has resumed its nuclear weapons program.[93] North Korea appears to have had a nuclear weapons program in the early 1990s, and failed to permit IAEA inspections as required under its safeguards agreement. It has still not per-mitted full IAEA inspections,[94] and in October 2002 admitted to an exist-ing program to develop nuclear weapons. The United States has also alleged that Iran has a nuclear weapons program, though the IAEA has declared Iran to be in compliance with its safeguard agreement.[95]

There has also been progress toward making the NPT universal, an objec-tive repeatedly referred to in review conference documents over the decades since 1970. South Africa relinquished its small nuclear arsenal and joined the NPT as a non-nuclear weapon state; Brazil and Argentina, both of which had nuclear weapons programs, did likewise; and former Soviet republics including Ukraine and Kazakhstan turned nuclear weapons on their territory over to Russia and joined the NPT as non-nuclear weapon states. However, the aim of including India, Pakistan, and Israel as non-nuclear weapon state parties has not been achieved, nor has there been any movement in that direction. It seems highly unlikely that India, and therefore Pakistan, would join the NPT or a subsequent regime absent a demonstrated practical process to achieve nuclear disarmament involving the five NPT nuclear powers. The prospects for Israel's joining the NPT as a non-nuclear weapon state seem dependent at least on achievement of a permanent peace settlement in the Middle East.

As for compliance with the Article VI disarmament obligation, in general there has been little progress since the Intermediate Nuclear Forces and Strategic Arms Reduction Treaties (START) agreements negotiated in the administrations of Ronald Reagan and the senior George Bush and that of Gorbachev as well as the 1991 Bush-Gorbachev parallel unilateral withdrawals of tactical nuclear weapons. France and Britain have trimmed back their arsenals. CTBT negotiations were concluded in 1996, and there has been no testing by a NPT-nuclear weapon state since 1996. At present, the CTBT has no prospect of entering into force due to opposition to ratification in the U.S. Senate and the Bush administration as well as the fact that India, Pakistan, and North Korea have yet to sign the treaty (see Chapter 3). U.S. plans announced in the Nuclear Posture Review (NPR) released in early 2002 and the May 2002 US-Russian Strategic Offensive Reductions Treaty signal that there will be reductions in deployed strategic nuclear arms by the United States and Russia. For reasons explained below, the reductions fail to meet criteria set forth by the 2000 Review Conference in significant respects. The NPR also expanded rather than contracted options for use of nuclear weapons against non-nuclear weapon states, a move condemned by the New York Times in an editorial entitled "America as Nuclear Rogue."[96] A more detailed analysis follows, with reference to the steps contained in the consensus 2000 final document.

US-RUSSIAN STRATEGIC ARMS REDUCTIONS

In the Nuclear Posture Review, the United States announced that it will reduce "operational" strategic deployed nuclear weapons to 3800 by 2007, and to 1700-2200 by 2012. Reflecting the U.S. plan, the short and starkly simple Strategic Offensive Reductions Treaty, signed on May 24, 2002 in Moscow (Moscow Treaty), requires the United States and Russia to limit "strategic nuclear warheads" to 1700-2200 by the year 2012.[97] The treaty will expire that same year unless it is renewed. It also is subject to termination on three months notice, based only on the exercise of "national sovereignty;" the typical nuclear weapons treaty provision for withdrawal in case of "extraordinary events" jeopardizing a state's "supreme interests" has been dropped.

The U.S.-Russian agreement and the two states' announced plans are positive at least in the sense that they advance the reduction process, which paradoxically has been stalemated since the Soviet Union disintegrated. But a force of about 2000 strategic nuclear arms for each side to be reached 10 years hence leaves in place the capability of destroying the entire opposing society, and indeed ending life on this planet as we know it. Beyond that fundamental point, there are several serious and interrelated ways in which the reductions fall short of what is envisaged by the NPT 13 steps.

First, the U.S. plan in general does not call for destruction of delivery systems or dismantlement of warheads, nor are these measures required by the Moscow Treaty. According to an analysis of the Nuclear Posture Review by the Natural Resources Defense Council, 50 MX missiles are to be deactivated, but their silos will be retained, as will missile stages and the warheads.[98] Four of 18 U.S. Trident submarines will be withdrawn from the strategic nuclear force, but will then be converted to carry conventional cruise missiles.[99] Beyond these measures, no additional strategic delivery platforms are scheduled to be eliminated from nuclear forces.[100] In contrast, START I requires, and START II would have required, the destruction of delivery systems, and the 1997 Helsinki commitment to START III additionally envisaged accounting for and dismantling of warheads. In addition, according to NRDC, the United States is planning "for a new ICBM [land-based intercontinental missile] to be operational in 2020, a new SLBM [submarine-launched ballistic missile] and SSBN [nuclear-armed submarine] in 2030, and a new heavy bomber in 2040, as well as new warheads for all of them."[101]

Second, beyond the operational deployed strategic forces, the United States plans to retain large numbers of warheads in a "responsive force" capable of redeployment within weeks or months. The Moscow Treaty does not prevent such storage. NRDC estimates that at the level of 1700 to 2200 operationally deployed strategic warheads to be reached in ten years, there would be an additional 1350 strategic warheads in the responsive force, as well as scores of "spares."[102] This approach is justified on the basis of a need for "flexibility."[103] It is contrary to the principle of irreversible disarmament included in the NPT 13 steps.

Third, the United States has made no indication that it plans to reduce the readiness level of the operationally deployed strategic arms. Today, both the United States and Russia each have about 2,000 warheads on high alert, ready for delivery within minutes of an order to do so. Projecting present practices forward, it has been estimated that at the 2012 level of 1700 – 2200 operationally deployed warheads, the United States would have about 900 on high alert.[104] One could see this as a sort of slow-motion de-alerting process, all the more so given that the "responsive force" planned by the United States essentially is in a de-alerted status. But there is no reason the reductions in operationally deployed forces have to be spread out over so many years. Nor should they be maintained in a high alert status whatever their numbers. The NPT commitments to "concrete agreed measures to further reduce the operational status of nuclear weapons systems" and "a diminishing role for nuclear weapons in security policies" should be applied to deployed as well as reduced warheads.

Fourth, the extent to which reductions will be transparent and verified remains to be determined. A non-binding Joint Declaration setting forth political commitments signed in connection with the Moscow Treaty states that START I provisions "will provide the foundation for providing confidence, transparency, and predictability in further strategic offensive reductions, along with other supplementary measures, including transparency measures, to be agreed."[105] Transparency issues (the term verification is nowhere mentioned in the treaty or declaration) may be dealt with in a consultative group established by the declaration, an implementation commission established by the treaty, or START I consultative bodies. Russia and the United States do not even have a common understanding of the meaning of the phrase "strategic nuclear warheads" used in the treaty. Further, it is unclear how transparency or verification will be achieved absent destruction of delivery systems or dismantlement of warheads. Destruction of delivery systems is the primary method of verification under START I.

Fifth, under START II, negotiations of which were completed but which has not entered into force, multiple warhead land-based missiles would have been banned. In contrast, the May 2002 US-Russian agreement places no limits on multiple warhead missiles or on any category whatever, providing instead that each party "shall determine for itself the composition and structure of its strategic offensive arms." That omission may prove to be destabilizing, especially in the context of the U.S. drive to develop and deploy missile defenses which may cause Russia to retain existing deployed multiple warhead missiles and to deploy new ones.[106] Such deployment in turn would push each state to continue to maintain its strategic forces on hair-trigger alert with the consequent risk of nuclear war by miscalculation.

Sixth, the rate of reduction is slower than under the START process. The U.S. plan anticipates 3800 deployed strategic arms by 2007, whereas START II would have reduced the number to 3000-3500 deployed strategic arms by 2007. The 1997 Helsinki commitment to START III anticipated reductions to 2000-2500 strategic warheads by 2007. A change in the counting formula (the Bush administration does not include warheads on submarines being overhauled, about 250 at any time, among "deployed" strategic warheads) makes the Helsinki numbers and the 1700-2200 range set by the Nuclear Posture Review and the May 2002 treaty roughly equivalent. Thus the new schedule of reduction to 1700-2200 deployed strategic warheads by 2012 pushes back the Helsinki target date by five years.

DIMINISHING ROLE FOR NUCLEAR WEAPONS IN SECURITY POLICIES

In the post-Cold War years the two largest nuclear powers, the United States and Russia, have integrated nuclear forces into their military strategies and expanded their role.

In 1993, Russia abandoned its policy of renouncing the first use of nuclear weapons, and its January 2000 Security Concept stated that nuclear weapons could be used to "repulse armed aggression, if all other means of resolving the crisis have been exhausted."[107] Since the 2000 Review Conference, Russia has made no moves to reverse or limit its reliance on a first use option.

The 2002 U.S. Nuclear Posture Review states that nuclear weapons will be "integrated with new non-nuclear strategic capabilities" including advanced conventional precision-guided munitions. The Nuclear Posture Review also enlarges the range of circumstances under which nuclear weapons could be used.[108] Classified portions obtained by the Los Angeles Times and the New York Times call for contingency planning for use of nuclear weapons against Russia, China, North Korea, Iraq, Iran, Syria, and Libya; identify possible "immediate contingencies" requiring U.S. nuclear use as "an Iraqi attack on Israel or its neighbors, a North Korean attack on South Korea, or a military confrontation over the status of Taiwan;" and indicate that nuclear weapons "could be employed against targets able to withstand non-nuclear attack," or in retaliation for use of nuclear, biological, or chemical weapons, or "in the event of surprising military developments."[109] The NPR options for use of nuclear weapons have not, so far as is known, been codified in a presidential directive (the last publicly known directive was that of President Clinton in 1998), and top U.S. officials have sought to downplay their significance. However, the NPR was signed by Secretary of Defense Rumsfeld, and certainly indicates at the very least a strong trend in U.S. nuclear planning. Thus, far from diminishing the role of nuclear weapons in security policies, as called for by the 2000 NPT 13 steps, the United States has expanded options for nuclear use.

The United States continues to plan for a massive retaliation or preemptive counterforce attack in response to an actual or imminent nuclear attack, and for first use of nuclear weapons against an overwhelming conventional attack. In the past, the United States had indicated that nuclear weapons could be used in retaliation to a chemical or biological weapons attack. Now that option has been stated plainly. But in addition, the United States has identified a circumstance for a preemptive first use of nuclear weapons against targets like underground bunkers containing command and control facilities or stocks of biological and chemical weapons.[110] This scenario had been referred to in previous military planning documents, but not in a document as authoritative as the Nuclear Posture Review. The new, catch-all category of "surprising military developments" could cover first use of nuclear weapons in a wide range of circumstances.

In addition to violating the NPT commitment to diminishing the role of nuclear weapons in security policies, the U.S. plans undermine the negative security assurance offered by the United States to non-nuclear weapon states parties to the NPT. Those assurances are at a minimum political commitments essential to the bargain underlying the NPT, and arguably have become legally binding, notably because they were reiterated in connection with the indefinite extension of the NPT in 1995.[111] Use of nuclear weapons against any NPT-compliant state not acting in association with a nuclear weapon state would violate the assurances. Yet the Nuclear Posture Review identifies five non-nuclear weapon states parties to the NPT, Iraq, Iran, North Korea, Libya, and Syria, as potential targets. None of these states has been authoritatively and conclusively determined to be presently in violation of the NPT by the IAEA, NPT states parties acting collectively, or the Security Council. As noted above, the NPR also identifies circumstances for first use of nuclear weapons not in response to a prior use of a nuclear, biological or chemical weapon.

Regarding nuclear use in response to a chemical or biological attack, the United States has indicated that it could be justified as a "reprisal," that is, an otherwise unlawful act carried out to prevent further unlawful acts by the state using chemical or biological weapons in violation of international law.[112] However, the use of nuclear weapons, or any weapon, including in reprisal, must always meet fundamental requirements of necessity, proportionality, and discrimination. Thus the International Court of Justice affirmed that states must "*never* use weapons that are incapable of distinguishing between civilian and military targets" (emphasis added).[113] Given that the radioactive effects of nuclear explosions are, as the ICJ observed, uncontainable in space and time,[114] there are no realistic situations in which nuclear weapons could meet these requirements.[115] Moreover, regardless of whatever hypothetical scenarios of retaliatory nuclear use with limited "collateral damage" can be conjured up, in general making nuclear weapons more usable as a matter of policy and operation undermines the nonproliferation regime and risks unleashing nuclear chaos in the world that among other unacceptable consequences could result in nuclear explosions on U.S. soil. As the *New York Times* editorialized,

> Where the Pentagon review goes very wrong is in lowering the threshold for using nuclear weapons and in undermining the effectiveness of the Nuclear Non-Proliferation Treaty.... Nuclear weapons are not just another part of the military arsenal. They are different, and lowering the threshold for their use is reckless folly.[116]

U.S.-Russian Non-Strategic Arms Reductions

Step 9c of the 13 steps calls for "further reduction of non-strategic nuclear weapons, based on unilateral initiatives and as an integral part of the nuclear arms reduction and disarmament process." There has been no publicly reported progress in this regard since 2000. Indeed, the 1991 Bush-Gorbachev parallel unilateral withdrawals of non-strategic arms from deployment have yet to be subjected to the requirements of the "reduction and disarmament process," that is, the withdrawals are not transparent, they are not irreversible, they have not been verified, and they have not been codified in legally binding form. The 2002 U.S. Nuclear Posture Review contains plans for further development of earth-penetrating, low yield nuclear warheads that could be deployed on tactical systems.[117]

MISSILE DEFENSES

The NPT does not deal with anti-missile systems, as such. However, the 2000 Final Document, in step 7, called for "preserving and strengthening the ABM Treaty" and described it as a "cornerstone of strategic stability and as a basis for further reductions of strategic offensive weapons." Relatedly, step 9 states that the several measures it sets forth are to be taken "in a way that promotes international stability, and based on the principle of undiminished security for all." A premise then of the 13 steps is that the development and deployment of missile defenses must not obstruct the process of nuclear arms control and disarmament and the total elimination of nuclear arsenals and must be consistent with international stability and the principle of undiminished security for all.

U.S. policy regarding missile defenses runs counter to the thrust of the NPT 13 steps. The United States withdrew from the ABM Treaty, and continues to stress the role of missile defenses in its overall military strategy. According to the Nuclear Posture Review, missile defenses together with advanced offensive nuclear and conventional strategic forces and a "responsive defense infrastructure" capable of developing and producing nuclear weapons and resuming nuclear testing form a "new triad," replacing the triad of nuclear-armed land-based missiles, submarine-based missiles, and heavy bombers.[118] The NPR reportedly anticipates limited deployment of strategic missile defenses by 2008.[119] This in itself is contrary to the call for preserving that treaty. It was well known, however, that the ABM Treaty, at least in its existing form, was in jeopardy from the U.S. drive for missile defenses. What is now lacking is any clear U.S. commitment to ensuring that missile defenses do not obstruct disarmament. In 2000 the Clinton administration tacitly approved Russia's future maintenance of large, alerted nuclear forces to counteract deployment of limited U.S. missile defenses.[120] The May 2002 Joint Declaration seeks to assuage Russian concerns regarding missile defenses by providing for information exchange, study of possible areas for cooperation on defenses, *etc.* However, there is little evidence that the Bush administration is prepared to make concrete practical commitments to restrict missile defenses or to subject plans for missile defenses to transparency and negotiation. Such steps are needed to facilitate U.S.-Russian elimination of multiple warhead land-based missiles and other reductions beyond those agreed in May 2002; to enable de-alerting; and to avoid stimulating a further

Chinese build-up of its arsenal and a consequent arms race in Asia (see chapter on ABM Treaty).

NUCLEAR TESTING

Of the five NPT nuclear weapon states, the United States and China have yet to ratify the Comprehensive Test Ban Treaty. All five, including the United States, continue to affirm the moratorium. General John Gordon, the head of the National Nuclear Security Administration in the U.S. Department of Energy, testified to Congress that "nothing in the NPR" changes U.S. support for the moratorium, explaining that "[o]ver time, we believe that the stewardship program will provide the tools to ensure stockpile safety and reliability without nuclear testing."[121] Gen. Gordon stated further, though, that "there are no guarantees" and that the United States will "enhance" its "test readiness program."[122] The U.S. stance is contrary to the 2000 step calling for early entry into force of the CTBT, and only qualifiedly consistent with the commitment to a moratorium. The importance of achieving entry into force of the CTBT to the integrity and viability of the NPT must also be underlined. The CTBT is referred to in the NPT preamble, it was understood to be an essential element of the "cessation of the arms race" prong of Article VI, and a commitment to its negotiation was central to the 1995 extension decision.

Also significant is that the United States is making large investments in a modernized nuclear weapons maintenance, research and development infrastructure.[123] In its recent $5.9 billion request to the U.S. Congress for nuclear weapons activities (not including delivery systems) in fiscal year 2003, the Department of Energy relied on the NPR as its primary budget justification, stating that it

> reflects a broad recognition of the importance of a robust and responsive nuclear weapons infrastructure in sustaining deterrence and dissuasion. In this connection, ... the flexibility to sustain our enduring nuclear weapons stockpile, to adapt current weapons to new missions, or to field new weapons, if required, depends on a healthy program for stockpile stewardship ... as well as a robust infrastructure for nuclear weapons production.[124]

The nearly $6 billion proposed budget is well above the average of $4.2 billion (in 2002 dollars) for comparable activities during Cold War years.[125]

The NPR, according to Gen. Gordon, recognizes "the need to revitalize nuclear weapons advanced concepts activity," and the Energy Department

> has taken an initiative, endorsed by the NPR, to reestablish small advanced warhead concepts teams.... The teams will carry out theoretical and engineering design work on one or more concepts, including options to modify existing designs or develop new ones. In some instances, these activities would proceed beyond the 'paper' stage and include a combination of component and subassembly tests and simulations.[126]

The New York Times reported that the NPR "cites the need to improve 'earth-penetrating weapons' that could be used to destroy underground installations and hardened bunkers" and calls for such weapons both with lower yields to lessen nuclear fallout and larger yields to attack deeply buried targets.[127] Research was slated to begin in April 2002 on "fitting an existing nuclear warhead into a new 5,000-pound 'earth penetrating' munition."[128] Already in 1996, the United States deployed a nuclear weapon modified to achieve an earth-penetrating capability, the B-61-mod 11.[129]

U.S. plans for long-term maintenance and modernization of its nuclear weapons infrastructure and its nuclear arsenal are contrary to the spirit of the CTBT, the 2000 commitment to a diminishing role for nuclear weapons in security policies, and the undertaking to eliminate nuclear arsenals pursuant to Article VI. In particular, research and development of new or modified weapons runs counter to the Article VI obligation of good-faith negotiation on "cessation of the arms race at an early date." Indeed, according to a declaration by France, Russia, the United Kingdom and the United States made at the Conference on Disarmament in anticipation of the 1995 extension conference, "the nuclear arms race has ceased."[130]

FISSILE MATERIALS ACCOUNTING, CONTROL AND DISPOSITION

For reasons explained above, the 1995 commitment to commence formal negotiation of a fissile materials treaty has not been met. Except for China, the NPT nuclear weapon states "have implemented unilateral and/or negotiated transparency measures of varying degrees."[131] U.S. estimates of Russian military fissile materials holdings reportedly are accurate only within plus or minus 30 percent, equivalent to more than 20,000 warheads.[132] U.S.-Russian plans to place some "surplus" military fissile material holdings under IAEA monitoring are proceeding slowly. Fissile materials holdings as well as warhead inventories of the non-NPT nuclear weapon possessing states are opaque. The imperative of accounting for and controlling fissile materials, including non-military stocks of weapon-usable plutonium, as well as warheads, is now widely understood after the September 2001 terrorist attacks which raised the specter of terrorist use of nuclear explosive devices. Much more remains to be done in this area.

NUCLEAR DISARMAMENT IN GENERAL

There is no sign that the Article VI obligation as now understood in light of its authoritative interpretation by the ICJ and the 2000 unequivocal undertaking to eliminate nuclear arsenals have been integrated into national nuclear planning. Rather its invocation seems to remain a rhetorical flourish for international settings. Thus Gen. Gordon testified that the Nuclear Posture Review "reaffirms that nuclear weapons, for the foreseeable future, will remain a key element of U.S. national security strategy."[133] With the exception of China's longstanding position of no first use, there is no evidence of a diminishing role for nuclear weapons, or of an effort to comply with the ICJ holding that threat or use of nuclear weapons is generally illegal, in the doctrines of the nuclear weapon states. No committee to deal with the nuclear disarmament process as a whole has been established in the Conference on Disarmament, contrary to the 2000 commitment. Nor have the NPT nuclear weapon states engaged in a multilateral process of reduction and elimination of nuclear forces. China, which proclaims its support of complete nuclear disarmament, and Britain have both stated their willingness to engage in such a process, but only when U.S. and Russian nuclear forces have reached much lower levels.

CONCLUSION

The nuclear weapon states long have understood the NPT as an asymmetrical bargain, imposing specific, enforceable obligations in the present on non-nuclear weapon states, while requiring of nuclear weapon states only a general and vague commitment to good faith negotiation of nuclear disarmament, to be brought to fruition in the distant future if ever. The 1995 and 2000 Review Conferences, reinforced by the 1996 International Court of Justice opinion, decisively rejected this view. It is now established that the NPT has a symmetry of obligations, and that Article VI is an obligation to be met in accordance with criteria of transparency, verification, and irreversibility, with specific measures embedded in legally binding agreements. Measured against these reasonable standards — adopted with U.S. support at the 2000 Review Conference — the nuclear weapon states, especially the United States, are failing to comply with the NPT disarmament obligation, not only due to the lack of progress in particular areas, but above all, by reason of the failure to make disarmament the driving force in national planning and policy with respect to nuclear weapons.

3

THE COMPREHENSIVE TEST BAN TREATY

BACKGROUND

A complete nuclear test ban has been a goal of the global movement for nuclear disarmament and the governments of many countries for half a century. It is a commitment that has repeatedly been made in treaties and other official pronouncements and documents by nuclear weapons states, including the United States and the Soviet Union/Russia.[134]

The first major step was taken in 1963, when the United States, the Soviet Union, and Britain signed the Limited Test Ban Treaty (LTBT), also frequently referred to as the Partial Test Ban Treaty, which banned nuclear weapons tests in the atmosphere, in space, underwater, or on the Earth's surface. Fallout over other countries was prohibited. The LTBT was promptly ratified and entered into force in October 1963. A number of other countries (including India, Israel, and Pakistan) also signed the treaty. France and the People's Republic of China did not sign it. The U.S. Senate did attach some conditions, called "safeguards," to its ratification, including maintenance of readiness to resume atmospheric testing.[135] That readiness was maintained for about a quarter of a century after the LTBT entered into force. Only underground tests were left out of the ban. France continued nuclear testing in the atmosphere until 1974 and China until 1980.[136]

The 1974 U.S.-Soviet Threshold Test Ban treaty limited the size of the tests to 150 kilotons. Article III of the treaty required negotiations on the subject of peaceful nuclear explosions, which were not covered by the Threshold Test Ban Treaty. There was also an official understanding on how "unintended breaches" of the treaty, in the form of relatively small exceedances of the 150 kiloton limit, would be handled. The United States wanted a completion of the negotiations on the latter issue as a precondition for submission of the treaty to the Senate for its approval of ratification. U.S.-Soviet negotiations regarding both issues were completed in 1976, whereupon the Threshold Test Ban Treaty and the treaty banning "peaceful nuclear explosions" were submitted to the Senate for ratification. Both treaties were ratified in December 1990.[137] By that time the Berlin Wall had come down and the Cold War was over.

The parties to the 1963 LTBT committed themselves, in the preamble, "to achieve the discontinuance of all test explosions of nuclear weapons for all time." They stated that they were "determined to continue negotiations to this end," and that they desired "to put an end to the contamination of man's environment by radioactive substances" – which is an inevitable accompaniment of nuclear weapons testing, including underground testing.[138] The three parties to the 1963 limited test ban again committed themselves to a comprehensive test ban in 1968 when they signed the Nuclear Nonproliferation Treaty (NPT). The NPT went into effect in 1970. In the NPT, the three nuclear weapons states that were parties to the LTBT reaffirmed their commitment to a comprehensive test ban and made specific reference to the prior 1963 commitment.[139]

At the review conference of the NPT in 1990, many non-nuclear parties expressed strong dissatisfaction at the failure of the nuclear weapons states to achieve a comprehensive nuclear test ban. The NPT was due to be renewed, and failing that, to expire in 1995. At a January 1991 conference, non-nuclear weapon states parties to the LTBT sought to amend that treaty to make the ban on testing comprehensive.[140] The amendment was not adopted due to opposition by the United States, whose consent was required by the terms of treaty, but the initiative added to the momentum for a comprehensive ban. The growing call for a test ban helped create the climate for a one-year test moratorium by the Soviet Union in October 1991. A year later, on October 2, 1992, the administration of President George H.W. Bush put into place a similar moratorium, which was extended by President Clinton in 1993 and again in 1995. Russia extended its testing moratorium in 1992, two weeks after the U.S. moratorium went into effect. France and China did not stop testing until January and July 1996 (respectively) – that is, until just before the last phase of the negotiations that led up to their signing of the CTBT in that same year. Test moratoriums by the nuclear weapon states that are parties to the NPT continue.

THE CTBT AND ITS CURRENT STATUS

The achievement of a comprehensive test ban treaty by 1996 was an explicit commitment made by the nuclear weapons states to all parties to the NPT, as part of the indefinite extension of the NPT in 1995. The extension document itself contains no conditions. The CTBT commitment was part of side understandings undertaken by parties to the NPT as part of the extension process (see NPT chapter). In October 1996, the five nuclear weapons states parties to the NPT, as well as more than 100 other countries, and Israel (not a party to the NPT), signed the CTBT. Article I of the CTBT bans all nuclear explosions, for any purpose, warlike or peaceful. It states:

> Each State Party undertakes not to carry out any nuclear weapon test explosion or any other nuclear explosion, and to prohibit and prevent any such nuclear explosion at any place under its jurisdiction or control.
>
> Each State Party undertakes, furthermore, to refrain from causing, encouraging, or in any way participating in the carrying out of any nuclear weapon test explosion or any other nuclear explosion (CTBT 1996).

It is important to note that Article I of the CTBT does far more than obligate parties to refrain from carrying out nuclear explosions. They are also enjoined from "causing, encouraging, or in any way participating" in such explosions. Finally, the treaty does not ban possession of nuclear weapons or other nuclear devices. It bans "the bang, not the bomb."

An important vagueness in the treaty is that it does not contain a formal definition of a nuclear explosion. Moreover, the CTBT does not ban all nuclear experiments involving sudden releases of nuclear energy. However, the negotiating history makes clear that for any nuclear experiments to be considered legal they must meet at least two criteria:

> The nuclear explosive yield should be far less than 4 pounds of TNT equivalent, the non-zero limit that the United States had sought before it decided to drop this exception and negotiate for a "zero-yield" treaty, and Nuclear fission experiments involving explosive compression of fissile materials should not achieve nuclear criticality.[141]

Peaceful nuclear explosions are included in the general ban on nuclear explosions, even if the specific devices being tested cannot be turned into weapons. China had wanted an exemption for PNEs and the United States had wanted an exemption for "hydronuclear" explosions. Various complications in reaching an agreement led President Clinton to announce (on August 11, 1995) that the United States would support a "zero-yield" test ban. China also dropped its demand for an exception for PNEs. Hence the treaty, as signed, bans all nuclear explosions.

Finally, the negotiating process also indicates that "sub-critical" nuclear tests, in which the mass of nuclear material does not achieve criticality, would not be considered nuclear explosions under the treaty. In sum, while the treaty does not actually provide a definition of a "nuclear explosion," the record makes clear that the room for argument as to this definition is very narrow and cannot include any exceptions for PNEs or for hydronuclear explosions. At the other end, some generation of nuclear neutrons in the process of sub-critical tests is allowed provided there is no nuclear criticality. There exists no comparable public negotiating record regarding thermonuclear explosions, which involve isotopes of hydrogen (see below).

The treaty applies equally to all parties. In other words, unlike the NPT, the CTBT does not distinguish in any way between those states that have nuclear weapons and those that do not. For this reason, the CTBT does not deal with nuclear devices, which are covered by the NPT, but with nuclear explosions as such. The CTBT does have two categories of signatories in regard to the conditions for entry-into-force, specified in Article XIV. That article refers to Annex 2 of the treaty, which contains a list of 44 countries that must sign and ratify the treaty before the CTBT can enter into force. Countries were included in this list because all of them have some form of nuclear capability, such as a research or commercial nuclear reactor. During the treaty negotiations in 1996, India repeatedly stated that it would not be a party to a treaty that, in its view, was not a disarmament treaty but only a nonproliferation treaty. This position had echoes of India's refusal to be a party to the NPT in the 1960s (see NPT chapter). Given that it was not going to sign, India asked that it should not be included in the list. Nonetheless, India is one of the 44 countries listed in Annex 2.

Article II sets up a CTBT Organization with a mandate for putting into a place an extensive global monitoring system to detect nuclear tests; Article II also provides for a variety of inspections. Article IV sets forth the rights and obligations of parties in regard to verification.

The goal of the monitoring system is to detect nuclear explosions. It is generally agreed that all explosions over one kiloton can be detected with a very high degree of reliability. Most assessments of the present and planned system indicate that tests considerably below this magnitude can also be reliably detected. By the same token, it is also generally agreed that very small tests of a few tens or hundreds of kilograms of TNT equivalent could escape detection by the monitoring system. The provisions for on-site inspections in the treaty are meant as a safeguard against such cheating. All parties to the treaty may request on-site inspections and the procedures for making the requests and the conduct of such inspections are specified. An independent commission on the verification question concluded as follows:

> The system is expected to detect with a very high level of confidence—and hence deterrence—a non-evasively conducted explosion of at least one kiloton (kt). Because of the real possibility of detection significantly below this yield, there is also a considerable deterrent effect against clandestine testing below one kt. The IMS [International Monitoring System of the CTBT] is expected to be able to determine the location of such events within 1,000 square kilometres, the maximum area permitted for an on-site inspection.[142]

Article IX gives any party "the right to withdraw from this Treaty if it decides that extraordinary events related to the subject matter of this Treaty have jeopardized its supreme interests." Six months notice to other states parties and the Security Council and an explanation of the circumstances are required.

The CTBT has not yet entered into force. Of the 44 countries that must sign and ratify it before it can do so, 31 have signed and ratified it as of March 2002, including Russia, France, and Britain. China and Israel have signed but not ratified it. The United States has signed it, but in October 1999, the U.S. Senate rejected ratification (see below). India, Pakistan, and North Korea (formally known as the Democratic People's Republic of Korea) have not signed it. It is clear that the United States Senate will not take up the treaty ratification question again in the near future. Whether and when it may ultimately do so is a matter of conjecture. The process of signature and ratification by other key states is likely to remain in limbo until the U.S. position becomes clearer. Since each one of the 44 states named in the treaty must ratify it before it can enter into force, it appears that the entry into force of the CTBT is unlikely until there is a substantial change in sentiment in this regard in the U.S. Senate.

Finally, there may be more to the treaty than is public. The Department of Energy, in response to questions from Senator Harkin about the legality of certain experiments involving thermonuclear reactions in the National Ignition Facility being built at Lawrence Livermore Laboratory, has stated that the "negotiating record itself is confidential."[143] In other words, there is a secret negotiating record.

It is unclear which countries were party to this secret record. During negotiations of security treaties, it has been the norm for caucuses of powerful states to meet apart from the whole group on some occasions. In the context of the CTBT, the question has arisen as to whether there was some kind of understanding among a small group of countries to allow laboratory thermonuclear explosions to be conducted while brushing the question of the legality of such explosions under the rug. The author of this chapter has met with several diplomats in the course of investigating this issue. These private conversations indicate that only some of the negotiating parties were aware of the potential controversy that might surround the legality of some proposed thermonuclear experiments (see below for more details).

THE U.S. SENATE'S REJECTION OF CTBT RATIFICATION

In his opening statement, Senator Jesse Helms, then Chairman of the Senate Foreign Relations Committee, at the Senate hearing on ratification of the CTBT on October 7, 1999, said:

> Perhaps we shall be reminded that it was not the Republicans who asked for this vote — it was forced upon us by the President and the 45 [Democratic] Senators on the other side of the aisle. But the fact remains, if this treaty is brought to a vote next Tuesday, I believe that it will be defeated. There is only one way the President can call off that vote: He must formally request in writing that (a) the treaty be withdrawn and (b) that the CTBT not be considered for the duration of his presidency.
>
> If the President does so, then the CTBT will be effectively dead - just as the SALT II Treaty was effectively dead after President Carter made a similar written request of the Senate. If Mr. Clinton does not submit a written request, we will proceed with the vote and I am confident that the CTBT will be defeated. The President will have the choice.[144]

In effect, Senator Helms gave notice to the Clinton administration that it could choose one of two ways for CTBT ratification to be defeated. Successful ratification, in his view, was not an option.

Despite the support for the CTBT by the Clinton administration and a wide array of military experts inside and outside the administration, the opponents of the treaty proved more formidable. They prevailed despite the six "safeguards" that the Clinton administration had agreed to in its submission of the CTBT for ratification.[145] These included the "stockpile stewardship program" to maintain the U.S. nuclear arsenal, maintaining a test site, presumably the Nevada Test Site, in a condition to resume testing, and annual certification by the U.S. Joints Chiefs of Staff and nuclear weapons laboratory directors that the U.S. nuclear arsenal was safe and reliable. If the arsenal was not certified, the understanding was that the United States could withdraw from the treaty and test. The stockpile stewardship program was also designed to maintain nuclear weapons design capabilities and further research into new nuclear weapons designs.[146]

The main argument of the official U.S. treaty proponents was that the CTBT was an instrument of horizontal nonproliferation – that is, it would make it difficult for non-nuclear countries to test to develop nuclear arsenals. Yet, proponents of the CTBT, from the 1950s to the time it was signed in 1996, were motivated by both nonproliferation and disarmament considerations. The historic hopes that the CTBT would be a factor in promoting nuclear disarmament were made a part of the preamble to the CTBT by its framers. The United States played a leading role in determining the content and detailed language of the treaty. Yet during the ratification hearings, the Clinton administration did not present the nuclear disarmament argument even once as a positive factor in favor of the treaty, U.S. commitments under the NPT notwithstanding. Consider for instance, a statement of then Undersecretary of State for Arms Control, John Holum, at a press briefing:

> For us, the main security value of this treaty is non-proliferation. The Comprehensive Test Ban Treaty strengthens the global standard against the spread of nuclear weapons, and makes it much harder for any country to make nuclear weapons, especially smaller, lighter designs that are easy to conceal and deliver — the kind that would be most threatened [sic] to us.
>
> On South Asia, both India and Pakistan have pledged at various times to sign. The CTBT there can help contain a deadly nuclear arms race between countries that aren't constrained by the nonproliferation treaty. If we get North Korea under the test ban they'll be less able to exploit their ballistic missile capabil-

ities against us. The same is true of Iran, and they have signed the Comprehensive Test Ban Treaty.

Nonproliferation is an urgent national priority. The United States is the leader of the global effort against the spread of weapons of mass destruction. A world in which the rogues have nuclear weapons would be a world of peril for all Americans. The Test Ban Treaty is not a silver bullet, but it's another valuable tool. Nonproliferation is hard, uphill work. The American people should not expect good results if the Senate denies us the means.[147]

That the treaty was an unequal one, which would impose restraints on the nuclear weapons "have-nots" rather than the "haves," was made clear in the same press briefing by Undersecretary of Energy Ernest Moniz:

One of the major issues in this debate, of course, is that of our ability to maintain a safe and reliable nuclear stockpile in the absence of testing. And, as Bob Bell said earlier, this remains a supreme national interest for this country. There are several challenges in this task: maintaining weapons as they age; establishing a capability to replace and certify new weapons components; training new weapons scientists; and reestablishing an operational manufacturing capability.

These challenges are being met today. I can say that with a confidence that is grounded, first of all, in our history. Our history, 50 years of experience of more than 1,000 nuclear tests, of 150 tests with modern weapon types, and over — or approximately 15,000 surveillance tests. This is really the grounding of our program. Each weapon in the enduring stockpile has been thoroughly tested and is subjected to regular, in-depth surveillance.

Now, seven years following our last testing experience, we have implemented, in this administration, an experimentally based, scientific program, using both experiment and computer simulation, to provide the integrating elements to sustain reliability. This program, I want to stress, already has had many successes. We have a detailed, coordinated, integrated weapons plan — one also integrated with military requirements. We have gone through three rigorous certification procedures involving the labs, STRATCOM, the Nuclear Weapons Council and others — including scientific advisors. We have resolved, today, stockpile problems that were not resolved in the years of testing.

> We have met new military requirements in the absence of test-
> ing — for example, requirements for a deep penetrating
> weapon, the so-called B-61-11. We have obtained new, critical
> scientific data using non-nuclear experiments — for example,
> we now know how plutonium behaves when it ages, one of the
> key questions for maintaining the stockpile.[148]

The desire of the United States to be able to confidently maintain nuclear forces over the long term, to be able to confidently deploy new or modified designs, and generally to go it alone with its own military preparations, prevailed despite these considerations. In fact, the modest disarmament implications that the CTBT might have for the nuclear weapons states, referred to in the preamble as a bow to longstanding promises made by the nuclear weapons states, became a tool in the hands of treaty opponents. Jeanne Kirkpatrick, the U.S. ambassador to the United Nations from 1981 to 1985, summarized the arguments of many treaty opponents succinctly in her Senate testimony on October 7, 1999. Prefacing her list of objections with the remark that "other regimes with little regard for the rule of law or human rights work to acquire weapons of mass destruction," she noted:

> First is the fact that our government takes its commitments seri-
> ously. If we were to sign this treaty, we would feel bound by its
> terms. We would not feel free to violate it at will as many gov-
> ernments will. We would not conduct explosive tests.
>
> Second, as everyone knows, this treaty cannot be verified. The
> CIA has recently publicly acknowledged that it cannot detect
> low-yield tests. It bothers me that we will not know when they
> are cheating and some will cheat.
>
> Third, I learned from my service on the Blue Ribbon and FARR
> Committees that the safety and reliability of our nuclear stock-
> piles cannot be taken for granted, but must be monitored.
> Testing (banned forever by this proposed treaty) is a vital part
> of ascertaining and maintaining the reliability and safety of our
> nuclear weapons. It is also a necessary step in modernizing our
> nuclear weapons.
>
> Testing is vital to maintaining the reliability and credibility of
> our nuclear deterrent.
>
> The authors of this treaty understand how important testing is
> to maintaining the viability of nuclear weapons. The Preamble
> to the Treaty states, and I quote:

> 'Recognizing that the cessation of all nuclear weapon test explosions and all other nuclear explosions, by constraining the development and qualitative improvement of nuclear weapons and ending the development of advanced new types of nuclear weapons, constitutes an effective measure of nuclear disarmament and nonproliferation in all its aspects,
>
> 'Further recognizing that an end to all such nuclear explosions will thus constitute a meaningful step in the realization of a systematic process to achieve nuclear disarmament.'

> Fourth, that deterrent has never been as important to the security of Americans as it is today with rogue states developing the capacity to attack our cities and our population. Americans and their allies are more vulnerable than we have ever been.

Her conclusion was that the United States "cannot rely on this treaty to prevent the countries that are actually or potentially hostile to us from acquiring and testing nuclear arsenals and ballistic missiles." Hence, the United States must maintain its nuclear arsenal because it "can rely only on its nuclear deterrent. We have no other defense."[149]

Opponents of the treaty also noted that testing was not required to develop nuclear weapons, pointing to the fact that the bomb that destroyed Hiroshima had not been tested prior to its wartime use.

During the consideration of the treaty by the Senate, there were worldwide appeals to the United States to ratify the treaty. The principal allies of the United States, East and West, including the Prime Minister of Britain, the President of France, and the Chancellor of Germany, made public appeals to the Senate to ratify the treaty. The Prime Minister of Japan sent a personal letter to the United States. Experienced U.S. commentators used strong language to warn of adverse diplomatic consequences. For instance, an opinion piece published by the *Washington Post* stated that if the United States did not ratify the treaty it "will be seen as the rogue state of proliferation."[150] All these appeals failed. Consistent with some previous major forks in the road between more weapons and unilateral military strength on the one hand and nonproliferation on the other, the United States once again chose the former.[151] The United States Senate rejected the CTBT by a majority. There were only 48 votes in favor of ratification, whereas 67 (two-thirds of the Senate) were required.

The treaty's failure relates less to the merits of the document itself; rather, it is the result of the general underlying argument that the United States should rely first of all and most importantly on its own military strength, including nuclear weapons, to address any particular proliferation situation.[152] This argument does not have any room for questioning whether the United States itself has any obligations to others. The merits of the CTBT as an instrument of nonproliferation and to a modest extent as an instrument of disarmament are reasonably clear. While the design of rudimentary nuclear weapons can be done without testing, it is essentially impossible to build an arsenal of the type that might be delivered accurately by intercontinental ballistic missiles without testing. Hence, in this regard, countries that have tested extensively, notably the five nuclear weapons states that are parties to the NPT, have an advantage in having previously tested nuclear weapons designs that can be put on intercontinental missiles. Tests of more than a few hundred tons of TNT are verifiable by technical means, and inspections are available for other suspect activities. That a treaty cannot have perfect inspection is no more an argument against it than to say that military force cannot achieve security objectives in every instance, therefore military force should be ruled out altogether under all circumstances. The issues at stake in the arguments against the CTBT are not technical ones, but an assertion by the United States of the right to continue over the long haul not only to possess but to further develop an already extensive nuclear weapons capability despite its commitments for disarmament under the NPT. This approach was most recently codified in the Bush administration's Nuclear Posture Review (see NPT chapter).

AFTERMATH OF THE SIGNING OF THE CTBT AND ITS REJECTION BY THE U.S. SENATE

The prospect that the CTBT would be restricted to a nonproliferation role, rather than a disarmament and nonproliferation role, emerged during the negotiations that led up to it. Nuclear weapons states seemed to be on a course to maintain their arsenals and to implement programs that would ensure the usability of the nuclear weapons in the absence of testing. Among the nuclear weapon states, only China appeared ready to undertake negotiations to achieve complete nuclear disarmament (though its readiness has never been put to the test by other nuclear weapon states).

The United States had already put into place the Stockpile Stewardship program, which is more expensive than the nuclear testing program during the Cold War. France and China continued to test nuclear weapons into 1996, the year the treaty was signed. India announced that it would not go along with such a treaty.[153]

In May 1998, India conducted several nuclear weapons tests. The decision was a complex one. One trigger was an election and the formation of a new government led by the Bharatiya Janata Party, which had long wanted India to become a declared nuclear weapons state. Pakistan followed India's tests with its own three weeks later.

The rejection of the CTBT by the U.S. Senate in October 1999 was preceded by a reaffirmation by NATO in April of the same year of the central role of nuclear weapons in NATO military doctrine, including possible first use of nuclear weapons against non-nuclear states. The 2000 Review conference of the NPT urged all states that had not done so to sign and/or ratify the treaty. But the United States has stepped farther back from the treaty since that time. President Bush said during his campaign that he did not support the CTBT, and his administration has maintained that posture since. The Bush administration has reaffirmed the continuation of the test moratorium, though no assurances have been given that this will continue indefinitely. The United States also appears to have explicitly embarked on new nuclear weapons design activities.[154] This makes it more likely that it will test nuclear weapons some time in the future and break the test moratorium. The dim prospects of the treaty in the U.S. Senate are made far poorer by the U.S. nuclear posture that includes new weapon designs. There has been little progress elsewhere among the 13 of the 44 states that have either failed to sign or ratify the treaty. How these failures will affect other treaties, notably the NPT, is a matter of conjecture at the present time.

COMPLIANCE STATUS

The Vienna Convention on the Law of Treaties, Article 18, provides that a state "is obliged to refrain from acts which would defeat the object and purpose of a treaty" when it has signed the treaty until it makes its intent clear not to ratify, or when it has ratified the treaty, providing that entry into force is not unduly delayed. The object of the CTBT is embedded in the Article I ban on nuclear explosions or causing, encouraging or participating in such explosions.

While the United States has not ratified the Vienna Convention, it is a signatory, and it has treated Article 18 as binding customary law, for example with respect to the SALT II treaty.[155] Consistent with Article 18, following defeat of the CTBT in the Senate, the Clinton Administration took the position, in a letter to heads of state from then Secretary of State Albright, that it would comply with its legal obligations as a signatory- in other words, that the basic obligation of no testing continues to apply.[156] The Vienna Convention requirement is reinforced by the fact that the United States has made commitments to the CTBT in connection with the legal decision to extend the NPT indefinitely and at the 2000 NPT Review Conference. Further, from the outset of the NPT, the CTBT has been viewed as an essential measure for implementation of the Article VI obligation to negotiate cessation of the nuclear arms race and nuclear disarmament.

The CTBT remains before the Senate Foreign Relations Committee, and the Senate could still choose to approve ratification of the treaty. The Bush administration has stated that it does not support ratification of the CTBT, but has not made a formal notification of an intent not to ratify to the UN Secretary-General, the depository for the treaty. As a matter of constitutional and international practice, only such a formal communication would suffice to terminate the U.S. obligation as a signatory not to defeat its object and purpose.[157] Other states that have signed or ratified the CTBT are also bound by the Article I prohibition.

The United States has not made such a formal communication. But we recognize that the issue is somewhat clouded by the Bush administration's policy regarding the CTBT. However, we believe that the United States is not only committed to observe the test ban by a moratorium that is legally in place but also under a prior process involving the entry into force of the NPT in 1970 and the indefinite extension of the NPT. There are no ambiguities in regard to other states that have signed or ratified the CTBT. They are bound by the Article I prohibition not to cause, encourage or participate in nuclear tests. Finally, our evaluation of the issue of laboratory thermonuclear explosions below is in the context of the U.S. claim that these do not violate the CTBT.

All nuclear weapon states, including the United States, are continuing their test moratoria. However, the United States and Russia continue to conduct "sub-critical" tests, in which the fissile material does not achieve nuclear criticality. These tests are permitted under the CTBT. Sub-critical tests provide for the kind of active experimentation that helps countries with test sites to keep the sites in a state of readiness to resume nuclear testing. Of the nuclear weapon states parties to the CTBT, only France has actually closed down its test site as a result of the CTBT. Britain has long had no test site of its own and used the Nevada Test Site in the United States on a mutually agreed basis. Hence, so long as the U.S. test site is in a state of readiness, it would presumably remain available to Britain. India and Pakistan are not signatories to the CTBT and maintain their test sites. Israeli contingency plans in relation to testing are unknown since it has not acknowledged having a nuclear arsenal.

Laser fusion explosions and compliance[158]

Inferences regarding the legality of pure thermonuclear explosions, that is, nuclear explosions that do not involve fissile materials, must be made from the history of the negotiations and from technical considerations. There is no public negotiating history regarding such explosions (as distinct from laser fusion experiments, also called inertial confinement fusion, ICF for short, that do not involve explosions, which like other similar activities, are permitted under the CTBT).

Our conclusion that the United States, France, Britain, Japan, and Germany appear to be violating Article I of the CTBT is based primarily on a 1998 analysis of the issue by the Institute for Energy and Environmental Research.[159] The United States and France are building laser fusion facilities called the National Ignition Facility (Livermore, California) and Laser Mégajoule (near Bordeaux) with the intent of producing pure thermonuclear explosions. Britain, Japan, and Germany are assisting the process (see below).

As noted above, the CTBT does not ban facilities or bombs, but it does enjoin parties from conducting nuclear explosions or "causing, encouraging, or in any way participating in the carrying out" of nuclear explosions. The intent of the United States and France in building these facilities is to carry out pure thermonuclear explosions triggered by lasers. They also intend that some of these planned explosions would achieve magnitudes of about ten pounds of TNT equivalent, which is clearly greater than the four pounds of nuclear yield prohibited under the ban on hydronuclear explosions (which are fission explosions).

Unlike the preparations to keep the Nevada Test Site ready for nuclear explosions in the context of a policy of maintaining the moratorium itself, the United States and France do not intend to build NIF and LMJ in order to maintain the capability for carrying out explosions. They are building them so as to put them into service when they are ready. Hence, building NIF and LMJ is a fundamentally different kind of activity from maintaining capability to carry out tests. Building these devices is part of a process of causing nuclear explosions, since such explosions would be carried out when the devices are ready. The United States and France are therefore actively preparing to violate the first paragraph of Article I of the CTBT, which bans all nuclear explosions. It also appears to us they are in violation of the second paragraph of Article I of the CTBT because they are engaging in activities designed to cause nuclear explosions in NIF and LMJ. Similarly, Britain also appears to be out of compliance with the CTBT because it is helping to finance the National Ignition Facility and intends to participate in explosive experiments there. Finally, Japan has done nothing to prevent a Japan-based corporation, Hoya, from supplying glass that is essential to the construction of NIF and LMJ.[160] Japan is therefore contributing to U.S. preparations for violating the CTBT. Japan also appears to be in violation of Article I because it is encouraging the United States and France to violate Article I. Similarly, a German-based company, Schott, is supplying glass to NIF and LMJ.[161] Germany is therefore in a situation analogous to Japan. Article III of the CTBT requires governments "to prohibit, in conformity with international law, natural persons possessing its nationality from undertaking any such activity [that is, activity prohibited to a state party under the treaty] anywhere." Japan and Germany thus are responsible for preventing their citizens from causing, encouraging, or participating in the carrying out of a nuclear explosion anywhere in the world.

The United States claims that NIF-produced explosions would not violate the CTBT because laser fusion facilities are exempt from the ban in Article I of the CTBT. The United States has claimed that an alleged exemption for these experiments under the NPT applies also to the CTBT.[162] However, the NPT permits peaceful nuclear explosions. The CTBT does not. The NPT bans possession of nuclear weapons or other nuclear explosive device by all states parties except five – that is, it has two categories of members. The claimed exemption has the effect of allowing non-nuclear weapon states to conduct such experiments without breaching their obligation not to acquire nuclear explosive devices. The CTBT applies equally to all parties and bans all nuclear explosions, as is clear from the straightforward text of Article I quoted in full above. The U.S. and French laser fusion facilities are to be used for weapons maintenance and design, and also for experiments that, it is claimed, would lead to electricity generation devices. In either case, explosions are not permitted, since the CTBT rules out all nuclear explosions, including those that may lead to peaceful applications. Moreover, it is possible that NIF and LMJ could contribute to the design of pure fusion nuclear weapons, even though they cannot themselves be made into weapons, since they are too large.

A Department of Energy's response to the letter from Senator Tom Harkin of Iowa failed to clarify the issues.[163] The DOE claims that NIF is not weaponizable. But the CTBT bans all nuclear explosions, so the potential for nuclear explosions to be made into weapons is irrelevant to compliance with Article I of the treaty. Moreover, NIF is publicly justified as contributing to capabilities of maintaining the U.S. nuclear arsenal and also designing new weapons. Finally, spread of laser fusion technology to other countries would greatly boost their ability to build thermonuclear bombs.

The DOE insists that the 1975 understanding based on the NPT that allows laser fusion research is valid for the CTBT. But it has cited no negotiating history that would allow such an interpretation of the CTBT. On the contrary, it has in this specific context asserted the secrecy of the negotiating history of the CTBT, as the following response to a question from Senator Harkin shows:

> Question 4: Official statements indicate that the DOE is using the Nonproliferation Treaty (NPT) Review Conference deliberations in its determination that NIF explosions would be legal under the CTBT. Is there a negotiating record in the CTBT process that allows the NPT exemptions on nuclear explosions to be carried over to the CTBT? If so, please provide me with the documentation of that negotiating record.

> Answer 4: While the negotiating record itself is confidential, there are public documents that support this position. For example, a comparison of the Rolling Text of September 26, 1995 to the final Treaty [CTBT] shows that a provision that would have ruled out ICF [Inertial Confinement Fusion] was specifically considered and rejected during the negotiations.[164]

As noted above, ICF experiments or devices are not banned under the CTBT, so that the response of the DOE to the question is an evasion of the issue, which relates to specific planned explosions in a specific ICF device, the National Ignition Facility. Absent an express exemption in the treaty, the language and intent of the CTBT rule out ICF explosions but permit non-explosive ICF experiments. The official argument that the planned explosions for NIF and LMJ would comply with the CTBT is further undermined by the fact that they are intended to support weapons programs.

In sum, the violation of the CTBT that we allege is not in relation to all laser fusion work. Indeed, all of the laser fusion work that has been done so far would be legal under the CTBT because it involves nuclear reactions at levels and in configurations that are clearly comparable to sub-critical fission tests. None has involved a nuclear explosion. The violation that the United States and France are committing is not in building NIF and LMJ but in planning to use these devices to carry out explosions of magnitudes that are greater than 4 pounds of TNT equivalent. The negotiating record that is public clearly indicates that whatever definition of a nuclear explosion that is eventually adopted, the largest permitted nuclear yield of any nuclear reaction that occurs in a very short period of time (i.e., an explosion) must be far less than 4 pounds of TNT equivalent. It is essential that the matter of laser fusion explosions be taken up explicitly by the parties to the CTBT, so as to reaffirm the complete ban on all nuclear explosions. In this connection, we also urge the publication of the secret negotiating history, which may not be known to all states.

4

THE ANTI-BALLISTIC MISSILE TREATY

BACKGROUND

The ABM Treaty was created by the United States and the Soviet Union in the context of a growing armory of missiles that had several warheads, each of which could be independently targeted – the so-called "multiple independently-targetable reentry vehicles" known as MIRVs (See for example, York 1970 and Spencer 1995). These weapons raised the theoretical possibility of a surprise first strike by one of the Cold War antagonists that might wipe out most of the strategic nuclear forces of the other side. It could then prevent nuclear warheads from harming its territory from a retaliatory strike by the remainder of the strategic forces by using anti-ballistic missile forces to defend itself. Thus, what appears on the surface and in nomenclature to be a "defensive" weapon was possibly a central element in a potential first strike strategy.

Since the threat of successful retaliation has been considered a cornerstone of nuclear deterrence, the combination of accurate first strike nuclear warheads and missile defenses created the prospect that the side without missile defenses would lose its deterrence capability or appear to lose it. The ABM treaty, which limited missile defense to two sites in each country with a maximum of 100 interceptors of incoming warheads at each site, was meant to ensure that both the Soviet Union and the United States retained enough retaliatory capacity after a first strike to threaten the cities of the other, thus preserving the nuclear deterrence between the Cold War superpowers. The treaty's preamble also stated the "premise" that the limitation on anti-ballistic missile systems "would contribute to the creation of more favorable conditions for further negotiations on limiting strategic arms."

The ABM treaty was unusual in also putting limits on future technological development in the interests of preserving the "strategic balance" between the United States and the Soviet Union. The Federation of American Scientists has summarized the provisions of the treaty as follows:

> Further, to decrease the pressures of technological change and its unsettling impact on the strategic balance, both sides agree to prohibit development, testing, or deployment of sea-based, air-based, or space-based ABM systems and their components, along with mobile land-based ABM systems. Should future technology bring forth new ABM systems "based on other physical principles" than those employed in current systems, it was agreed that limiting such systems would be discussed, in accordance with the Treaty's provisions for consultation and amendment.[165]

The ABM treaty provides for a five-yearly review by both parties (Article XIV). It permits withdrawal from the treaty by either party "if it decides that extraordinary events related to the subject matter of this Treaty have jeopardized its supreme interests." (Article XV). There is no penalty for withdrawal, which requires six months notice to the other state.

In 1974, the ABM treaty was amended when the United States and the Soviet Union signed a protocol reducing the number of allowed missile defense sites from two to one (ABM Protocol 1974).

Since the disintegration of the Soviet Union in 1991, some U.S. leaders, including Senator Jesse Helms, questioned whether there was a valid ABM Treaty on the ground that the treaty was between the United States and a country, the Soviet Union, which had ceased to exist.[166] There was no real question regarding Russia, because Secretary of State James Baker had publicly affirmed in Russia that the United States regarded Russia as an ABM Treaty successor state and that the treaty remains in force.[167] In light of the question regarding the other former Soviet republics, the United States, Russia, Ukraine, Belarus, and Kazakhstan signed an agreement designating all these states as successor states to the ABM Treaty in 1997.[168]

President Clinton did not submit the 1997 agreement regarding successor states to the U.S. Senate for ratification, presumably because Senator Helms, then-chairman of the Senate Foreign Relations Committee, had promised to use the occasion of the consideration of the agreement for ratification to kill the ABM treaty altogether.[169]

The Bush administration and other supporters of the withdrawal of the United States from the ABM treaty have claimed that the treaty is obsolete since it essentially codifies nuclear deterrence ideas dating from the Cold War. For instance, Senator Jon Kyl noted that:

> A changed world requires different approaches to ensure the safety and security of American citizens. As missile technology proliferates and terrorists continue plotting new and more deadly ways to harm us, our nation remains highly vulnerable to nuclear and biological attack. We must move away a treaty that requires us to leave our towns and cities deliberately defenseless to missiles fired by rogue nations or terrorists. The ABM Treaty is a straitjacket irrelevant in the post-Cold War era.

And that:

> The ABM Treaty does not protect us from Iraq, nor has it deterred dictatorships in Iran or North Korea from attempting to build a nuclear arsenal. The treaty does not protect our nation against accidental missile launches or attacks from terrorists who commandeer a nuclear missile. In short, it is a relic - and the world will not miss its passing.[170]

Those who have argued against U.S. withdrawal from the ABM treaty, while still supporting the idea of a missile defense, have argued along the lines of Senator Biden on the eve of President Bush's notice of intent to withdraw from the treaty:

> In my view, invoking this [withdrawal] clause is a bit of a stretch, to say the least. No new enemy has fielded an ICBM missile, which is the only missile our national missile defense is intended to stop. Tactical missile defense is not barred by the ABM Treaty, and Russia has said it would even amend the treaty to permit an expanded United States testing program. So where is the jeopardy to our supreme interest?

> The administration has said it wants to conduct tests that would breach the ABM Treaty, but the head of the Ballistic Missile Defense Organization in the Pentagon told Congress earlier this year that no breach was needed to do all the tests that were needed and scheduled.

> Informed scientists say the features added to the test program that might breach the treaty, which the Defense Department presented to the Armed Services Committee several months

ago, are far from necessary, especially at this time. Phil Coyle, the former chief of testing for the Pentagon, says we can conduct several years of needed testing without having to breach the treaty's terms.[171]

On December 13, 2001, the Bush administration informed Russia that the United States intended to withdraw from the treaty. He said:

> Today, I have given formal notice to Russia, in accordance with the treaty, that the United States of America is withdrawing from this almost 30 year old treaty. I have concluded the ABM treaty hinders our government's ability to develop ways to protect our people from future terrorist or rogue state missile attacks.
>
> The 1972 ABM treaty was signed by the United States and the Soviet Union at a much different time, in a vastly different world. One of the signatories, the Soviet Union, no longer exists. And neither does the hostility that once led both our countries to keep thousands of nuclear weapons on hair-trigger alert, pointed at each other. The grim theory was that neither side would launch a nuclear attack because it knew the other would respond, thereby destroying both.
>
> Today, as the events of September the 11th made all too clear, the greatest threats to both our countries come not from each other, or other big powers in the world, but from terrorists who strike without warning, or rogue states who seek weapons of mass destruction.[172]

The withdrawal went into effect on June 13, 2002.

ANALYSIS OF THE U.S. NOTICE OF WITHDRAWAL FROM THE ABM TREATY

Widespread official questioning of the ABM treaty began in the United States in March 1983, when President Reagan announced his commitment to a research program, known later as the "Strategic Defense Initiative" and popularly called "Star Wars," whose goal was to create a shield over the United States that would protect it from nuclear attack. Since such a shield would also protect it from nuclear retaliation, it clearly put into question the very principles on which the ABM treaty was created. A few months later, the United States questioned the legality of a radar at Krasnoyarsk (in Siberia) being built by the Soviet Union. The Soviet Union denied that this was an illegal installation. In January 1984, the

United States declared the Soviet radar to be out of compliance with the terms of the ABM treaty. As the Cold War wound down, the Soviet Union agreed that the Krasnoyarsk radar was illegal under the ABM treaty. In September 1989, the Soviet Union agreed unconditionally to dismantle the radar. [173]

For the rest of the 1980s, the United States continued to discuss with the Soviet Union the possibility of replacing the ABM Treaty with an agreement that would permit a variety of missile defenses, including space based defensive weapons, with the idea that defense was better than deterrence. These arguments have not addressed the potential of missile defenses to be used as part of a first strike arsenal, or as part of an arsenal that would negate the deterrence capacity of some or all nuclear weapon states.

Negation of deterrence would provide the United States with a free hand in using conventional military forces in a manner of its choosing, for instance in Taiwan, without fear of nuclear devastation. This potential of missile defenses has recently been pointed out by *New York Times* columnist Bill Keller:

> The schemers in the current debate [on missile defenses] fear that any nation with a few nuclear weapons can do to us what we did to the Soviets [during the Cold War] – deter us from projecting our vastly superior conventional forces into the world. This could mean Iraq, or North Korea or Iran, but most importantly it means China.
>
> ...
>
> 'The logic of missile defense is to make the stakes of power projection compatible with the risks of power projection,' says Keith B. Payne [President of the National Institute for Public Policy], a deterrence theory expert and an ardent supporter of missile defense. Missile defense, in other words, is not about defense. It's about offense.[174]

The offensive capacity of missile defenses also relates to an increase in nuclear first strike capability, especially in relation to vulnerable and/or small arsenals of a potential adversary. Consider China, for instance. China currently has about 20 long-range ballistic missiles, which are liquid fueled. If most of these are wiped out in a first strike, then the remaining could be dealt with by even a limited missile defense (presuming it worked).[175]

Toward the end of the 1980s, the United States abandoned as unworkable the initial expansive idea of a complete missile shield of the Reagan-era, which would have included nuclear weapons. That is, the defense system was partly based on nuclear explosions in space.[176] In the 1990s, non-nuclear devices designed to destroy incoming missiles or warheads became the center of the program and the idea of space based nuclear weapons as part of a missile defense system was abandoned. In 1999, the United States adopted a law requiring that a missile defense would be deployed as soon as technologically feasible. This law came in the context of a 1998 test of a medium-range rocket by North Korea that had the potential to be turned into a missile that could reach Japan.

During the late 1990s, the United States and Russia engaged in intense negotiations to arrive at some post-Cold-War agreement on reduction of nuclear weapons, implementation of weapons reduction agreements, verification, disposition of stocks of weapon-grade plutonium that had been declared as surplus to weapons requirements after the end of the Cold War, as well as missile defenses. The disagreements had not been bridged by the time of the U.S. presidential election of 2000. President Bush had stated during the election campaign that he favored U.S. withdrawal from the ABM Treaty.

The December 13, 2001 notice of withdrawal from the treaty came in a context that is important:

- It was done about three months after the attacks of September 11, with the argument that defenses were now more important because there were clearly parties that aspired to have weapons of mass destruction that could not be deterred, even on pain of death.

- The withdrawal was in the face of continued Russian opposition. However that opposition has so far been muted.

- Russian cooperation in the War on Terrorism had no effect on the Bush administration's approach to the ABM Treaty in terms of actually securing Russia's assent before withdrawal.

- China's strategic interests in the issue were set aside. China's reaction has also been one of muted opposition.

- The United States has rejected other treaties, including the Kyoto Protocol and the CTBT.

The decision of the United States to withdraw from the ABM Treaty without a negotiated agreement with Russia is difficult to understand in terms of missile threats and defenses. First, it is possible to carry out a variety of tests within the framework of the treaty.[177] An effective system cannot be deployed for many years, and perhaps not for decades, if ever. The tests carried out so far have resulted in many failures and, in some cases, modest successes. It is generally agreed that the "successful" interceptors could be overcome in a real-world situation by decoys. At the same time, the non-missile threats relating to weapons of mass destruction, notably nuclear weapons, have grown and are now recognized as far more perilous than before September 11. For instance, according to the most recent National Intelligence Estimate, "the Intelligence Community judges that U.S. territory is more likely to be attacked with WMD [weapons of mass destruction] using nonmissile means [than ballistic missiles]."[178] Yet the resources being devoted to missile defenses ($8 billion per year)[179] are far greater than those devoted to preventing a nuclear bomb in a truck or ship or programs to put plutonium or highly enriched uranium into non-weapons usable form so as to prevent its theft. This set of priorities corresponds less to defense as such and more to the Nuclear Posture Review, which seeks to maintain large numbers of nuclear weapons on alert or standby for many different kinds of war-fighting capabilities, including first use of nuclear weapons under a variety of circumstances. The U.S. annual budget for nuclear weapons design and testing is currently larger than the average during the Cold War. Internationally, it is widely agreed that the ABM Treaty withdrawal will impede further U.S.-Russian arms reductions. Russia has already announced a withdrawal from its commitments under the START II arms reduction treaty (not yet in force) in the wake of the U.S. withdrawal from the ABM Treaty. Other adverse effects include stimulating or reinforcing a Chinese buildup of its arsenal, with attendant ripple effects on India and Pakistan and perhaps even Japan; making de-alerting all weapons much more difficult to implement; and opening the way to weaponization of space. On the latter point, the ABM Treaty prohibited space-based systems including radar usable for missile interception that would also be necessary to strike satellites or air or ground targets.

By unilaterally withdrawing from the ABM Treaty in the absence of any immediately compelling reason to do so, the United States is acting in a cavalier manner toward its legal obligations. However, there appears to be no way to challenge the withdrawal other than through the U.S. political and legal systems. Congress has shown little inclination to do so, but a lawsuit filed by members of Congress claims that the withdrawal is invalid due to a lack of congressional approval. The United States has provided the needed six months notice and a statement of the alleged "extraordinary events" motivating the withdrawal. No more is required, there is no process of judging the merit of the claims within the framework of the treaty, and Russia has not objected that the withdrawal clause has been violated. Yet, the U.S. withdrawal does raise a broader question about treaty adherence and the rule of law. It is the first formal unilateral withdrawal of a major power from a nuclear arms control treaty after it has been put into effect. A precedent has been set for the United States and other states to cite parallel provisions in other important security treaties, among them the NPT, the Biological and Chemical Weapons Conventions, and the Comprehensive Test Ban Treaty. If the United States can withdraw unilaterally from a treaty that is regarded as a cornerstone of strategic stability, then what is to keep other states from withdrawing from treaties as they see fit? The NPT, for instance, requires a three-month notice of withdrawal. Like the ABM treaty, it specifies no penalty for withdrawal. Unlike the ABM Treaty, the NPT does require notice to the Security Council, which could then act if it finds a threat to international peace and security. But the Security Council would be prevented by the veto of any of the permanent members from acting with respect to them or states they wish to protect. Similarly, a withdrawal from the CTBT also requires notice to the Security Council.

While the provision regarding notice to the Security Council does not contain an explicit authorization of any action in response to a withdrawal, the potential for such action is present provided that the permanent members collectively decide that such action is warranted. They are unlikely to act against their own countries or their allies of course. This asymmetric power of the nuclear NPT nuclear weapons states already violates the principle of equality before the law. The decision of the United States to unilaterally withdraw from the ABM Treaty further undermines it. It makes action with respect to other states that withdraw from treaties even less legitimate, since the United States has itself unilaterally cited "extraordinary events" as a basis for withdrawal from a security treaty.

The U.S. withdrawal from the ABM Treaty occurs at a time when the United States expects other countries to adhere to their commitments, especially in connection with the "War on Terrorism." The United States has also made a list of countries that may be targeted with nuclear weapons. One of the rationales in the targeting strategy is the possession of weapons of mass destruction by countries contrary to their treaty commitments. But what if any of the target countries currently party to the NPT decide to withdraw from the NPT and build nuclear arsenals because they feel their national survival threatened by U.S. policy? North Korea, having just admitted to developing a nuclear program, may be at risk of doing so. These events raise a whole host of questions as to how long the existing NPT regime may endure.

The problem of preventing the use of weapons of mass destruction deliberately or by accident is a complex one. The risks of the use of weapons of mass destruction by terrorist groups or by states that do not now possess them are real. But so are the risks that nuclear weapons states would use them. The risks of large-scale nuclear war by accident or miscalculation have grown[180] – and this is arguably the most serious risk of all since it threatens global destruction. The United States and Russia would potentially be in the center of such a catastrophe. A unilateral withdrawal from the ABM Treaty will, at the very least, perpetuate the risks of accidental nuclear war by causing the maintenance of nuclear weapons on hair trigger alert. As noted above, the U.S. missile defense program does not address the main threats of nuclear weapons use by non-state groups or by non-nuclear weapons states in the near- to medium-term. When taken in combination with other factors, such as the nuclear posture of the United States, it jeopardizes the most important treaty that prevents the spread of nuclear weapons and nuclear materials – the NPT.

In the context of complete verified de-alerting of nuclear weapons and a commitment to complete disarmament, including missile control, it is possible to imagine missile defenses, globally applied, as theoretically positive, though it is not clear whether that would be a worthwhile priority even then. But the present context of the U.S. withdrawal is quite different. Highly influential elements within the U.S. government are advocating the U.S. domination of space.[181] The U.S. nuclear posture includes possible first use of nuclear weapons in a variety of circumstances and does not rule out a first strike. At the present time, justifying a unilateral withdrawal from the ABM Treaty as an act of defense stretches credibility beyond the limit, especially when taken in combination with the U.S. record on other treaties detailed in this book, as well as the technical reality that a functioning missile defense system would enhance the ability of the United States to carry out a first strike with reduced damage to itself.

5

THE CHEMICAL WEAPONS CONVENTION

BACKGROUND

The use of chemical weapons in war has been legally prohibited since the Geneva Protocol of 1925.[182] The Chemical Weapons Convention (CWC) enhances this prohibition by banning the development, production, stockpiling and transfer of chemical weapons, by monitoring each member state's chemical industry, and by increasing transparency.

The CWC was negotiated over a period of more than a decade within the United Nations Conference on Disarmament. The United States played a significant role in negotiations, advocating a treaty broad in scope and with a thorough verification and inspection regime.[183] The CWC was completed and opened for signature on January 13, 1993.

The CWC contains three basic obligations that each state party must undertake:

(1) Prohibition of Weapons. States parties agree to never develop, acquire or use chemical weapons or transfer them to anyone;

(2) Destruction of Weapons. States parties agree to destroy all their existing chemical weapons production facilities and stockpiles;

(3) Declarations and Inspections. Each state party must declare any chemical weapons facilities or stockpiles. States parties are not restricted in the use of chemicals and facilities for purposes other than the manufacture/use of chemical weapons, but must allow routine inspections of declared "dual-use" chemicals and production facilities that could be used in a manner prohibited

by the convention. The annexes of the Convention set forth the
list of such chemicals and facilities.[184]

In addition to the routine inspections, the treaty also gives states parties
the right to request a challenge inspection of any facility, declared or
undeclared, on the territory of another state party that it suspects of possible non-compliance (Article IX). A requested inspection may be blocked
by a three-quarters vote of an Executive Council of member states if the
request is judged to be frivolous or abusive.

The CWC established an independent agency, the Organization for the
Prohibition of Chemical Weapons (OPCW), to oversee all aspects of the
execution of the convention. One subpart of the chemical weapons, the
Technical Secretariat, carries out inspections; the Executive Council
(made up of 41 member states) oversees implementation of the treaty provisions (including investigations of non-compliance) and the Conference
of the States Parties is the principal decision-making organ made up of all
CWC members, with duties including setting the budget and policies, and
overseeing the other organs.

The CWC also created a legal mechanism to assist in the prevention of terrorism because states are required to outlaw the production, transfer and
use of chemical weapons for their nationals, and because the treaty prohibits the transfer of the most dangerous chemicals to non-member
states.[185]

The CWC has successfully increased transparency, with declarations of
existing chemical weapons stockpiles by India, South Korea, Russia, and
the U.S., which are all destroying, or preparing to destroy, existing chemical weapons materials and facilities. But the treaty has not been used to
its fullest potential. It is not universal: 29 signatories to the treaty have not
ratified it, some of the non-member states (e.g. Iraq, North Korea, Libya,
Egypt, Syria, Israel) are believed to maintain chemical weapons programs,
and at least one state party, Iran, has been accused by the U.S. government
of continuing a chemical weapons program.[186]

Moreover, in its implementing legislation for the Convention, the United
States placed restrictions on the application of certain treaty provisions, so
that it is not complying with the full requirements of the text. The decision
to implement the treaty in a limited manner risks erosion of some of the
most valuable aspects of the treaty, including the verification regime.

U.S. RATIFICATION AND IMPLEMENTATION OF THE CWC

DIFFICULTIES IN SENATE APPROVAL OF THE CWC

The CWC, like all treaties, was reviewed by the Senate Foreign Relations Committee before it was put to a vote for ratification. At the time, Senator Jesse Helms was the chairman of the Committee. Helms advocates a school of thought, increasingly prominent in U.S. government, that participation in such treaties constrains the options of the United States and undermines the role of the United States as the world's only superpower.[187] The opponents argued that the CWC would injure U.S. businesses because it would compromise trade secrets and would require costly monitoring systems. Also, opponents argued that the CWC would not be effective because it would not fully prevent states parties from cheating, because it may not catch all cheaters, and because countries that have developed or seek to develop chemical weapons programs would not join.[188]

Because chemical weapons ingredients have commercial uses and chemical weapons production facilities can be hidden, no law prohibiting chemical weapons is going to catch all potential violators. No treaty is foolproof, but increased transparency improves the ability to prevent the development, production, transfer, and use of chemical weapons. The CWC verification regime includes a mechanism for routine inspections of declared dual-use facilities, challenge inspections in cases of suspected non-compliance, and information sharing. Members of the treaty are required to criminalize illicit behavior within their regimes, and those countries that do not join are prevented from legally acquiring dual-use materials from party members, thus depriving them of significant trade opportunities. Moreover, safeguards within the treaty, including the Annex on the Protection of Confidential Information, protect confidential and proprietary information. These and other compelling arguments led to support from the Reagan, Bush, and Clinton Administrations, the intelligence community, the chemical industry (contradicting the position that the industry would be overburdened by reporting and inspection obligations), and the American public.[189]

U.S. EXCEPTIONALISM IN RATIFICATION OF THE CWC

The United States signed the treaty in 1993, but then largely ignored it, allowing opposition to the treaty to gain momentum. In October 1996, the issue of ratification finally became a priority of the Clinton Administration after Hungary became the 65th country to ratify the convention; under Article XXI of the CWC, the treaty enters into force six months from the date of the 65th ratification. The United States recognized the need to join the treaty before its entry into force to avoid being shut out of the role of a founding member, which would include a seat on the Executive Committee and the right to draft the rules of the treaty's enforcement.[190]

The Senate Foreign Relations Committee threatened to hold up the treaty in deliberations indefinitely. The Clinton Administration was forced to make considerable compromises with the Foreign Relations Committee to secure the treaty's release from the committee for a floor vote by Senate.[191] The Foreign Relations Committee aimed to secure additional safeguards with respect to constitutionality, cost, and security. The Committee could not attach reservations to the treaty, because Article XXII prohibited subjecting the articles of the treaty to reservations. Instead, when the Foreign Relations Committee finally released the treaty for a floor vote, it had attached 28 "conditions." These conditions were not subject to further debate. That is, the Senate could either agree to the treaty with the conditions, or could reject the treaty in its entirety. After the Senate approved ratification of the treaty subject to the 28 conditions, Congress added further limitations when the treaty was translated into domestic law (the "implementing legislation").[192]

Some of these restrictions dealt solely with domestic issues, such as requiring the President to report to the Senate, funding, and U.S. constitutional "safeguards," but several restrictions amounted to a refusal to comply with certain terms of the CWC and its Verification Annex. Under Article VI of the CWC, states parties are required to subject toxic chemicals and their precursors and facilities related to such chemicals (as enumerated in the CWC annexes) to verification measures as provided in the Verification Annex. Pursuant to the implementing legislation, however, the President has the right to refuse inspection of any U.S. facility upon the determination that the inspection may "pose a threat to the national security interests." [193] Another restriction narrows the number of facilities that are subject to the inspection and declaration provisions.[194] Also, the United States refuses to allow samples to be "transferred for analysis to any laboratory outside the territory of the United States,"[195] even though the Verification Annex permits, if necessary, "transfer [of] samples for analysis off- site at laboratories designated by the [OPCW]."[196] As discussed below, these unilateral actions restrict the U.S.'s compliance with the CWC and set a dangerous precedent for other treaty members.

Meanwhile, as the United States continued to deliberate on the implementation of the convention, it could not meet its treaty obligations. The United States was required to make initial declarations of activity relating to proliferation-risk chemicals 30 days after the treaty's entry into force (i.e., by the end of May 1997). As described above, as a result of Congressional disagreements, the implementing legislation, which gives the treaty obligations legal effect within the United States, did not pass both houses of Congress until October 1998. Then, regulations needed to establish the manner in which the treaty obligations would be managed within the government were not issued until December 1999.[197]

Without the domestic law setting out the requirements for declarations of chemical industry facilities, inspections of U.S. industry could not take place. This delay created problems for the CWC Secretariat's budget and the allocation of inspectors. More significantly, the delay encouraged other countries to drag their feet until the United States finally made its industry declaration in March 2000, almost three years after it was due.[198] Iran, which is also believed to maintain a chemical weapons program, held off on declaring; Italy, China, France, Germany and other countries threatened to suspend inspections of their industrial facilities until the United States complied.[199]

EFFECTS OF U.S. NON-COMPLIANCE

As described above, the United States created limits on its compliance with the CWC due to substantial opposition within the Senate. The three main limitations on U.S. compliance are: a prohibition on analyzing U.S. chemical samples in laboratories outside of the United States, the presidential right to refuse an on-site inspection, and the limitation of the scope of industrial facilities to be declared.

The refusal to allow sampling outside of the United States could interfere with successful verification of compliance, and the provision is senseless given the safeguards of confidential information in the treaty.[200] The decision to limit the scope of facilities to be declared also risks weakening the ability to monitor and detect non-compliance. "It should be recalled that both Russia and Iraq concealed their chemical weapons program with large industrial sites."[201] Thus, "by shrinking the pool of industrial facilities to which OPCW inspectors are granted routine access," facilities that are not complying may slip past inspection.[202] Other CWC members "will not allow the United States to create a separate and less rigorous verification regime for itself."[203] Some countries will place the same restrictions on inspections. For example, India, in its implementing legislation, prohibits taking samples out of the country, and Russia also proposed similar legislation.[204]

With respect to the conduct of inspections, Dr. Amy Smithson of the Henry L. Stimson Center, who has monitored the implementation of the CWC since its entry into force, observed that the United States officials behaved in an inflexible and uncooperative manner toward the international inspectors, perhaps due to wariness left over from the days of bilateral inspections with the Soviet Union, or perhaps to mask some inaccuracies in reporting. Whatever the reason, the behavior has created a "domino effect of uncooperative behavior during CWC inspections" of other countries.[205] For example, after the United States restricted inspection procedures on tagging and sampling and analysis of chemical munitions, Russia and South Korea, both declared possessors of chemical weapons, imposed the same restrictions during inspections on their territory. India also applied restrictions to its inspections, "citing the U.S. example."[206]

FAILURE TO USE THE CHALLENGE INSPECTION MECHANISM AND CHANGES TO THE OPCW

Since the entry into force of the CWC, no country has invoked the provision allowing challenge inspections in the case of suspected development, production or stockpiling of chemical weapons. Use of the challenge inspection mechanism would bolster the treaty as a tool for gathering information and deterring the spread of chemical weapons, and would address concerns that treaty violations by member states do exist. For example, the United States has alleged that treaty member Iran maintains a chemical weapons program.[207] Iran, which has made declarations and has allowed inspections of former chemical weapons production facilities, claims to have ended its chemical weapons production, but U.S. intelligence sources believe that Iran is continuing to develop chemical weapons and has sought assistance from CWC members Russia and China to assist with its program.[208]

Critics contend that the United States should invoke the challenge inspection procedures of the CWC to address Iran's suspected treaty violations. The reason for failing to do so may be fear of a retaliatory challenge inspection request or to avoid revealing the sources of its information. In March 2002, Under Secretary of State for Arms Control and International Security John Bolton explained that before invoking the challenge inspections, the United States needed to resolve "management issues" of the OPCW, which he called a "troubled organization" that may not be capable of undertaking the burden of challenge inspections.[209]

After announcing its intention to make management changes, the United States achieved the controversial removal of the head of the OPCW, José Bustani, who had held that position since the beginning of the organization. CWC member states voted to remove Mr. Bustani mid-term, 48 votes to 7, with 43 abstentions. Mr. Bustani had been re-elected for a four-year term in 2000 with support from the United States.[210] This is believed to be the first instance where the head of an international agency was dismissed mid-term. The United States argued that its decision was due to "financial mismanagement, demoralisation of the Technical Secretariat staff, and what many believe are ill-considered initiatives."[211] OPCW officials and delegates agreed that Mr. Bustani's aggressive style offended member states, and observers pointed to Mr. Bustani's questionable financial priorities, including his battle to significantly increase his paycheck.[212] Another possible reason was Mr. Bustani's effort to persuade Iraq to join the Convention, which some believe encroached on the way in which the United States plans to address Iraq's suspected possession of weapons of mass destruction.[213] U.S. foreign policy, as of mid-2002, includes the goal of overthrowing the Saddam Hussein government that rules Iraq.

The United States was viewed as pressuring other states to achieve the management change. U.S. criticisms of Mr. Bustani were accompanied with threats not to pay its dues unless Mr. Bustani was voted out.[214] The U.S. pays over 20% of the OPCW budget. Also, the U.S. ambassador reportedly threatened to dismantle U.S. chemical weapons independently of the OPCW if its demands were not met.[215] Irrespective of the merits of the U.S. complaints, the manner in which the United States achieved the removal of the head of the OPCW reveals its desire to dominate and control the structure of treaties and their implementing bodies. Decisions relating to international bodies that must serve all their member states should be made outside of the context of financial threats and threats of withdrawal.

Whatever the goal, the OPCW faces further U.S.-led changes. Although critics of the U.S. actions, including Mr. Bustani, believe that the motivation for these initiatives is to increase U.S. control over the organization, the United States has expressed its desire for a stronger OPCW to help eliminate chemical weapons.[216] If U.S. protestations are to be viewed as sincere, then it is time for the United States to remove the loopholes it opened to restrict or prevent inspections of U.S. facilities. The United States should also use the challenge inspection mechanism to address concerns of non-compliance. The longer the challenge inspection goes unused, the less credible the treaty will appear as a protection for the international community.[217]

THE LEGACY OF THE CWC

The opposition that surfaced during the CWC ratification process had once been an undercurrent of dissent, but is now the prevailing view of the current administration. Opponents of the CWC included Vice President Dick Cheney (former Secretary of Defense under President George H. W. Bush) and Secretary of Defense Donald Rumsfeld (former National Security Advisor under President Gerald Ford). The arguments against the CWC were recycled during the negotiations of the Protocol to the Biological and Toxin Weapons Convention, and that agreement was killed before its drafting was even completed (see next chapter).

Now that the CWC has been implemented, one of the main concerns about the treaty, the potential disclosure of national security and proprietary information, was put to rest by the State Department Special Negotiator for Chemical and Biological Arms Control: "The Chemical Weapons Convention inspections already conducted on both Department of Defense facilities and at commercial firms have thus far demonstrated our ability to fulfill the obligations of the Chemical Weapons Convention without sacrificing sensitive national security or commercial proprietary information."[218]

6

THE BIOLOGICAL WEAPONS CONVENTION

BACKGROUND

With the terrorist attacks of September 11 and the ensuing anthrax attacks, the United States suffered a chilling reminder of the dangers of biological weapons. The anthrax mailings that resulted in five deaths served as a warning that the United States needs comprehensive measures to respond to the use of biological weapons and to treat victims. But equally if not more important, all states need to prevent the diversion of materials and equipment for the development of biological weapons. After September 11, the Bush administration reiterated its support for the Biological Weapons Convention (BWC) as a legal mechanism to aid in preventing the proliferation and use of biological weapons by terrorists or rogue nations.[219]

The BWC was signed in 1972 and came into force on March 26, 1975. Article I states that:

> Each State Party to this Convention undertakes never in any circumstances to develop, produce, stockpile or otherwise acquire or retain:
>
> 1. Microbial or other biological agents, or toxins whatever their origin or method of production, of types and in quantities that have no justification for prophylactic, protective or other peaceful purposes;
>
> 2. Weapons, equipment or means of delivery designed to use such agents or toxins for hostile purposes or in armed conflict.

Article II states that:

> Each State Party to this Convention undertakes to destroy, or to divert to peaceful purposes, as soon as possible but not later than nine months after the entry into force of the Convention, all agents, toxins, weapons, equipment and means of delivery specified in article I of the Convention, which are in its possession or under its jurisdiction or control. In implementing the provisions of this article all necessary safety precautions shall be observed to protect populations and the environment.[220]

Taken together, these two articles require that all parties to the BWC should have destroyed all of the stocks of biological weapons or removed them from military jurisdiction into peaceful applications by December 26, 1975, except for those small amounts needed to develop vaccines and other defensive measures. Also, Article IV requires the parties to the BWC to prohibit the manufacture or development of biological weapons within their jurisdictions. This means that states are required to pass laws restraining individuals and corporations within their jurisdiction or control from developing or possessing biological weapons.

Lacking verification procedures and mechanisms to monitor compliance, the BWC is significantly flawed as an enforceable commitment. Russia exposed the weakness of the treaty in 1992, when it publicly admitted to the existence of its fully developed biological weapons program, established a year after the Soviet Union signed the BWC.[221] Similarly, UN inspections after the Gulf War revealed that Iraq, then a BWC signatory, had created a secret and extensive offensive biological program.[222] Since the BWC allows possession of biological weapon materials in small amounts needed for defensive purposes, such as development of vaccines, the need for a verification arrangement has long been evident.

HISTORY OF THE NEGOTIATIONS FOR A PROTOCOL TO STRENGTHEN THE BWC

The efforts to strengthen the BWC to prevent violations and to detect them more readily when they occurred began over ten years ago. At the third BWC review conference in September 1991, states parties established an Ad Hoc Group of Governmental Experts (VEREX) to identify and examine potential verification measures from a scientific and technical standpoint.[223] In 1994, a special conference of states parties established an Ad Hoc Group, which is open to all states parties, to consider appropriate measures to strengthen the BWC, and to draft proposals to be included in a legally binding instrument.

The Ad Hoc Group began formal protocol negotiations in 1995, and transitioned to a draft Protocol text (the rolling text) in 1997. By fall 2000, the negotiations slowed due to difficulties in reaching compromises. In March 2001, the Chairman of the Ad Hoc Group, Ambassador Tibor Tóth of Hungary, presented a Composite Text "to address the remaining outstanding issues,"[224] in the hope of facilitating completion of the negotiations on a protocol before the Fifth BWC Review Conference, held from November 19-December 7, 2001.

CONTENTS OF THE BWC VERIFICATION PROTOCOL

DESCRIPTION OF THE PROTOCOL

The Protocol offered three principal mechanisms to strengthen the BWC:

1. Declarations of national bio-defense programs, facilities with high biological containment, plant pathogen facilities and facilities working with certain toxic agents;

2. Promotion of the accuracy of the declarations through random site-check visits and clarification visits;

3. Challenge inspections to investigate allegations of non-compliance.

The Protocol's declaration and verification regime is designed to address the "dual-use" nature of disease agents and technology. The same microorganisms that may be diverted for use in biological weapons are studied by defense and pharmaceutical/biotechnology firms to develop defenses against a natural outbreak or a deliberate attack.

For years, the United States and its allies supported the mechanisms set forth in the Protocol as the basic elements needed to strengthen the BWC. For example, in 1998, the United States and twenty-eight other states submitted a paper to the Ad Hoc Group supporting declarations, clarification visits, and investigations into concerns over non-compliance as measures to strengthen the convention.[225]

The Protocol offers several types of visits aimed at increasing confidence and resolving questions relating to the accuracy of states' declarations. The visits would also enhance the transparency of declared facilities.

According to Tibor Tóth, Chairman of the Ad Hoc Group: "The transparency provisions in the Protocol will, over time, create a climate of openness and candor around significant dual-use activities. We are about creating light where there is darkness. This is an environment in which proliferators may well find it more difficult to operate [and] flourish." [226]

The provision for challenge inspections would install a permanent legal mechanism for thorough inspections of suspected cheaters. Additional benefits include the detailed provision for sharing scientific information and the requirement that each state party adopt penal legislation criminalizing actions prohibited under the BWC. The provision for penal legislation may help to prevent bioterrorism, as each country would be required to prosecute anyone within its jurisdiction suspected of developing any such program.

None of these mechanisms currently exists in the BWC. Although it is valued for codifying the norm that biological weapons should not be developed or used, the BWC does not require countries to enact laws prohibiting biological weapons activities by its citizens, there are no mandatory reporting requirements for any state's biodefense program,[227] or provisions for on site visits. These measures are the first basic steps in preventing a diversion of microorganisms from peaceful to military use, and in expanding our knowledge of the current threat so that we may attempt to develop responses. The provisions of the Protocol could also be crucial in discovering whether the original parties to the BWC met their commitments to destroy all but small amounts of biological weapon materials before the end of 1975, or whether, like the Soviet Union and Iraq, they violated them.

CRITICISMS OF THE PROTOCOL AND RESPONSES

Verification Measures Are Not Strong Enough

Treaty negotiators, scientists, and arms control advocates recognize that inherent difficulties exist in monitoring biological agents. The subject agents are utilized in a variety of industries, and facilities may be able to rid themselves of agents without detection. In order to verify use of the agents, therefore, inspections must be thorough and broad in scope. Critics of the Protocol argue that the declaration and inspection system proposed in the Protocol does not go far enough to ensure transparency.

Some analysts found that too many facilities are exempted from inspection.[228] "A state could therefore keep much of its biodefense operations legally exempt from routine international scrutiny, subject only to the unusual process of facility investigation that will be difficult to initiate."[229] The Protocol also places limits on the information that is subjected to inspection and verification. For example, although the Protocol included random visits as a means of promoting accurate declarations, the number of random visits a year is limited, "making the likelihood of such visits quite low for any given facility."[230]

The visits are limited largely to protect the biotechnology industry's proprietary information and states parties' biodefense programs.[231] Negotiators agreed to permit the inspected party to determine access during a visit. But experts feared that the protections against intrusiveness during inspections "could readily compromise the overall degree of transparency actually achieved and would certainly diminish the impression of transparency even among cooperative parties."[232]

As part of its Chemical and Biological Weapons Nonproliferation Project, the Stimson Center assembled a panel of experts to explore the technical prospects of an inspection regime. Most panelists agreed with the basic monitoring tools of the Protocol's inspection regime but had concerns with the quality of visits, including the amount of time and limited staffing. According to the summary report, *House of Cards*, "the draft protocol appears to have bent over backward to minimize the inconvenience and intrusiveness of inspections to host facilities. While it is important to hold down the burden of inspections, skimping on inspection manpower and time on site could yield poor results."[233]

There is clearly a tension between transparency of inspections and their thoroughness on the one hand and the protection of proprietary information on the other at least in some cases. The Stimson Center panel favored more thorough inspections than provided for in the Protocol, which would promote better assurances of compliance and create a greater likelihood of detecting violations. As we show below, the United States played a key role in weakening the inspections provisions.

U.S. Role in Weakening the Protocol's Inspection Regime

The United States now claims that the provisions of the Protocol are too weak to provide value, but several observers of the negotiations note that the United States was partly responsible for creating the weaker provisions. For example, the United States insisted on loopholes to limit the declaration of biodefense facilities, opposed the declaration of production facilities other than vaccine plants, and argued to prohibit sampling during visits.[234] The United States also resisted defining the purpose of random visits as ensuring the *accuracy* of declarations; instead it insisted on their characterization as "increasing confidence in the consistency of declarations."[235]

The United States sought more limited inspections to safeguard its confidential biodefense information and industrial proprietary information. Supporters of the Protocol believe that this information could be adequately safeguarded, and a working paper from Germany to the Ad Hoc Group applying the methods of the Protocol concluded that "information can be achieved without intrusive on-site activities, without compromising confidential proprietary or national security information and without checking any quantitative data."[236] Instead of weakening inspections, the United States should have conducted more research and testing to improve both the methods of collecting information and safeguarding the systems. Yet the United States did not conduct extensive tests during the negotiations, or when it undertook a review of its Protocol policy, even though the U.S. was required to undertake such tests by a 1999 law.[237]

U.S. REJECTION AND THE END OF THE PROTOCOL

The United States never took a leading role in the negotiations of the BWC Protocol under either the Clinton or Bush administrations.[238] The United States put forward only 16 out of the 450 working papers submitted to the Ad Hoc Group.[239] Some observers of Protocol negotiations believe that the lack of U.S. leadership toward the Protocol might be explained by its mixed reception within the U.S. government from the beginning. For example, the commerce department and national security officials reportedly opposed the treaty for its potential risk to trade secrets and lack of ability to catch cheaters.[240] And as mentioned above, neither administration conducted thorough field tests to determine the efficacy of the monitoring regime. Nevertheless, toward the end of the Clinton Administration, Ambassador Donald Mahley, U.S. Special Negotiator for Chemical and Biological Arms Control Issues, testified that then Secretary of State Madeline Albright and then Under Secretary of State for Arms Control and International Security Holum "still hope[d] a satisfactory Protocol can be achieved by the [November] 2001 target date."[241]

THE BUSH ADMINISTRATION POLICY REVIEW AND DECISION TO SCRAP THE PROTOCOL

When the Bush administration took office, it soon began to review its policy toward the Composite Text.[242] The review was completed in May 2001. Although the conclusions were not released publicly, the review committee found thirty-eight problems with the Protocol and "concluded that the verification measures in the treaty were unlikely to detect cheating" and that "these same provisions might be used by foreign governments to try to steal American secrets."[243] The administration did not at this time abandon the Protocol, and some hope remained that the U.S. would work with the existing text so that some agreement to strengthen the BWC would survive.

Two days after the opening of the 24th and final scheduled session of the Ad Hoc Group, the United States announced its rejection of the draft Protocol. Ambassador Mahley announced to the Ad Hoc Group that the United States is "unable to support the current text, even with changes, as an appropriate outcome of the Ad Hoc Group efforts."[244] The United States thus rejected the draft Protocol, and any effort to improve on the existing text. Mahley further indicated that instead of the Protocol, the United States "intends to develop other ideas and different approaches" to strengthen the BWC.

Allies in the European Union and other states registered disappointment at the U.S. decision, and disagreed with the conclusion that the costs of the Protocol would outweigh its benefits.[245] Nevertheless, the Ad Hoc Group determined not to go forward with negotiating the Protocol without U.S. participation.

REASONS GIVEN FOR THE DECISION TO OPPOSE THE PROTOCOL ARE NOT VALID

In his address to the Ad Hoc Group, Ambassador Mahley offered the following explanation for rejecting the draft: "[The draft Protocol] will not improve our ability to verify BWC compliance. It will not enhance our confidence in compliance and will do little to deter those countries seeking to develop biological weapons. In our assessment, the draft Protocol would put national security and confidential business information at risk."[246]

This explanation offered a disingenuous representation of the purpose and contents of the Protocol.

"Verification" flaws

The theory that the Protocol failed to meet its objectives relies on the false assumption that one of its main objectives was "to uncover illicit activity."[247] The United States had not previously argued that the Protocol would be designed to detect cheaters, and knew that there were considerable limitations in creating such a protocol.

The very nature of biological weapons makes their detection exceptionally difficult. As stated by Dr. Edward Lacey, Acting Assistant Secretary of State, Bureau of Verification and Compliance, the elements used to create biological weapons are dual use in nature: "both they and the facility at which they are conducted could be used for legitimate purposes or for offensive biological warfare purposes."[248] Only small amounts of material are needed to create a militarily significant program, making detection even more difficult. "Whereas many tons of chemical agent are needed for a militarily significant chemical warfare capability, a comparable biological warfare capability would be measured in pounds of agent."[249] Adding further difficulty to the possibility of detection is that "the equipment needed to produce such amounts of biological agent could be housed in a relatively small space inside a building without specific distinguishing features."[250]

The fact that this Protocol could not be used to smoke out all violations was well known to the negotiators and to the U.S. government. Ambassador Mahley, less than a year before the speech to the Ad Hoc Committee, explained to the House Government Reform Committee, Subcommittee on National Security, Veterans Affairs and International Relations that the Protocol "is not an issue of verification." Verification "involves being able to make a judgment of high confidence in detecting a violation before it can become a militarily significant threat." But because even a small almost undetectable program could pose a threat, the United States "has never, therefore, judged that the Protocol would produce what is to us an effectively verifiable BWC."[251]

Even recognizing that the treaty could not detect all instances of cheating, through its provisions for declarations and clarifications, a protocol would promote transparency of a state's biological activity. Mahley testified that there is "real value" in increasing this transparency: "What we have sought in the negotiations is greater transparency into the dual-capable activities and facilities that could be misdirected for BW purposes. This could, in our view, complicate the efforts of countries to cheat on their BWC obligations."[252]

The Defense Department supported the approach set forth by Ambassador Mahley:

> We do not believe that the Protocol being negotiated will be able to provide the kind of effective verification that exists in other arms control treaties. That is, it will not provide a high degree of confidence that we could detect militarily significant cheating. We therefore recognize that this Protocol will not "solve" the problem of biological weapons proliferation, even among the BWC States Parties who opt to join. But it can contribute to the more limited goal of strengthening confidence in BWC compliance by enhancing international transparency in the biological sphere. We see this as an important and useful contribution to our nonproliferation efforts.[253]

In September 2000, therefore, the U.S. objective for the Protocol was "to enable us to gain more information about and insight into activities of potential concern."[254] The ability to detect all "illicit activity" was not, and for practical reasons could not be, the U.S. objective in negotiating the Protocol.

Security and Confidentiality of U.S. Information

Another alleged problem with the draft Protocol, according to Ambassador Mahley's July 25, 2001 statement, is that safeguards to protect information not relevant to the BWC are insufficient, and that the U.S. biodefense programs and biotech industry would not be adequately protected.

The current U.S. position is factually inconsistent with the content of the Protocol, with earlier U.S. views on the subject, and with experience in safeguarding such information. In testimony submitted to the House Government Reform Subcommittee in September 2000, Ambassador Mahley expressed confidence that U.S. security information would be secured in the Protocol. He noted a parallel with the inspections under the Chemical Weapons Convention,[255] which had succeeded in "demonstrat[ing] our ability to fulfill the obligations of the Chemical Weapons Convention without sacrificing sensitive national security or commercial proprietary information." Mahley explained that the lessons of the CWC were being used to explore ways to achieve an equal level of protection for biological inspections "and we are confident we can do so by the time any BWC Protocol is in place."

Thus, quite contrary to the assertion that the risks to U.S. information outweigh the benefits of the Protocol, Mahley had, less than a year earlier, concluded that "the impact on U.S. facilities should be manageable, while the value of on-site activity in other countries to transparency and our BW nonproliferation efforts is real."[256]

The draft Protocol in fact contains more mechanisms for safeguarding information than the CWC, and the United States has been a party to that treaty since 1997. "Unlike the CWC, the protocol text does not require routine visits, it allows no sampling and analysis in non-challenge visits, and it gives control of access to the host country."[257] States parties are not required to provide either confidential or commercial proprietary information in declarations.[258] The draft Protocol also "exempts many defense facilities and most pharmaceutical facilities from declaration," adding further security to U.S. information. Concerns about the security of information are particularly dubious because many of the facilities covered under the draft Protocol are already covered under the CWC and subject to challenge inspection.[259]

Given its prior statements, the existing overlap with the inspection mechanisms of the CWC and the Protocol's safeguards for information, the U.S. position with regard to security and confidentiality of the Protocol holds little weight.

The Value of the Protocol

The United States now argues that because the Protocol will not be able to catch cheaters, and risks compromising security information, there is little value to what the Protocol seeks to accomplish. As discussed above, this assertion is at odds with the seven years of negotiations undertaken by the United States before it announced its withdrawal of support.

The United States had previously recognized the value of the Protocol even with its imperfect ability to detect violators, particularly because it creates a regime of transparency. In the face of the legally binding declaration requirements, the cost of a state's noncompliance or incomplete disclosures would greatly increase. And the value of the declaration provisions is obvious when compared with the current state of information on other states' biological facilities; "without the Protocol all that any country has to go on are press reports and intelligence estimates and so on," but the Protocol would require mandatory declarations "with the means to clarify any ambiguities, uncertainties, anomalies or omissions, providing hard evidence as to activities and facilities within the State Party."[260]

As recently as September 2000, Ambassador Mahley acknowledged the value of the Protocol: "I do not wish to convey the impression that there is no potential benefit from a satisfactory Protocol, nor that it is a hopeless technical problem. It is extraordinarily difficult, but that makes it a worthy challenge."[261]

ALTERNATIVES PROPOSED BY THE UNITED STATES TO STRENGTHEN THE BWC

The July 25 statement rejecting the draft Protocol assured the Ad Hoc Group that the United States would soon propose alternative measures to strengthen the BWC.

On November 19, 2001, when the Fifth BWC Review Conference convened in Geneva, John Bolton, U.S. Under Secretary of State for Arms Control and International Security, reiterated the U.S. concern that certain BWC states parties were not complying with the treaty,[262] and set forth potential measures to strengthen the BWC in the alternative of the Protocol:

- Criminalization of Offenses: Called for each state to enact national criminal legislation with respect to biological weapons offenses;

- Security Standards: Urged parties to adopt voluntary security standards for certain pathogens and voluntary reporting of biological releases or events that could affect other countries;

- Biosafety procedures and Assistance to Victims: Urged enhanced cooperation with the World Health Organization to adopt strict biosafety guidelines, and cooperation on medical assistance in the event of an outbreak;

- Investigation of Outbreaks and Compliance Concerns: Called for a mechanism for international investigations of suspicious disease outbreaks and/or alleged BW incidents, upon determination by the UN Secretary General that such inspections should take place. The United States would also support a

>   mechanism, on a strictly voluntary basis, for "clarifying and
>   resolving compliance concerns by mutual consent," including
>   information exchanges and voluntary visits.[263]

When the Fifth Review Conference of the BWC reviewed the policies proposed by the United States, several countries "generically referred positively to 'new ideas' and supported steps such as the criminalisation of activities by individuals that ran counter to the Convention, bio-safety measures, and limiting access to dangerous pathogens, all of which were included in the U.S. proposals."[264] But while states parties expressed a willingness to work with the U.S.-proposed measures, they did not support the proposals as an alternative to the Ad Hoc Group's fulfilling its mandate to negotiate an all encompassing legally-binding agreement to strengthen the BWC.[265]

BWC states parties did not accept the U.S. proposals as a viable alternative to a comprehensive multilateral agreement. The Protocol required legally binding measures that would be applicable to all members of the protocol; the U.S. proposals lack international legal enforcement and do not sufficiently expand on the existing system.

The Bush administration calls for states to implement criminal legislation to prosecute people committing biological weapons offenses, but offers no legally binding mechanisms to require countries to adopt the legislation. Moreover, it opposes the International Criminal Court, whose Statute could be amended to expressly criminalize use of biological weapons (provisions of the Statute already generally prohibit such use). With respect to monitoring non-compliance, the Protocol had proposed challenge inspections under an Organization for the Prohibition of Bacteriological (Biological) and Toxin Weapons as a means of redress for compliance concerns. As an alternative, the United States suggests measures under the Secretary General. But this proposal merely extends a system that is already in place. "In 1987, the UN General Assembly called upon the secretary-general to carry out investigations in response to reports by any UN member state concerning the use of chemical or biological weapons. The resolution also asked the secretary-general to convene a group of qualified experts to develop guidelines and procedures and to identify laboratories that could be used for these investigations—all that work was completed in 1989."[266]

The suggestions for voluntary visits, exchanges of information, and other voluntary compliance mechanisms maintain the status quo; they do not meet the transparency goals that would be achieved by a protocol, and would do little to improve the measures already in place. As explained by one observer, "Article V of the BWC already says the states parties should consult and cooperate with one another to resolve problems, and previous review conferences have agreed on consultative procedures to implement that part of the convention. So it's difficult . . . to see how the administration has moved the ball forward on this issue."[267]

THE SUSPENSION OF MULTILATERAL EFFORTS TO STRENGTHEN THE CONVENTION

The initial session of the Fifth Review Conference of the BWC was held from November 19 to December 7, 2001, pursuant to the terms of the BWC, which requires a review conference of states parties every five years. This conference was intended to be the time at which BWC parties received the negotiated draft Protocol. But the U.S. had recently rejected the Protocol, and on the final day of the meeting, the United States proposed to terminate the Ad Hoc Group whose stated purpose was to create a legally binding mechanism to strengthen the BWC.[268] The United States advocated as an alternative that BWC member states should meet annually to assess implementation of any agreed-upon measures and consider new measures. Annual meetings were favored by many other states parties, but not in conjunction with disbanding the Ad Hoc Group; the United States was the only country to favor terminating the group's mandate. The decision "enraged" some of the U.S.'s closest allies and "heated corridor discussions revealed a general sense of the U.S. action as a deliberate last-minute attempt to derail the Conference."[269] The committee suspended work on its draft final report, agreeing to re-convene a year later to complete its final declaration.[270] As of September 2002, the United States has been seeking to delay all further discussion on measures to strengthen the BWC until 2006 (Slevin 2002). The U.S. resistance to legal measures to address bioweapons seems mindless of the 2001 anthrax attacks and wholly inconsistent with the administratoin's goal of strengthening protections against weapons of mass destruction.[271]

THE U.S. BIODEFENSE PROGRAM

The United States does not endorse a mandatory declaration regime to further transparency of states' biological programs. The rationale may be largely explained by the U.S. commitment to biodefense work, and the belief that the declaratory regime risks its security information and biotechnology firms' intellectual property. In fall 2001, reports surfaced of U.S. biodefense programs carried out in secret to replicate offensive biological measures and arms control experts began questioning whether these biodefense measures are in compliance with the fundamental obligations of the BWC.

In the book *Germs* and the corresponding *New York Times* article, authors Judith Miller, Stephen Engelberg, and William Broad reported that the United States undertook a secret program in the late 1990s to construct a model biobomb, build a bioweapons lab, and replicate a super-strain of anthrax.[272] And since the anthrax attacks in September 2001, the U.S. program to make weapons-grade anthrax also came to light. After the terrorist attacks, the United States became more determined to conduct secret research in the area of biodefense, and has made efforts to broaden the scope of confidentiality of scientific research. Secrecy is necessary, government officials argue, to prevent use of the information for making weapons or detecting vulnerabilities in U.S. biological defenses.

Secrecy may also shield the fact that the research has reached the outer limits of compliance with the BWC. Because fellow states parties do not know the extent of the programs, they cannot assess U.S. compliance. This situation puts the prohibition of biological weapons in a precarious state: apart from assurances that the projects are for defensive purposes, they are not easily distinguishable from offensive measures that a country might take to develop bioweapons. If another state were to commit to similar endeavors, would the United States rely on assurances that they are for defensive purposes without any evidence?

RECENT U.S. BIODEFENSE RESEARCH

The Germ Bomb

In 1997, the CIA began a secret study of Soviet bioweapons systems, which spawned a project called Clear Vision that built and tested a model of a Soviet biological bomblet. The model bomb was constructed to test a bomb's dispersal characteristics to see how it might be used in an attack. The project did not build fully operational weapons; they lacked fuses so they could not be detonated and were filled with simulants instead of live agent.

The Bioweapons Production Plant

The Pentagon, meanwhile, was conducting its own secret projects for biodefense. In 1998, the Pentagon began a project to see whether it was possible to construct a bioweapons facility out of commercially available materials. The project "built a functioning facility that had turned out two pounds of 'product' – anthrax simulants –in test runs."[273] No infectious biological agent was produced.

The Superbug

While the other two operations have been completed, the super-anthrax project, also made public in 2001, is still in effect. Russian scientists published a scientific report in 1997 that they had transferred a toxin gene from *Bacillus cereus*, an organism that causes food poisoning, into the anthrax microbe. The CIA planned to replicate the work, and then the project was taken over by the Pentagon in 2001. The stated purpose of the project is to see if the anthrax vaccinations given to American soldiers would work against the superbug. Although the project was delayed as a result of the September 11 attacks, it was reportedly reapproved in October 2001.[274] Whether or not a clear violation of the BWC, critics contend that such genetic engineering research on bio-weapons is highly dangerous.[275]

Weapons-Grade Anthrax

In December 2001, the U.S. army admitted that it had manufactured "weapons-grade" anthrax. Weapons-grade anthrax is created when spores are processed fine enough: 1 to 5 microns, so that they can be readily inhaled and trigger the most serious form of the disease, inhalation anthrax. It was the first acknowledgement that the government had weaponized anthrax since the United States committed to banning biological weapons in 1969. The details of the program have been withheld from the public, even though it appears likely that the Army's weaponized anthrax is the source of the anthrax used in the fall 2001 U.S. anthrax attacks.[276]

THE LEGALITY OF U.S. BIODEFENSE ACTIVITIES UNDER THE BWC

The BWC allows states parties to develop and maintain biological agents for "prophylactic, protective or other peaceful purposes," but flatly prohibits the "weapons, equipment or means of delivery designed to use such agents or toxins for hostile purposes or in armed conflict."[277]

The construction of the biobomb prompted U.S. government review of whether the project complied with the terms of the BWC. The interagency review did not come to a resolution. The CIA argued that its project was defensive and thus permitted under the treaty because it responded to specific intelligence about threats from adversaries. The State Department, on the other hand, "argued that the treaty ruled out any tests involving weapons."[278] The State Department is correct. BWC scholars agree that making devices for the delivery of biological weapons, even for defense assessment purposes, is not permitted under the BWC.[279]

The development of weapons-grade anthrax also might be viewed as being outside the parameters of the treaty. The army processed anthrax spores to such a degree that the particles are small enough to be easily inhaled into the lungs and cause inhalation anthrax, without any additional means of delivery. The anthrax itself thus constitutes a weapon, in this view.

The other two projects, the production plant and the super-bug, are not likely to be viewed as violating the BWC, but the United States would probably be required to report them in a protocol aimed at transparency. The U.S. decision not to endorse the Protocol might therefore be explained as an attempt to preserve the ability to run these types of covert programs.

If BWC states parties cannot assess whether their fellow treaty members are in compliance, confidence in the effectiveness of the treaty will inevitably erode. That was the heart of the argument for a transparency mechanism that, until recently, the United States advocated. If states doubt U.S. compliance, they may be less willing to cooperate with the United States to prevent biological weapons proliferation. Or states may undertake their own secretive biodefense programs, also asserting that they comply with the BWC because they are "defensive" in nature. As Clinton administration officials said, "Simultaneous experiments involving a model of a germ bomb, a factory to make biological agents and the development of more potent anthrax, would draw vociferous protests from Washington if conducted by a country the United States viewed as suspect."[280]

CONCLUSION

The stated reasons for the U.S. withdrawal from the protocol are suspect at best and do not stand up to serious scrutiny. They are contrary to the very positions taken by the U.S. government over a considerable period while the Protocol was being negotiated. The central issue during the negotiations was never the complete detection of cheating but greater transparency that would promote nonproliferation. The other parties to the BWC were willing to entertain U.S. demands for national laws for prosecuting individuals violating the BWC and other voluntary measures. Yet the United States not only rejected the specific text for the Protocol under consideration, it advocated the complete abandonment of strengthening the BWC through a legally binding agreement. There is general agreement that the Protocol as it stood could have been improved in a variety of ways to enable better detection of non-compliance. But the United States made no specific proposals in this regard. On the contrary, when it came to inspections, it appeared to be more concerned about protecting commercial information. Finally, even that issue seems moot in many cases, since the facilities in question are already subject to inspection under the verification provisions of the Chemical Weapons Convention. Walking away from negotiations and advocating abandonment of negotiations is exactly the opposite of the behavior that one would expect from a country that was engaged in good faith in promoting compliance with the BWC.

Recent revelations about the U.S. development of biological weapons capability, including highly dispersible anthrax as well the means of their delivery, raise the question as to whether the rejection of the Protocol might not be related to its desire to prevent inspections of its own facilities. Such inspections could pose the risk of revealing past U.S. violations of the treaty, if they had taken place.

When we view the entire, complex set of facts, it is difficult to accept that the United States walked away from the Protocol because it was defective or because it wanted a stronger and more transparent verification process. That would have been desirable and could have been achieved by agreeing to the Protocol with the proviso that it be strengthened in certain areas, notably in regard to the detection of non-compliance. That is the course we believe the United States should have taken. The fact that it abandoned the Protocol and the negotiating process points rather to the conclusion that the United States would like to be completely exempt from oversight by any other party, while creating its own ways to enforce others to comply with its wishes on an ad hoc basis.

7

TREATY BANNING ANTIPERSONNEL MINES

MINE BAN TREATY OVERVIEW

There are an estimated 60-70 million antipersonnel landmines in over seventy countries,[281] killing or maiming thousands of men, women and children each year.[282] Anti-personnel mines are indiscriminate weapons that lay dormant until triggered by footsteps and cannot distinguish between civilians and soldiers. They continue to kill or injure long after fighting has stopped. "Mines also render large tracts of agricultural land unusable, wreaking environmental and economic devastation."[283]

Mines have also caused nearly 100,000 U.S. Army casualties since 1942.[284] One-third of all U.S. Army casualties in Vietnam were the result of mine incidents.[285] Thirty-three percent of U.S. personnel killed in action and fourteen percent of the wounded in action during the 1990-1991 Persian Gulf War were the result of mine incidents.[286] Peacekeeping operations in Somalia, Bosnia, and Kosovo have all resulted in U.S. mine casualties. In 2001, U.S. military personnel were injured in mine incidents in Afghanistan, Kosovo, and South Korea.[287]

The international outcry against these weapons prompted the rapid negotiation and enactment of the Convention on the Prohibition of the Use, Stockpiling, Production, and Transfer of Anti-Personnel Mines and On Their Destruction (Mine Ban Treaty). States parties are required to make implementation reports to the UN Secretary-General within 180 days, destroy stockpiled mines within four years, and destroy mines in the ground in territory within their jurisdiction or control within 10 years.[288] The Mine Ban Treaty also requires states parties to take appropriate domestic implementation measures, including imposition of penal sanctions for violation of its provisions.

The International Campaign to Ban Landmines (ICBL) considers the Mine Ban Treaty the only viable comprehensive framework for achieving a mine-free world. It is evident that the treaty, and the ban movement more generally, are making a significant difference. A growing number of governments are joining the Mine Ban Treaty, there is decreased use of antipersonnel mines, a dramatic drop in production, an almost complete halt to trade, rapid destruction of stockpiled mines, fewer mine victims in key affected countries, and more land demined.

A total of 145 countries have signed or acceded to the Mine Ban Treaty as of August 31, 2002, and a total of 125 of those countries have ratified or acceded, thereby fully committing to all the provisions of the Mine Ban Treaty. After achieving the required 40 ratifications in September 1998, the Mine Ban Treaty entered into force on March 1, 1999, one of the fastest entries into force of a multilateral treaty. Considering the relatively short time that this issue has been before the international community, the number of signatories and accessions — nearly three-quarters of the world's countries — is exceptional. This is a clear indication of the widespread international rejection of any use or possession of antipersonnel mines. But there are major exceptions, notably India, which placed large numbers of mines along its border with Pakistan after the terrorist attack on India's Parliament on December 13, 2001.

EVOLUTION OF U.S. POLICY

In October 1992, at the initiative of Senator Patrick Leahy, the strongest advocate of a ban in the U.S. government, the United States enacted a one-year moratorium on the export of antipersonnel mines. In 1993, the U.S. State Department produced *Hidden Killers: The Global Problem with Uncleared Landmines*, the first comprehensive study of the mines crisis. In September 1994, President Clinton became the first world leader to call for the "eventual elimination" of antipersonnel mines, and the United States sponsored a UN General Assembly resolution endorsing the eventual elimination of mines which was passed in December 1994. In 1995, the Senate passed an amendment requiring a one-year moratorium on use of antipersonnel mines, except along international borders and demilitarized zones. It was signed into law in February 1996, and was to take effect three years later, but was much diluted in 1998 when Congress gave the President the authority to waive the moratorium.

During 1995 and early 1996, the United States turned its attention to the Review Conference of the Convention on Conventional Weapons (CCW) and its Protocol II.[289] Protocol II regulates and restricts the use of anti-personnel landmines but does not call for their elimination. The United States emerged from the Review Conference as the major promoter of so-called "smart" mines that automatically self-destruct — and was criticized by the ICBL for seeking a technical solution to the mines crisis that fell far short of embracing a comprehensive ban. The CCW review ended on May 3, 1996, with adoption of Amended Protocol II. The ICBL and the International Committee of the Red Cross strongly criticized the protocol, but U.S. officials hailed it as a major accomplishment. By this time, some three-dozen governments had publicly expressed support for an immediate, total ban on antipersonnel mines, and the United States found itself falling behind many other truly pro-ban governments.

In what was billed as a major landmines policy statement on May 16, 1996, President Clinton said the United States would "lead a global effort" to ban mines, and "seek a worldwide agreement as soon as possible to end the use of all antipersonnel landmines." But the policy was not a comprehensive ban; rather it made a distinction between dumb mines (which do not self-destruct) and smart mines (which destroy or deactivate themselves). The United States committed not to use dumb mines, except in Korea. Also, the United States agreed to stop producing and destroy its stockpile of dumb mines. But the United States "reserve[d] the option" to use smart mines until an international ban takes effect, and did not limit the production or stockpiling of smart mines.[290]

In November 1996 the United States introduced a UN General Assembly resolution urging states "to pursue vigorously" an international ban treaty "with a view to completing the negotiation as soon as possible." The resolution also called on governments unilaterally to implement "bans, moratoria or other restrictions" on production, stockpiling, export, and use of antipersonnel mines "at the earliest date possible." [291] The resolution was passed on December 10, by a vote of 155-0, with ten abstentions. Meanwhile, Canada had launched the Ottawa Process, the effort to negotiate and sign an international treaty banning antipersonnel mines. The U.S. did not join in the Ottawa Process initially, attending meetings as an observer. Instead of proceeding with the Ottawa Process, the United States chose to pursue a global ban at the UN Conference on Disarmament (CD). It claimed to prefer the CD because two of the largest antipersonnel mine producers, Russia and China, both CD members, opposed the Ottawa process.[292] The decision was criticized by the U.S. Campaign to Ban Landmines as an effort to avoid rapid progress toward a ban, given the notoriously slow pace of the CD. When the CD was unable to put the issue of the mine ban on its agenda in a timely fashion, the U.S. switched its position and announced that it would participate in the Ottawa Process for the final round of negotiations in Oslo in September 1997.

When the United States joined the Ottawa Process, it laid out a series of demands, or prerequisites for its support of the treaty. Chief among these were a geographic exception for continued use of antipersonnel mines of all types in Korea, a change in the treaty's definition of antipersonnel mine so that U.S. antipersonnel mines contained in "mixed" systems with anti-tank mines would not be banned, and an optional nine-year deferral period for compliance with the treaty's key prohibitions. During the negotiations, the other governments rejected these demands.

On the closing day of negotiations, September 17, 1997, President Clinton announced that the United States would not be signing the treaty, but then stated that the United States would unilaterally stop using antipersonnel mines everywhere but Korea by 2003, and in Korea by 2006.[293] Other officials clarified that this would not apply to antipersonnel mines contained in mixed munitions, because the United States no longer considered them antipersonnel mines, but rather submunitions.[294] President Clinton's May 1998 landmine policy announcement refined this commitment.

CURRENT U.S. POLICY

In 1998 President Clinton committed the United States to cease using antipersonnel mines, except those contained in "mixed systems" with anti-tank mines, everywhere in the world except for Korea by the year 2003. By the year 2006, if alternatives have been identified and fielded, the United States will cease all use of all antipersonnel mines, including those in mixed systems, and will join the Mine Ban Treaty.[295]

The Bush Administration is currently conducting a review of U.S. mine policy. As of the time of this writing, is not known when a decision will be made. It is not known if the Clinton Administration's policy toward anti-personnel landmines remains in effect either in part or as a whole.

In late November 2001, Department of Defense officials recommended that the United States abandon its standing commitment to join the 1997 Mine Ban Treaty by 2006 if alternatives to antipersonnel mines are identified and fielded.[296] The Pentagon's review is one component of a multi-agency landmine policy review. Officials from the Department of State and the National Security Council will also participate in the mine policy review prior to a decision by President Bush.

U.S. officials are fond of stating that "our mines are not the problem."[297] Regrettably, that is not the case. The United States was, in the past, one of the biggest exporters of antipersonnel mines. From 1969 through 1992, the United States exported 4.4 million antipersonnel mines to at least thirty-two different countries.[298] U.S. mines have been planted in the ground and have caused civilian casualties in more than two-dozen countries.

U.S. JUSTIFICATION: SMART MINES ARE BETTER

A large part of the basis for the "our mines are not the problem" contention is a distinction made by the United States between "smart" mines and long-lasting "dumb" mines. Following the Vietnam conflict, the United States — in response to a perceived military, not humanitarian, need — procured self-destructing, scatterable mines (dropped from aircraft or shot out of artillery). More than eighty percent of the current U.S. stockpile consists of ADAM artillery-delivered antipersonnel mines, and the United States has several other types of smart mines as well. All smart mines are designed to self-destruct between four hours to fifteen days after their use depending on the setting selected and mine type. If the mines fail to self-destruct, they are also designed to "self-deactivate" within 120 days, as a result of their battery dying. Because of the short lifespan of these mines, U.S. officials claim that the mines "pose little, if any, humanitarian threat to noncombatants."[299]

Smart mines are not without humanitarian impact. There is danger in the period between when the mines are armed and when they self-destruct or self-deactivate, which may be a period of hours, days, or up to seventeen weeks. Because most U.S. smart mines are remotely delivered and not required to be marked, fenced, or monitored, they threaten civilians and livestock when used in populated areas. These mines are also a danger to friendly forces that may maneuver through the mined area during the course of subsequent combat operations. Some of the smart mines will fail to arm at all, and others that arm will fail to self-destruct. From a deminer's perspective, all mines encountered must be treated as though they are live. The smart mines must be cleared one at a time using the same procedures used to clear dumb mines. As a result, the U.S. posture is misleading, because even smart mines cause substantial humanitarian impact.

Moreover, one result of the attempt to distinguish between dumb and smart mines is that many countries feel justified in keeping all antipersonnel mines, whether dumb or smart, as a countervailing measure. Some countries point out that because smart mines have a limited operational lifespan, they are not viable for the long-term defense of borders or fixed installations and therefore one needs to keep dumb mines. Thus, the overall impact of the U.S. position is to encourage continued use of a variety of mines.

U.S. JUSTIFICATION: MINES ARE CRITICAL IN DEFENDING KOREA

President Clinton cited the situation in Korea as the paramount reason for not signing the treaty in September 1997. Accepting the advice of the Joint Chiefs of Staff, the President declared that antipersonnel mines were critical to the defense of South Korea and its capital, Seoul. The defense strategy for Korea appears to rely on a system of obstacles and minefields emplaced by U.S. and South Korean forces to slow an invasion, thus allowing other powerful weapons to be brought to bear on North Korean forces. The United States plans to lay more than one million additional dumb mines in South Korea — not in the existing DMZ,[300] but throughout the twenty-mile area between the DMZ and Seoul.[301] In addition, numerous self-destructing mines would be scattered by aircraft and artillery.[302]

Several retired military leaders have questioned the utility of antipersonnel mines in Korea, citing the overwhelming technological superiority of U.S. weapons being able to compensate for having no antipersonnel mines. Lt. General James Hollingsworth, former commander of U.S. forces in Korea, has said, "There is indeed a military utility to [antipersonnel mines], but in the case of U.S. forces in Korea it is minimal, and in some ways even offset by the difficulty our own [antipersonnel mines] pose to our brand of mobile warfare.... Not only civilians, but U.S. armed forces, will benefit from a ban on landmines. U.S. forces in Korea are no exception."[303]

Additionally, according to information obtained by Human Rights Watch from the U.S. Army Material Command in a Freedom of Information Act request, 45 percent of the 1.2 million long-lasting "dumb" (non-self-destructing) antipersonnel mines retained for use in Korea are stored at depots in the continental U.S.[304] Another 50 percent are in Korea, but at the onset of conflict will be handed over to South Korean troops for their use.[305] The United States earmarks only the remaining 5 percent of the mines for immediate use by U.S. troops in South Korea.[306] The United States has repeatedly said that these mines are needed to stop a massive surprise attack by North Korea but their utility is questionable if they are sitting in warehouses in the United States weeks if not months away from Korea.

PROGRAMS TO DEVELOP ALTERNATIVES TO ANTIPERSONNEL MINES

It appears increasingly unlikely that the Pentagon will meet the 2006 target date for identifying and fielding alternatives for antipersonnel mines. The Pentagon was directed by President Clinton and the Secretary of Defense on May 16, 1996 to begin to "undertake a program of research, development and other measures needed to eliminate the requirement [for exceptions in Korea and mixed systems] and to permit both the United States and our allies to end reliance on [antipersonnel mines] as soon as possible."[307] A target date of 2006 was established in 1998 by linking the success in identifying and fielding alternatives to antipersonnel mines with the United States joining the Mine Ban Treaty.[308]

While the United States policy requires research into alternatives, compliance with the Mine Ban Treaty is not a criterion for any of the alternatives programs. In 1999, as a condition of ratification of CCW Amended Protocol II, President Clinton agreed that the search for alternatives to AP landmines would not be limited by whether they complied with the Mine Ban Treaty. The text of the certification reads,

> I will not limit the types of alternatives to be considered on the basis of any criteria other than those specified in the sentence that follows. In pursuit of alternatives to United States anti-personnel mines, or mixed anti-tank systems, the United States shall seek to identify, adapt, modify, or otherwise develop only those technologies that (i) are intended to provide military effectiveness equivalent to that provided by the relevant anti-personnel mine, or mixed anti-tank system; and (ii) would be affordable.[309]

The contradiction between the policy objectives established under President Clinton and the subsequent interpretation of his instructions is jeopardizing the overall success of the alternatives program and threatens the 2006 target date.

In its fiscal year 2001 budget, the Department of Defense proposed a multi-year, $820 million program for pursuing three "tracks" of alternatives. [310] However, elements of the alternatives program are being impacted by the Bush Administration mine policy review. *Inside the Army*, a weekly newsletter on Army affairs, reported that the Army has zeroed-out funding in its 2003-2007 spending plan for one of the three tracks of the landmine alternatives program — the NSD-A and RADAM programs.[311] The Pentagon in its recommendations for the mine policy review is also proposing to abandon a second track of its alternatives program — the search for alternatives for so-called mixed systems. Notably, these mixed systems contain anti-personnel and antivehicle mines, so they would violate the treaty.

U.S. CONTRIBUTION TO GLOBAL DEMINING PROGRAMS

Apart from its failure to commit to a complete mine ban, the United States has been a major contributor to programs for demining and mine action awareness. The United States has contributed an estimated $390 million in global mine action activities.[312] In 2000, 37 countries received funding for mine action (demining programs). The U.S. Department of Defense has provided training and assistance for national demining programs in 42 countries, including in Kosovo, Somalia, Afghanistan, and Cambodia.[313]

IMPACT OF U.S. MINE POLICY ON THE IMPLEMENTATION OF THE TREATY

Article 1 obligates states parties to "never under any circumstance... assist, encourage or induce, in any way, anyone to engage in any activity prohibited to a State Party under this Convention" and, pursuant to Article 9, states parties are required to "take all appropriate legal, administrative and other measures, including the imposition of penal sanctions, to prevent and suppress any activity prohibited" by the treaty. The United States has antipersonnel landmines stockpiled in at least five states that are states parties to the Mine Ban Treaty: Germany, Japan, Norway, Qatar, and United Kingdom at Diego Garcia, as well as treaty signatory Greece.[314] States parties' allowing other states to stockpile anti-personnel mines in their territory arguably violates the Article 1 prohibitions. U.S. antipersonnel mine stockpiles have been removed from Italy and Spain.

Germany, Japan, and the United Kingdom do not consider the U.S. mine stockpiles to be under their jurisdiction or control, and thus not subject to the provisions of the Mine Ban Treaty or their national implementation measures. Norway, through a bilateral agreement with the United States, has stipulated the mines must be removed by March 1, 2003, which is the deadline for Norway to comply with its obligation for destruction of antipersonnel mines under its jurisdiction and control. Qatar has yet to comment on the issue.

A state party's participation in the anti-terrorism coalition also may raise questions of compliance with the Article I obligation not to assist in any prohibited activity. For example, while the United Kingdom has expressed the view that U.S. stocks of antipersonnel mines contained in ammunition pre-positioning ships at Diego Garcia are not under U.K. jurisdiction or control, this leaves open the question of the legal interpretation if those mines were moved ashore and loaded on aircraft operating from the base at Diego Garcia for use in Afghanistan.

In order to comply with the fundamental treaty obligations, states parties must insure that munitions destined for Afghanistan or elsewhere transiting their territory do not contain antipersonnel mines. In 1999 U.S. Army engineer units deployed to Albania with antipersonnel mines and their delivery systems (MOPMS and Volcano mixed mine systems) as part of Task Force Hawk to support operations in Kosovo. Most of the U.S. Army units deployed from bases in Germany. At the time of this deployment, Albania was a signatory to the Mine Ban Treaty and Germany was a state party to the treaty.

CONCLUSION

As the U.S. policy currently stands, the United States keeps company with Russia, China, Iran, Iraq, Libya, North Korea, Burma, Syria, India, Pakistan, Cuba and others by refusing to join the Mine Ban Treaty. The United States joins Turkey as the only members of NATO not to have signed the treaty, though Turkey has pledged to accede to the accord. It is one of just fourteen countries that have not forsworn production of mines. In sum, the United States is part of a very small minority opposing a comprehensive ban. The dangers and costs of antipersonnel mines are now well known, and the United States should accede to the treaty. In the meantime, it should take immediate steps to comply with its provisions.

8

THE UNITED NATIONS FRAMEWORK CONVENTION ON CLIMATE CHANGE AND THE KYOTO PROTOCOL

The 1992 United Nations Framework Convention on Climate Change (UNFCCC) and the 1997 Kyoto Protocol are linked treaties relating to climate change.[315] Evaluation of compliance with treaty obligations in the area of climate change therefore must consider these two treaties together. The UNFCCC is the fundamental treaty on climate change, since it sets forth the framework of obligations and basic considerations relating to climate change. The Kyoto Protocol was signed pursuant to those obligations. As such it can be considered as one instrument, albeit a crucial one, in the fulfillment of commitments under the UNFCCC. Moreover, the UNFCCC is a treaty that is already in effect and hence considerations of compliance in relation to climate change must necessarily take account of it.

THE UNFCCC

The mid-to-late 1980s saw rising concerns worldwide about the potential for severe disruption of the world's climate due to increasing concentrations of greenhouse gases in the Earth's atmosphere. The most important of these gases is carbon dioxide; and others include methane, nitrous oxide, and halogenated hydrocarbons, such as the materials that are commonly used as refrigerants. This period also saw dramatic and definitive evidence of ozone layer depletion in the form of an "ozone hole" developing each Antarctic spring. A severe depletion of the ozone layer would threaten life on Earth by increasing deadly ultraviolet radiation.[316]

In 1992, during the administration of President George H.W. Bush, a number of countries, including the United States, ratified the United Nations Framework Convention on Climate Change. The Convention, which entered into force in 1994, recognized that:

> human activities have been substantially increasing the atmospheric concentrations of greenhouse gases, that these increases enhance the natural greenhouse effect, and that this will result on average in an additional warming of the Earth's surface and atmosphere and may adversely affect natural ecosystems and humankind.

It created the objective of stabilizing greenhouse gas concentrations:

> The ultimate objective of this Convention and any related legal instruments that the Conference of the Parties may adopt is to achieve, in accordance with the relevant provisions of the Convention, stabilization of greenhouse gas concentrations in the atmosphere at a level that would prevent dangerous anthropogenic interference with the climate system. Such a level should be achieved within a time-frame sufficient to allow ecosystems to adapt naturally to climate change, to ensure that food production is not threatened and to enable economic development to proceed in a sustainable manner.

In view of the risks, the convention obligated the parties to take action despite some uncertainties:

> The Parties should take precautionary measures to anticipate, prevent or minimize the causes of climate change and mitigate its adverse effects. Where there are threats of serious or irreversible damage, lack of full scientific certainty should not be used as a reason for postponing such measures, taking into account that policies and measures to deal with climate change should be cost-effective so as to ensure global benefits at the lowest possible cost.

Scientific evidence about global climate change mounted throughout the 1990s and grew to the point that by the end of the decade there was overwhelming agreement that climate change was occurring and that some component of this climate change was due to anthropogenic emissions of greenhouse gases, with carbon dioxide being responsible for about fifty percent of the total emissions.[317]

The UNFCCC recognized that "the largest share of historical and current global emissions of greenhouse gases has originated in developed countries, that per capita emissions in developing countries are still relatively low," and therefore put the burden of taking the lead in reducing those emissions on the developed countries:

> Accordingly, the developed country Parties should take the lead in combating climate change and the adverse effects thereof.

The UNFCCC recognized the sovereignty of states to pursue their own economic development and their own environmental rules within their jurisdictions, but it also explicitly put limits on that sovereignty when it came to effects outside state borders:

> [S]tates have, in accordance with the Charter of the United Nations and the principles of international law, the sovereign right to exploit their own resources pursuant to their own environmental and developmental policies, and the responsibility to ensure that activities within their jurisdiction or control do not cause damage to the environment of other States or of areas beyond the limits of national jurisdiction.

The implications of climate change and sea level rise for small island countries are explicitly discussed in the UNFCCC.

The UNFCCC codifies the obligations of countries, and especially the countries named in Annex I, to take action to prevent or mitigate climate change. Article 4 of the UNFCCC requires developed countries to take the lead in adopting policies and taking action to curb greenhouse gas emissions and climate change and recognizes that such actions were desirable in the short term (i.e. within the decade of the 1990s) in view of the rising threat of climate change. Referring to the developed countries (*i.e.* those listed in Annex I) it provides:

> Each of these Parties shall adopt national policies and take corresponding measures on the mitigation of climate change, by limiting its anthropogenic emissions of greenhouse gases and protecting and enhancing its greenhouse gas sinks and reservoirs. These policies and measures will demonstrate that developed countries are taking the lead in modifying longer-term trends in anthropogenic emissions consistent with the objective of the Convention, recognizing that the return by the end of the present decade to earlier levels of anthropogenic emissions of carbon dioxide and other greenhouse gases not controlled by the Montreal Protocol [which controlled ozone depleting compounds] would contribute to such modification....

THE KYOTO PROTOCOL

In light of mounting evidence of climate change during the 1990s, the parties to the UN Framework Convention on Climate Change, including the United States, convened in Kyoto, Japan in late 1997, and on December 11, 1997 signed a historic document on reducing emissions of greenhouse gases. That treaty has come to be known as the Kyoto Protocol. The precedent for this document was the Montreal Protocol for ozone layer protection signed in 1987, and strengthened several times since then.

The major provisions of the Kyoto Protocol are as follows:[318]

Article 3 specifies that countries listed in Annex B of the protocol (39 countries in all), generally the highly industrialized ones with relatively high per person income, must meet certain targets for greenhouse gas emissions by the 2008-2012 period relative to their emissions in 1990. The overall target for reduction for the group (the "Annex B" countries) is five percent. The United States commitment was to reduce greenhouse gas emissions by 7 percent.

Article 12 creates a process by which developed countries could assist the rest in creating sustainable development via a "clean development mechanism." The article specifies a list of industrialized countries (the "Annex I" countries) that would be allowed to meet their targets for greenhouse gas emissions by taking actions to reduce emissions in countries not on this list. The idea is to get the largest reductions at lowest cost and to encourage developing countries to join the process of emission reductions, even though they had no specific reduction targets. This list is almost the same as the Annex B list. The United States and all large developed countries, such as Japan, Germany, Britain, etc., are on both lists.

Article 17, created largely at the insistence of the United States, allows for emissions trading: "The Parties included in Annex B may participate in emissions trading for the purposes of fulfilling their commitments under Article 3 of this Protocol. Any such trading shall be supplemental to domestic actions for the purpose of meeting quantified emission limitation and reduction commitments under that Article." However, the methods and terms of such trading were not specified and left to later negotiations.

Article 6 allows countries on the Annex I list to reduce their emissions by taking credit for reductions achieved through investments in other Annex I countries.

The protocol would enter into force when 55 countries had ratified it, including Annex I countries that had among them a total of 55 percent of greenhouse gas emissions of all parties listed in that Annex. This provision did not give the United States a veto over entry into force, but it made entry into force very difficult without the United States, given that it had the largest emissions in the world by far (about one-fourth of the world's total).

Article 20 sets forth the amendment procedure. Amendments were to be made preferably by consensus, failing which, they would be by a vote of three-fourths of the "Parties present and voting at the meeting."

A few months prior to the U.S. signing of the Kyoto Protocol, the U.S. Senate passed a sense of the Senate resolution stating that the United States should not become a party to a treaty that imposed limits of greenhouse gases emissions on industrialized countries unless it required "new specific scheduled commitments to limit or reduce greenhouse gas emissions for Developing Country Parties within the same compliance period." The Senate also advised the President in the same resolution that United States should not become party to a treaty that "would result in serious harm to the economy of the United States."[319]

While the resolution was advisory, it was a powerful statement, given the fact that the U.S. Senate would have to ratify any treaty that emerged from the Kyoto negotiations. The resolution also put into question the U.S. commitment under the UNFCCC, which recognizes that the wealthy industrialized countries are disproportionately large emitters of greenhouse gases (on a per person basis), and that they should bear a corresponding burden in reducing emissions.

STATUS OF THE KYOTO PROTOCOL AND THE U.S. POSITION

The Clinton Administration did not submit the Kyoto Protocol to the U.S. Senate for ratification in the face of a clear intent by the Senate Foreign Relations Committee chairman, Senator Jesse Helms to defeat the treaty, which did not meet the criteria set forth in the Senate resolution. In January 1998, Senator Helms sent a letter to President Clinton asking him to submit the Kyoto Protocol as well as the ABM treaty understandings (see Chapter 4) for ratification. He notified the administration that he would not allow consideration of the ratification of the CTBT until the other two had been submitted.[320] Given the Senator's prior positions on all three issues, it was a notice that the prospects for all three treaties were grim, at best. Senator Frank Murkowski, another opponent of the Kyoto Protocol, introduced a bill in 1999 (S.882, 106th Congress, 1999) that would have adopted the approach of sequestration of carbon dioxide (that is capturing and storing carbon dioxide) rather than increasing efficiency of energy use or replacing fossil fuels with non-fossil fuels. It was basically a bill that would have fostered research into and development of sequestration technologies as well as voluntary efforts to reduce emissions. It had 21 co-sponsors, including Democrats and Republicans. However, the bill was not voted on in the committee that was considering it, though hearings were held.[321] Senator Murkowski opposed the Kyoto Protocol approach because:

- It would let developing countries "off the hook," which would eventually "doom" the treaty's efforts to stabilize the concentrations of greenhouse gases in the atmosphere.

- "Even if we could eventually halt all emissions from the 35 industrial nations required to limit them under the Kyoto Protocol, emissions from the 134 developing nations would continue to grow and atmospheric concentrations of greenhouse gases would continue to increase."

- "The Kyoto approach would erode U.S. sovereignty, punish U.S. consumers and do nothing to enhance the global environment."[322]

These arguments were fairly typical of the ones used to oppose the Kyoto Protocol in the United States. And opposition to it was broad and deep in the U.S. Senate.

During his campaign, Presidential candidate George W. Bush seemed to indicate a different direction for U.S. policy toward reducing carbon dioxide emissions, if not to the specific timetable set forth in the Kyoto Protocol. For instance a September 2000 campaign policy paper stated that a Bush administration would "establish mandatory reduction targets for emissions of four main pollutants: sulfur dioxide, nitrogen oxide, mercury and carbon dioxide."[323]

In March 2001 the new Administrator of the EPA, Christine Todd Whitman, announced that the United States would soon put forth a plan to achieved carbon dioxide reductions to implement the commitment that President Bush had made during his campaign.[324] This very public commitment by the EPA Administrator quickly became the focus of an intense internal debate within the Bush administration, at the end of which the commitment to reducing carbon dioxide emissions was put on hold. The administration said it would present a new plan on the global warming question[325] and also asked the National Academy of Sciences (NAS) to review the matter.

The NAS came to the conclusion, as so many other scientific bodies had done, that emissions of greenhouse gases due to human activities were causing increases in greenhouse gas concentrations and that the rising temperatures "over the last several decades are likely mostly due to human activities, but we cannot rule out that some significant part of these changes is also a reflection of natural variability."[326] Despite the findings of the NAS study, the Bush administration presented no alternative plan to reduce greenhouse gases. On the contrary, in May 2001, it issued an energy policy report that implied continued increases in carbon dioxide emissions for the foreseeable future.[327] Not until a May 2002 report submitted to the UN pursuant to the reporting requirements of the UNFCCC did the Bush administration acknowledge the NAS finding that the burning of fossil fuels is primarily responsible for recent global warming and that substantial environmental changes are very likely to occur in the coming decades.[328] Even then, the United States did not propose any new initiatives to decrease emissions, rather it emphasized the "challenge of adaptation"[329] to changing climate conditions.

Meanwhile, in August 2001, 38 countries, that is, all countries required to limit greenhouse gas emissions except the United States, agreed to limit their greenhouse gas emissions to achieve a collective 5.2 percent reduction from 1990 levels, or just over the limit required by the Kyoto Protocol. The agreement was signed by 178 countries in all.[330] The agreement was finalized in Morocco on November 10, 2001, by the end of the seventh meeting of the Conference of Parties (COP-7),[331] by which time the United States had dropped out of the process.

At Morocco, the parties to the Kyoto Protocol achieved the goal of a detailed agreement regarding the exact size and mode of reductions in greenhouse gas emissions, of the methods of trading, and the components of the "clean development mechanism." (Nuclear power has been excluded as a possible component). This agreement set the stage for ratification of the Kyoto Protocol by the parties that would be obligated to make the main reductions – that is, the countries with high per capita income and emissions, except for the United States.

The Australian government described the outcome of the meeting in Marrakesh as follows:

> COP-7 took as a starting point the Ministerial agreement reached in Bonn, Germany, during COP-6 Part II earlier this year. Negotiations covered a broad range of issues, including flexibility mechanisms, sinks, compliance, and the development of a pathway for the participation of developing countries. The end result was the adoption of the Marrakesh Accords, a 245-page compilation of the rules and procedures through which the Protocol can be implemented.
>
> The rules for the operation of the flexibility mechanisms provide for the creation of a relatively open and effective international market in emission credits, a market that will encourage affordable emission abatement activity. Credits generated through the mechanism will be fully fungible, meaning that each type of credit produced by the mechanisms represents the same amount of emission abatement activity, with no restrictions on the transferability of these units between countries. A 'commitment period reserve' will act to limit the volume of units that any country can transfer so as to address concerns about possible overselling by any country.
>
> . . . .
>
> Further progress was made towards encouraging the flow of financial and technological support to developing countries as well as clarification of how developed countries could cooperate with developing countries on emission abatement activity through the Clean Development Mechanism. However, there was no substantial discussion of emission reduction targets for developing countries themselves. There is a general perception that momentum is building for this issue to be addressed once the Protocol has entered into effect.[332]

The final agreement contained large elements of what the United States had wanted, but not everything. The process of ratification and entry into force is now expected to be completed in 2002 without the United States.[333]

ANALYSIS OF COMPLIANCE WITH THE UNFCCC AND THE KYOTO PROTOCOL

The compliance status of the United States (or any other party) with respect to the Kyoto Protocol must be considered together with that regarding the UNFCCC, which sets the basic framework of obligations of states parties. While internal economic issues and the lack of agreement on the issue of developing country emissions made it almost a foregone conclusion that the United States would not ratify the Kyoto Protocol, it is interesting to note that U.S. compliance with its treaty obligations under the UNFCCC has not been an important feature in the official internal U.S. debate on climate change. This is somewhat parallel to the lack of consideration for the fulfillment of U.S. disarmament obligations under the Nuclear Nonproliferation Treaty in regard to a test ban when the ratification of the CTBT was being debated.

While there are some differences between the U.S. Senate's implicit rejection of the Kyoto Protocol (by prior notice through a resolution) and its failure to ratify the CTBT, there are clear U.S. obligations in both cases. The achievement of a comprehensive test ban was a repeated and long-standing explicit commitment of the nuclear weapons states to the world under prior treaties in force. The CTBT was an explicit commitment, reaffirmed repeatedly in treaty-related documents as well as official pronouncements over decades. By contrast, the UNFCCC did not explicitly require a further treaty for the fulfillment of the obligations of the parties to it. Yet the UNFCCC did require action and leadership on the part of the developed countries. Hence, a judgment on the compliance status of the parties to the UNFCCC must necessarily be contextual, rather than directly relating only to the position of the parties to it in relation to the Kyoto Protocol. It concerns whether the parties to UNFCCC have taken the actions they promised in order to mitigate the threat of climate change.

For a number of reasons, that context leads us to conclude that the United States may be regarded as being in violation of the UNFCCC, which obligates the wealthy countries with high per capita incomes and emissions to take action to reduce greenhouse gas emissions in order to reduce the human impact on climate, especially in light of the growing evidence of serious impact of greenhouse gas emissions on climate.

The scientific conclusion in regard to human activities and climate change of the Intergovernmental Panel on Climate Change (IPCC) in its most recent comprehensive report on the subject, issued in 2001, the year in which the United States abandoned its commitment to the Kyoto Protocol, was as follows:

> In the light of new evidence, and taking into account the
> remaining uncertainties, most of the observed warming over

the last 50 years is likely to have been due to increase in green-house gas concentrations.[334]

Until June 2002, the Bush administration refused to acknowledge the scientific consensus that human activities were responsible for climate change. One indication of the opposition to this viewpoint was the successful campaign to remove Robert Watson as chair of the IPCC at the end of his term in 2002. Dr. Watson failed in his campaign to win re-election as chair and was voted out in April 2002.[335] The IPCC was established in 1988 by the United Nations Environment Programme and the World Meteorological Organization "to assess the scientific, technical and socio-economic information relevant for the understanding of the risk of human-induced climate change."[336]

The Bush administration finally conceded the responsibility of human behavior on climate change. The Climate Action Report acknowledged the finding of the NAS that "human induced warming and associated sea level rises are expected to continue through the 21st century."[337]

The Bush administration, regardless of these findings, has not implemented a policy to reduce the amount of greenhouse gas emissions. Yet there is little if any room for error or delay. Stabilization of carbon dioxide concentrations at levels significantly below a doubling of natural levels will require a reduction of emissions of greenhouse gases by about 50 percent or more over the course of this century. Most of this will have to come from those countries that have the largest absolute and per person emissions. By contrast, U.S. emissions are growing. Even China has been reducing its emissions, though it is not obligated to do so by the Kyoto Protocol, mainly as a byproduct of its drive to increase energy efficiency and reduce urban air pollution.[338] It is not so much the failure of the United States to ratify the Kyoto Protocol by itself that puts it in violation of the spirit and possibly the letter of its commitments under the UNFCCC, but a series of factors, of which the non-ratification of the Kyoto Protocol is only one:

- U.S. carbon dioxide emissions have grown at 1.3 percent per year since 1990, the reference year under the Kyoto Protocol,[339] while those of the European Union have fallen[340] (despite the fact that the European Union had lower emissions per unit of economic output to start with).

- The Bush administration's energy plan implies growing fossil fuel consumption and growing carbon dioxide emissions for the foreseeable future and contains no policy measures to ensure that the increases might be reversed at some point. The plan projects out to the year 2020.

- The Bush administration several times stated that it would come up with an alternative plan for reduction of carbon dioxide emissions, but has not done so.

- A bill that may have led to a policy of carbon dioxide sequestration (Senate Bill S. 882, 106th Congress) was considered by the Senate, but it was never enacted into law.

- The Senate has explicitly rejected the approach that requires the countries with the greatest current and historical per capita emission to take the lead and act first in reducing emissions.

- Many large U.S. based corporations have adopted internal goals for reductions of carbon dioxide emissions, but this has not had an impact on official policy.[341]

- Not only has the Kyoto Protocol not been ratified, but it was essentially rejected even before consideration of its ratification without any compensating method or set of policies to reduce the U.S. contribution to greenhouse gas accumulations.

There is now a vast amount of evidence of anthropogenic impact on climate, including that which was conceded by the U.S. As a result there is little question that major reductions of carbon dioxide emissions will be required in the decades to come to prevent severe disruption of climate. There is some risk of a variety of terrible catastrophes not yet incorporated into models of climate change, such as a shutting down of the Gulf Stream or vast increases in methane emissions due to permafrost melting, because they are not understood well enough.[342] A report of the United States National Research Council states:

> Abrupt climate changes were especially common when the climate system was being forced to change most rapidly. Thus, greenhouse warming and other human alterations of the earth system may increase the possibility of large, abrupt, and unwelcome regional or global climatic events. The abrupt changes of the past are not fully explained yet, and climate models typically underestimate the size, speed, and extent of those changes. Hence, future abrupt changes cannot be predicted with confidence, and climate surprises are to be expected.[343]

Action despite uncertainties is necessary because definitive proof can only be provided by the occurrence of catastrophe, by which time it will be far too late for effective action. As noted above, the UNFCCC explicitly asks states parties to take preventive action in the face of uncertainty.

Moreover, there is overwhelming evidence from the experience of industry, government, and commerce in many countries, including the United States, that there exist vast opportunities for economical reduction of emissions if sound energy efficiency polices are adopted.[344] In this context it is difficult to escape the conclusion that the United States is in violation of its treaty commitments under the UNFCCC.

9

THE ROME STATUTE OF
THE INTERNATIONAL CRIMINAL COURT

BACKGROUND

In July 2002, the Rome Statute of the International Criminal Court entered into force, ushering in an era of accountability for "the most serious crimes of concern to the international community as a whole"[345] much sooner than even the most optimistic observers dreamed possible a decade ago.[346] Adopted and opened for ratification by an overwhelming majority of countries in July 1998, the ratifications have since logged in at an astounding rate given the complexities of the treaty that endows the world's first permanent criminal court with jurisdiction to try individuals for genocide, war crimes and crimes against humanity, and eventually aggression.

The establishment of the International Criminal Court (ICC) caps off more than a half century of efforts to ensure accountability for such crimes in a permanent international tribunal. Until the ICC became a realizable goal, these efforts were geared primarily toward the creation of *ad hoc* military or criminal tribunals created to address specific situations. At the end of World War II, the Allied Powers established international military tribunals for Nuremberg and the Far East to address the war crimes and atrocities committed by the Nazis and the Japanese Imperial Army, respectively.[347] Almost 50 years later, the United Nations Security Council moved to create the International Criminal Tribunal for the former Yugoslavia in 1993 and then followed in 1994 with the creation of the International Criminal Tribunal for Rwanda.[348]

While such efforts have contributed to a growing body of international criminal law and have helped foster a global movement for justice and accountability, they have also been assailed as exercises in "victor's justice" or selective enforcement.[349] Thus, a permanent, standing court was needed to avoid *ad-hocism* and overcome the systemic inequality before the law that have been part and parcel of past efforts when tribunals are created by one group of countries, whether the Allied Powers or the Security Council, to prosecute the acts committed by nationals of other countries.

After World War II, in the context of an unprecedented flurry of activity at the international level, including the establishment of the United Nations and the International Military Tribunals for Nuremberg and the Far East (1945), and adoption of the Universal Declaration of Human Rights and the Genocide Convention (1948) and the four Geneva Conventions of 1949, there was hope that a permanent international criminal court would soon be a reality as well. In its resolution adopting the Genocide Convention, the UN General Assembly invited the International Law Commission "to study the desirability and possibility of establishing an international judicial organ for the trial of persons charged with genocide."[350] In fact, there was such expectation that a Court would soon be a reality that Article 6 of the Genocide Convention provided for trial of persons accused of genocide in "such international penal tribunals as may have jurisdiction." [351] But the Cold War set in, derailing the process for another 50 years.

With the end of the Cold War came the opportunity to revisit the idea of an international criminal court amidst new circumstances in the post-modern era. The idea was re-introduced in 1989 by Trinidad and Tobago as a means of dealing with difficult issues of extradition and prosecution in drug trafficking and related crime.[352] This event, coupled with the creation by the Security Council of the *ad hoc* tribunals for the Former Yugoslavia in 1993 and for Rwanda in 1994, provided the momentum necessary for serious deliberations toward a permanent international criminal tribunal.

Negotiations began in earnest by 1996 after the UN General Assembly created a Preparatory Committee to continue drafting the statute for an international criminal court.[353] By July 17, 1998, after two years of intensive, high-speed negotiations, the Statute of the International Criminal Court was adopted by an overwhelming majority of countries, leaving the United States and six other countries to vote against the historic development.

SOME BASICS ABOUT THE ROME STATUTE

The Rome Statute sets out the contours of a Court that will prosecute individuals for genocide, war crimes and crimes against humanity.[354] The Statute also provides that the Court will have jurisdiction over the crime of aggression once a definition of that crime is adopted as an amendment to the Statute.[355] The Statute recognizes no immunities for crimes within the Court's jurisdiction, even if those crimes are deemed official acts or are committed by a head of state.[356] Thus, the ICC is intended to help "end the culture of impunity," the assumption that atrocities can be committed without fear of legal consequences. It is expected that when combined with associated improvement of capabilities in national legal systems, the ICC will bolster global security by deterring the commission of serious human rights violations and atrocities.

Early in the negotiations, it was widely hoped that the Rome Statute would have a "universal jurisdiction" scheme and that the ICC would thus be able to prosecute all crimes of genocide, war crimes and crimes against humanity.[357] In international law, universal jurisdiction is deemed to apply to crimes considered so serious that they offend the international community as a whole and any state has not only a right, but a duty, to prosecute such acts no matter where they are committed or by whom.[358]

The Geneva Conventions of 1949 apply this principle, and provide that each state party "shall be under the obligation to search for persons alleged to have committed, or to have ordered to be committed, such grave breaches, and shall bring such persons, regardless of their nationality, before its own courts."[359] Examples of the "grave breaches" include willful killing; torture or inhuman treatment, including biological experiments; willfully causing great suffering or serious injury to body or health; and extensive destruction and appropriation of property, not justified by military necessity and carried out unlawfully and wantonly.[360]

As a result of heated and difficult negotiations in Rome, rather than unfettered universal jurisdiction, one of two conditions must be met for the Court to exercise jurisdiction in most cases: (1) the state where the crimes occurred ("territorial state") is party to the Rome Statute or consents to the jurisdiction of the Court; *or* (2) the state of nationality of the accused is party to the Statute or consents to the jurisdiction of the Court.[361] These "pre-conditions" do not apply when the UN Security Council refers a case to the ICC acting under Chapter VII of the UN Charter.[362]

It is important to point out that under this scheme nationals of non-party states could still wind up before the ICC through the Court's jurisdiction over crimes occurring on the territory of states parties. Thus, if a national of a non-party state is suspected of having committed crimes within the jurisdiction of the Court on the territory of a country that is party to the Rome Statute, then the ICC could act against the suspect.

The Rome Statute also corrects some historic inadequacies with respect to accountability for violence against women during armed conflict as well as in times of so-called peace. Whereas prior codifications of humanitarian law address sexual violence in terms of the need to protect honor or dignity and not as a grave breach under the Geneva Conventions, the Rome Statute explicitly concretizes rape, sexual slavery, enforced prostitution, forced pregnancy, enforced sterilization and sexual violence as war crimes and crimes against humanity.[363] In addition, trafficking in "persons, in particular women and children," and gender-based persecution are included as crimes against humanity.[364]

The Rome Statute strongly reinforces the existing taboo against use of weapons of mass destruction. The Statute expressly bans use of chemical weapons.[365] Use of biological, nuclear, and other weapons of mass or indiscriminate destruction is generally prohibited by several provisions, including those criminalizing attacks upon civilians and attacks which disproportionately kill or injure civilians and damage the environment.[366]

The ICC will be an independent institution and not an arm of the United Nations.[367] The ICC will also be largely independent of the Security Council. This is in contrast to the *ad hoc* international criminal tribunals for the former Yugoslavia and Rwanda. As Security Council creations, these *ad hoc* tribunals are dependent on the Security Council for their mandate, jurisdiction and funding.[368] As such, they are limited in the cases that can be brought there. The post-World War II military tribunals were also limited in jurisdiction and scope in that they were created for specific purposes amid special circumstances at the insistence of the Allied Powers and dismantled once these tasks were complete.[369]

The International Criminal Court derives its jurisdiction and authority from the Rome Statute, a negotiated treaty that required at least 60 ratifications and which entered into force on July 1, 2002. The ratifying states sit in an Assembly of States Parties to handle matters such as budgeting for the Court, nomination and election of judges, selection of the prosecutor and deputy prosecutors and oversight of activities of the Court.[370]

After the adoption of the Statute in 1998, negotiations continued on several supporting instruments necessary for the implementation of the Statute and the establishment of the Court. These included, among others, an Elements of Crimes Annex to further define the crimes within the Court's jurisdiction, Rules of Procedure and Evidence, a relationship agreement between the Court and the United Nations, rules of procedure for the Assembly of States Parties, and a first-year budget. Negotiations also continued toward a definition of the crime of aggression during this phase.[371] The negotiations were concluded in July 2002 and the Assembly of States Parties met for the first time in September 2002 at UN Headquarters in New York. The Court is expected to be operational in 2003.

"THE ICC IS INDEED A MONSTER..."[372]

When 120 countries voted to adopt the Rome Statute of the International Criminal Court on July 17, 1998, the United States was not among them. Rather than being part of the rising global tide toward a fair and effective system of international justice, the United States joined with China, Libya, Iraq, Israel, Qatar and Yemen to reject the treaty.[373]

Among U.S. conservatives, opposition to the International Criminal Court has often taken the form of misleading and erroneous allegations concerning the due process protections in the Rome Statute and invasion of U.S. sovereignty. U.S. Senator Jesse Helms has been perhaps the most vocal opponent of the Court. He observed at one point: "The ICC is indeed a monster – and it is our responsibility to slay it before it grows to devour us."[374] With Helms at the lead, conservatives in Congress pursued legislation hostile both to the future Court and to countries that support it.

But conservatives were not alone in their resistance to a more democratic international judicial arrangement. During the Clinton administration, the line of thinking was that there were "significant flaws" in the treaty that required correction before the United States would consider coming on board.[375] Ultimately, opponents on all sides seemed to agree on, or deeply fear, the essential nature of the main "flaw" – the idea that U.S. nationals could conceivably be brought before the ICC with or without the consent of the United States. They differed, however, in their approaches to the issue.

U.S. CRITICISMS AND CONCERNS

Limited Security Council Role

The United States had long hoped that the Court would be made dependent on the UN Security Council for the cases that could come before it.[376] However, the role of the Security Council was greatly circumscribed in the final text of the Rome Statute. It is this aspect – the degree of independence of the Council – that led the United States to oppose the permanent Court at the same time that it fully supported the creation and maintenance of the *ad hoc* tribunals. Had the ICC been made more dependent on the Security Council for the cases that could come before it, the United States, as one of the five permanent members with veto power, would have been situated nicely in terms of its ability to insulate its nationals and political allies from the jurisdiction of the Court. [377]

The Superpower Complex

Once it became clear that the ICC would not be dependent on the Security Council, the United States then pursued the possibility of explicit exceptions for nationals of non-states parties. In the quest for special treatment in the new scheme of international justice, U.S. officials argued that, as the sole remaining superpower, the United States was expected to deploy its military to "hot spots" more often than other countries.[378] That would make it more vulnerable to politically motivated accusations and prosecutions.[379] This concern was addressed by other delegations in the negotiations and was the reason for several articles in the Statute intended to provide a series of checks and balances with respect to the prosecutor's authority to self-start cases.[380]

As a result, the prosecutor must obtain the authorization of the pre-trial chamber prior to formally beginning an investigation on her own initiative.[381] In addition, the Security Council may elect to defer the investigation of a specific case for a period of 12 months.[382] While these mechanisms were added largely in response to U.S. concerns, it eventually became clear that none of the concessions would suffice unless the United States got a complete and explicit assurance that its nationals would never be subject to the Court's jurisdiction.

It is important to emphasize that the idea that a foreign court might have jurisdiction over persons who commit crimes on foreign territory is not a new concept nor unique to the ICC. Indeed, territorial jurisdiction, the ability of a state to prosecute crimes that occur in its territory, is one of the oldest and most sound bases of jurisdiction.[383] Territorial jurisdiction is often only superceded by an express agreement. It is for this reason that countries and international organizations often pursue explicit language bestowing criminal jurisdiction on the state of nationality of an accused for acts committed on foreign territory in bilateral or multilateral treaties such as Status of Forces Agreements.[384]

The ICC is a variation on this principle. When states join the Rome Statute, they extend jurisdiction over crimes of genocide, war crimes and crimes against humanity occurring on their territory to an international tribunal at the same time as confirming their own jurisdiction over such acts. Thus, if a national of Country A, a non-state party, commits crimes that are within the jurisdiction of Country B, a state party, the acts would fall within the jurisdiction of both Country B and the ICC. Thus, the ICC operates in a similar way to foreign jurisdictions.

The irony is that had the United States been successful in its attempts to correct the purported flaw in the treaty, *i.e.* had the flaw been "fixed" so that nationals of non-party states could never be brought before the ICC without the consent of the state of nationality if they committed crimes on the territory of a state party, there would be every incentive for the United States and other countries to remain outside the Statute.[385]

Due Process

Another argument put forward by U.S. opponents was that the Rome Statute did not provide the level of due process protections required by the U.S. Bill of Rights, such as the presumption of innocence, right to remain silent, right to trial by jury, right to defense counsel of one's choosing, right to speedy and public trial and cross examination. This argument is also unsupportable; many U.S. observers and legal experts have found that the protections in the Rome Statute meet or exceed those of the U.S. Constitution.[386] In a report published in connection with a resolution calling for the United States to accede to the Rome Statute, the American Bar Association commentators observed:

> The due process provisions of the Rome Statute are somewhat more detailed and more comprehensive than those found in the Bill of Rights... They are derived almost verbatim from the Article 14 of the International Covenant on Civil and Political Rights, which the US has ratified. These rights are also substan-

tively similar to the rights protected by the European Convention on Human Rights. Both of these post-World War II instruments were heavily influenced by the American Bill of Rights. *It is safe to say that the list of due process protections contained in the Rome Statute is the most comprehensive which has so far been promulgated* (emphasis added).[387]

Invasion of National Sovereignty

U.S. opponents have also wrongly asserted that the Rome Statute would invade national sovereignty and deny governments the right to try their own nationals for crimes within the jurisdiction of the Court. In a letter published after the Rome Statute was adopted, Sen. Helms alleged:

> ...The International Criminal Court declares that the American People are under its jurisdiction – no matter what the US government says. The delegates in Rome included a form of 'universal jurisdiction' in the court statute, which means that, even if the US never signs the treaty, or if the Senate refuses to ratify it, the countries participating in this court will still contend that American soldiers and citizens are within the jurisdiction of the court.[388]

Former U.S. Secretary of State Henry A. Kissinger has also made similar mischaracterizations of the ICC and has skipped over the nuances of its jurisdiction in complaining that because it has territorial jurisdiction, it has universal jurisdiction.[389] Arguments such as these overlook the Rome Statute's carefully crafted complementarity scheme which situates the ICC as a court of last resort which would come into play only when the national system has been unwilling or unable to act.[390] They also overlook the preconditions of territoriality and nationality that were built into the statute as a curb on outright universal jurisdiction.[391] Thus, the Court is intended to complement national systems rather than infringe upon them while narrowing the jurisdictional gaps, practical and substantive, that have long allowed for impunity.[392]

U.S. PARTICIPATION IN THE ICC NEGOTIATIONS

Even before formal negotiations commenced on the draft statute in 1996, the United States attempted to thwart altogether the process toward a permanent and independent court. In his accounts of the early stages of the resurrection of the idea in the corridors of the United Nations, Professor Michael Scharf describes his efforts as a State Department official to make the initiative "go away."[393] To do so, the United States pushed to have the issue diverted to the International Law Commission, which is well known for its snail-like pace.[394] But the eruption of violence in the former Yugoslavia and later in Rwanda served to intensify the demand for a permanent institution and to speed up the process, despite U.S. objections.

Once the process seemed likely to lead to a treaty, the United States participated intensively. On the positive side, the U.S. delegation to the ICC negotiations made significant contributions to various parts of the Rome Statute (including many aspects of the statute's "due process" and penalty provisions). But it also vigorously tried to ensure as strong a role as possible for the Security Council and a procedural and/or jurisdictional scheme that would, in practice, leave U.S. nationals outside the Court's reach. The U.S. efforts to rope its nationals off from the jurisdiction of the Court persisted even after the Rome Statute was adopted and into the subsequent negotiations of the supplemental texts.

In Rome, U.S. efforts threatened to unravel more than two years of work and five full weeks of around-the-clock negotiations at the diplomatic conference.[395] As the Rome conference came down to the wire, the U.S. delegation demanded a vote on an amendment it had proposed to the draft statute. The amendment sought to limit the Court's jurisdiction over nationals of non-states parties and require consent of such states prior to exercising jurisdiction over officials and military personnel.[396] The last minute move added an element of suspense to the negotiations as onlookers awaited the response of government delegations to the "check" played by the world's sole remaining superpower. The U.S. amendment was swiftly and overwhelmingly defeated via a no-action motion and the conference moved on to the business of adopting the Statute.[397]

Immediately thereafter, the United States called the Statute itself to a vote.[398] The chair and leadership of the Conference had hoped to avoid a vote on the Statute, preferring to have it adopted by consensus. Having just breezed past the U.S. last-ditch effort to get an exemption, the coalescence of governments in favor of a fairer and more independent system of international justice held sway and the Statute was adopted by an overwhelming majority of 120 countries, with 21 abstentions and 7 no-votes.[399]

Even after losing the battle at the Rome Conference, the U.S. delegation to the Preparatory Commission[400] continuously pursued more of a role for the Security Council and the ever-elusive 100% exemption for all U.S. nationals.[401] This was done through a highly technical and complicated two-part proposal that involved the Rules of Procedure and Evidence and the Relationship Agreement between the United Nations and the ICC, which was negotiated subsequent to the Rules.[402] Essentially, the goal of the U.S. post-Rome proposals was to bind the Court to extradition agreements between states and ensure that the Court would be required to obtain state consent prior to seeking the surrender of persons suspected of crimes within the Court's jurisdiction and who were found on foreign territory.[403]

The U.S. delegation's efforts in Rome and afterward were accompanied by an intensive Defense Department strategy of pressuring its counterparts in other countries to support U.S. positions on the ICC. In a now famous exchange during the Rome negotiations, William Cohen, then U.S. Defense Secretary, was reported to have contacted his German counterpart to indicate that non-support of U.S. positions would have implications for U.S. military support in Europe.[404] The German delegation at the time was arguing for the ICC to have universal jurisdiction. According to various news reports, the U.S. Secretary of Defense threatened that the U.S. might "retaliate by removing its overseas troops, including those in Europe" if Germany succeeded in its effort to obtain universal jurisdiction.[405]

In the post-Rome negotiations on the Rules of Procedure and Evidence and the Elements of Crimes Annex, the State Department commenced a formal démarche on other governments. A letter by Secretary of State Madeleine Albright again used the threat of future U.S. opposition to the ICC, albeit more subtly than Cohen, in the event U.S. "objectives" were not taken seriously in the talks.[406] Throughout the negotiations, the U.S. delegation and U.S. State and Defense Department officials repeatedly pointed out the enormous financial support and technical assistance the U.S. provided to the existing tribunals to suggest that lack of U.S. support for the Court would lead to its demise.[407]

POST-ROME U.S. STRATEGIES AND TACTICS TO UNDERMINE THE COURT

Despite the U.S. rejection of the Statute at the Rome Conference, intensive diplomatic pressure tactics and ongoing efforts to alter the Statute long after it had been adopted, President Clinton opted to sign the Rome Statute hours before the period for signature expired on December 31, 2000. In treaty law, signature of a treaty signifies an intent to ratify and carries an obligation not to engage in acts that would "defeat the object and purpose" of the treaty.[408] In a last minute political maneuver, the outgoing President simultaneously backtracked from the prospect of U.S. ratification at the same time that he authorized signature of the treaty.

In his statement made on the occasion of signature, Clinton stated, "I will not, and do not recommend that my successor submit the Treaty to the Senate for advice and consent until our fundamental concerns are satisfied."[409] The fundamental concerns were the "significant flaws" of the Statute which would mean that the Court, once it came into existence, "will not only exercise authority over personnel of states that have ratified the Treaty, but also claim jurisdiction over personnel of states that have not."[410] Though the act of signing was not a full-fledged show of support for the treaty, Senator Helms assailed President Clinton's decision to sign the Statute of an "international kangaroo court" as "outrageous" and vowed that the "decision would not stand."[411]

When the Bush administration entered office, it undertook a high-level policy review of the Statute. The events of September 11, 2001, put the decision on hold, but by that time there was reportedly a growing consensus toward "unsigning" the Statute.[412] On May 6, 2002, the Bush administration did just that when it transmitted a letter to UN Secretary-General Kofi Annan, which stated that the U.S. did not intend to ratify the treaty and therefore had "no legal obligations arising from its signature of December 31, 2000."[413] Under the laws governing treaty making, now that the United States has expressed its intention not to be bound by its signature, it is no longer required to refrain from actions that would defeat the object and purpose of the treaty and the Court.[414] Bush's official renunciation of the treaty effectively cleared the path for a variety of measures aimed at undermining the Court.

Status of Forces Agreements Clauses, "Article 98 Agreements," and Peacekeeping Missions

Soon after the Rome Statute was adopted, the United States began seeking ways to guard its military personnel from the Court's jurisdiction. It introduced provisions prohibiting the extradition of U.S. personnel to the ICC in negotiations of Status of Forces Agreements (agreements providing for the placement of U.S. military personnel in other countries), also known as SOFAs.[415] South Korea is among those countries party to a SOFA containing a promise not to extradite U.S. nationals to the ICC.[416]

In the absence of existing or renegotiated SOFAs, the United States is now seeking separate agreements that deal solely and specifically with the issue of extradition to the ICC.[417] These agreements are often referred to as "Article 98" agreements. Article 98 of the Rome Statute introduces potential restrictions on the Court's ability to gain access to suspects if found on the territory of a State which has a pre-existing agreement with the state of nationality of the accused not to extradite to the ICC. [418] Critics protest that the U.S. agreements are not consistent with the terms of Article 98, and would require states parties to violate the Rome Statute.[419]

The United States has also begun seeking similar clauses in UN Security Council resolutions authorizing the renewal of various peacekeeping missions. In May 2002, the United States sought to include language in a Security Council resolution renewing the peacekeeping mission in East Timor that would shield peacekeeping personnel from the jurisdiction of any national or international tribunal.[420] The U.S. proposal was defeated at that time in the UN Security Council.[421] However, the United States resumed this strategy and redoubled its efforts as the renewal of the Bosnian peacekeeping mission surfaced on the Council's agenda. At this point, the United States threatened to veto the mission altogether if its efforts to gain exemptions for peacekeeping personnel from non-ICC member states was rejected. The U.S. proposals for blanket immunity were rejected by the Security Council. In response, on June 30, 2002, the day the mission was set to expire and the eve of the Rome Statute's entry into force, the United States resorted to vetoing the renewal of the Bosnian mission.[422]

The Security Council authorized an emergency extension of the Bosnian mission to allow for further discussions. The U.S. efforts to hold the Bosnian mission hostage in exchange for exemption from the ICC met with fierce opposition from even its closest allies who resented the cynical strategy of pitting peacekeeping against justice. Critics argued that such efforts would undermine the legitimacy of the world's first permanent criminal court if one country were able to use the Security Council to carve out special treatment for its nationals.[423] However, two weeks of intensive negotiations and high-pressure by the United States in capitals all over the world resulted in a separate and controversial Security Council resolution dealing solely with the issue of exemptions for peacekeeping personnel from non-ICC member states.[424] The relevant language of Security Council Resolution 1422 states:

> *Acting* under Chapter VII of the Charter of the United Nations
>
> [The Security Council] [r]equests, consistent with the provisions of Article 16 of the Rome Statute, that the ICC, if a case arises involving current or former officials or personnel from a contributing State not a Party to the Rome statute over acts or omissions relating to a United Nations established or authorized operation, shall for a twelve-month period starting 1 July 2002 not commence or proceed with investigation or prosecution of any such case, unless the Security Council decides otherwise, and expresses the intention to renew the request for each 12 month period as necessary.[425]

The resolution is ostensibly linked to Article 16 of the Rome Statute.[426] Article 16 of the Rome Statute safeguards the Security Council's unique role in the maintenance or restoration of international peace and security. It is intended to allow the Council to defer the Court's investigation and prosecution of a specific case for renewable 12-month periods on a case-by-case basis in the event an action by the ICC would jeopardize the Council's efforts in a precarious security situation.[427]

However, the Security Council exceeded the narrow deferral provision by adopting the sweeping omnibus resolution that covers any case that might arise within the next year involving peacekeepers from non-party states.[428] The terms of the resolution's language not only insulate "officials and personnel" of non-states parties involved in UN peacekeeping missions but also military and government personnel engaged in operations that have been approved or authorized by the United Nations, such as the NATO force in Bosnia or the mission in Afghanistan, albeit for one year. The resolution could also be argued to extend beyond peacekeeping missions to shield policymakers and soldiers engaged in a UN authorized war, like the 1991 Gulf War. Proponents of the Court denounced the Council action as illegitimate under the UN Charter and inconsistent with the Rome Statute, and urged governments to ensure that the resolution does not get renewed next year.[429]

In Congress

On August 2, 2002, President Bush signed into law the American Servicemembers' Protection Act (ASPA).[430] The anti-ICC legislation had been in play in various guises beginning in 2000 at the insistence of Sen. Jesse Helms. The legislation does the following: (1) prohibits any U.S.

state or federal agency cooperation with the future ICC; (2) prohibits military assistance to most countries that are parties to the Rome Statute; (3) restricts the transfer of law enforcement or national security information to countries that ratify; (4) bars U.S. participation in UN peacekeeping missions unless assurances are granted exempting U.S. personnel from the Court; and (5) authorizes the President to use "all means necessary and appropriate" to free individuals held by or on behalf of the ICC.[431] At the same time, the legislation contains broad waiver provisions for the President that can be utilized in the "national interest."

The language of "all means necessary and appropriate" is typically understood to include the use of force. Because of this portion of the legislation, opponents of the legislation have dubbed the ASPA the "Hague Invasion Act" (the Court will be officially seated in The Hague, which would make the Netherlands a prime target), although any state that would hold an American on behalf of the ICC would be vulnerable under this provision. When the legislation surfaced a year earlier, some governments expressed their outrage at the bill and viewed it as unilateralist and counterproductive in light of administration efforts to build a "coalition against terror."[432] In a letter to Secretary of State Colin Powell dated October 30, 2001, German Foreign Minister Joschka Fischer warned that "adopting the ASPA would open a rift between the U.S. and the European Union on this important issue." He also advised that "In view of the international effort against terrorism, it is particularly important for the United States and the European Union to act in accord in this field too."[433] Belgian Foreign Minister Louis Michel sent a letter on the same day on behalf of the European Union to Secretary Powell and Senator Tom Daschle echoing the concerns expressed by Germany.[434]

The U.S. Senate has also pursued this track with respect to two anti-terrorism related treaties which it approved in December 2001, the International Convention for the Suppression of Terrorist Bombings and the International Convention for the Suppression of the Financing of Terrorism.[435] In adopting both treaties, the Senate included reservations that prohibit the transfer of any person, or consent to the transfer of any person extradited by the United States, to the International Criminal Court.

CONCLUSION

The Rome Statute was designed to focus on the types of international crimes, *i.e.*, the world's worst, that have been the subject of international tribunals since the end of World War II, but to do so in a way that would provide equality before the law, relatively independent of the power, economic strength, or political influence of the country of which the accused might be a citizen. As recent developments clearly demonstrate, civil society and states parties to the Rome Statute will need to guard the Court fiercely to ensure that the independence and impartiality of this historic institution are not undermined from within or without.

The reasons for the rejection of the ICC demonstrate with startling clarity the double standard unabashedly applied by the United States. At the end of the day, the U.S. opposition boils down to one problem: U.S. nationals could be subject – along with the rest of the world – to the jurisdiction of an international court. While the United States has viewed this as an entirely acceptable and at times morally imperative predicament for other countries, successive U.S. governments have found the thought that it could also be applied to its own nationals entirely unpalatable. Recent efforts by Argentine, Chilean and French officials to question former Secretary of State Henry Kissinger regarding his role or awareness of various events such as the 1973 military coup in Chile or a plan targeting Latin American leftists in the 1970s have only intensified the feeling among the U.S. establishment that the world is closing in.[436]

In the wake of September 11 and a rapid unfurling of executive orders and anti-terrorism legislation widely viewed as incompatible with the U.S. Constitution, U.S. positions with respect to the ICC seem even more disjointed and indicative of a double standard, particularly U.S. allegations of due process failings in the ICC and fears of politically motivated prosecutions.[437] Though the ICC will not have jurisdiction over acts which occur prior to entry into force of the Rome Statute, many government officials and observers all over the world have pointed to the Court as an appropriate forum for atrocities on the scale of September 11, and in some cases the best forum for bringing perpetrators of such acts to fair trial on the world stage.[438] Still, the current administration and forces in the U.S. legislature have intensified their opposition to the Court at the same time as welcoming the trial of suspected terrorists in military commissions without basic due process protections.[439]

As it currently stands, the array of U.S. legislation and policy with respect to the ICC has pitched the United States in a hostile stance against the vast majority of countries in the world. The recent official renunciation of the U.S. signature effectively cleared the path for a string of tactics designed to thwart efforts toward a fair and effective system of international justice. The current direction of U.S. policy is not only to keep U.S. citizens out of the Court's jurisdiction but also to make it as difficult as possible for participating countries to cooperate with the Court. With the anti-ICC American Servicemembers' Protection Act as law, the United States is particularly bent on making cooperation with the ICC especially difficult for developing countries, which need U.S. support in other arenas.[440]

Still, since garnering the ratifications necessary for entry into force, the Court is now a reality – despite the enormous obstacles thrown in its path along the way. It is highly significant in the development of the idea of the rule of law in global affairs that even intense pressure by the "sole remaining superpower" has not impeded the trek to a system of international justice. That accomplishment is a testament to the level of commitment in different parts of the world to a fair and effective criminal court and, indeed, a recognition of the urgent need for such an institution.

10

TREATIES AND GLOBAL SECURITY

INTRODUCTION

The evolution of international law since World War II is largely a response to the demands of states and individuals living within a global society with a deeply integrated world economy. In this global society, the repercussions of the actions of states, non-state actors, and individuals are not confined within borders, whether we look to greenhouse gas accumulations, nuclear testing, the danger of accidental nuclear war, or the vast massacres of civilians that have taken place over the course of the last hundred years and still continue. Multilateral agreements increasingly are the primary instruments employed by states to meet extremely serious challenges of this kind. If the United States continues on its present path of rejecting this approach, the consequence could be a frightening international order based more on the rule of force than the rule of law – with the United States the primary wielder of force – and a global system that is increasingly unable to effectively address common global problems.

The existing system of treaties is far from perfect. Across a broad range of objectives, including peaceful resolution of disputes, protection of human rights, nuclear disarmament, and global environmental protection, there is ample room for improvement in the system of international law and of treaties in particular. But the actions and policies of the United States that we have detailed in this book are taking the world in a direction contrary to an improvement of the system. They tip the scales further in the direction of the use of military force and reduce the ability of the weak to get redress even when their cause may be just.

THE ROLE OF MULTILATERAL TREATIES
IN BUILDING SECURITY

Multilateral treaties are certainly not the only means to address issues of global concern. Alternatives include unilateral measures, agreements within a region or among a few states, or an informal political process that proceeds on a case-by-case basis. However, global treaties have several advantages for addressing certain kinds of problems.

First, they clearly and publicly embody a set of universally applicable expectations, including prohibited and required practices and policies. In other words, they articulate important global norms, for instance against genocide, aggressive war, or weapons of mass destruction. They enable the prosecution of war criminals. They help to promote human rights. The Montreal Protocol, for example, is a treaty that has been central to the protection of the ozone layer on which life on Earth depends.

Second, treaties and the regimes they establish are a "framework for collective action to meet common challenges."[441] They provide a measure of predictability and accountability and promote learning. Treaties "contribute to the development of international consensus on both goals and methods for important international goals, … provide important reference points and criteria to guide States' activities and domestic legislation and provide a focal point for discussion and negotiations on the subject matter of the convention."[442] Progress on a particular issue can be measured over time in relation to the norms and objectives embedded in the treaties. Treaty review processes, as UN Under-Secretary-General for Disarmament Affairs Jayantha Dhanapala explains, "provide a vehicle for the candid expression of views about the operation of the respective regimes [and for] assessing the health of the underlying norms."[443]

Treaties also provide a foundation for further progress. States are able to accumulate expertise and confidence by participating in the structured system for pursuing a particular policy of mutual or collective benefit. This experience and confidence, in turn, will help to shape further development and implementation of the policy. Concepts such as trust or confidence-building are naturally elusive and impossible to quantify, but they are crucial factors in the development of treaty regimes. Of necessity, establishing and developing such regimes also requires some risk-taking since states are seeking to institute or strengthen confidence where it has been lacking. Taking such a risk is less likely without the prior discussion and careful agreement that take place during the treaty negotiation process.

TREATY COMPLIANCE AND CREATION

Government is instituted among individuals so that there may be a means to restrain any one person or group of persons from trampling on the rights of others, and in case of such transgression, to secure redress. In return, in a democracy, people willingly give up certain freedom of action when it would harm their neighbors. They also agree that courts are the venue of last resort for the settlement of disputes. The balance between freedom of action and restraint is struck precisely to increase common security. In any such arrangement there is necessarily a tension between freedom of action and restraint. No arrangement guarantees that transgressions on the part of members of the community will not occur. Indeed, the rule of law anticipates such transgressions and functions to prevent even the most serious transgressions from leading to mob rule, vigilante violence, and chaos.

The principles of international cooperation and security are no different for the most part, though the context of states being the contracting parties instead of individuals raises many practical questions. As Canadian Minister of Foreign Affairs Bill Graham stated:

> Our societies are based on the rule of law, and the sustainable, shared global future we seek must have the same basis, however difficult it may be to obtain universal acceptance of the rules and establish effective means of enforcement. Examples close to home illustrate the point: we do not dispense with domestic law because we know some will defy the law; homeowners do not consider stronger locks an adequate substitute for the law.[444]

International cooperation is hindered, however, if there is considerable distrust of treaty partners. Senator John Kyl, who has argued for reliance on U.S. military strength above all, has said that "a more successful and realistic strategic posture for the United States would rely less on the goodwill of bad actors than what we ourselves can control – our own defenses."[445] This argument would have merit if most countries were habitual violators of their security treaty commitments. Yet it has been observed that "the dictum that most nations obey international law most of the time holds true today with greater force than at any other time during the last century."[446] As in the case of national law, there are violations, but they are exceptions, not the rule. There will always be violators of laws in any legal system. And, as noted above by Minister Graham, legal regimes are not abandoned because some actors do not comply. The record with respect to treaties discussed in this book supports the view that compliance is the routine, and violation infrequent. For instance, among parties to the NPT, non-compliance appears to be confined to a few states, including the nuclear weapon states as well as North Korea and Iraq.

Opponents also resist international treaty commitments because they do not believe treaties impose true legal obligations. John Bolton, the Under Secretary of State for Arms Control and International Security, is, significantly, an advocate of this view.[447] According to Bolton, to the extent that treaties govern relations among countries, they do not involve legal obligations because a regularized enforcement framework analogous to that of courts and police in national legal systems is lacking. He writes:

> [According to the U.S. Supreme Court, a] treaty is primarily a compact between independent nations. It depends for the enforcement of its provisions on the interest and the honor of the governments that are parties to it. If these fail, its infraction becomes the subject of international negotiations and reclamations, so far as the injured party chooses to seek redress, which may in the end be enforced by actual war.[448]

Bolton then states:

> This is not domestic law at work. Accordingly, there is no reason to consider treaties as "legally" binding internationally, and certainly not as "law" themselves.[449]

Accordingly, treaty compliance is only a matter of policy choice:

> There may be good and sufficient reasons to abide by the provisions of a treaty, and in most cases one would expect to do so because of the mutuality of benefits that treaties provide, but not because the United States is "legally" obligated to do so.[450]

This doctrine is wrong because it fails to appreciate the normative expectation specific to legal obligations that they shall be observed, and also because it underestimates the incentives for compliance and capacity for enforcement in the international sphere (see below). It has dangerous practical implications for international cooperation and compliance with norms. U.S. treaty partners do not enter into treaties expecting that they are only political commitments by the United States that can be overridden based on U.S. interests. If that were the case, what is the incentive for the treaty in the first place? For example, when the United States made changes in its tax code that overrode provisions of tax treaties with several European states, the European treaty partners protested. "The violation of [the] treaty by unilateral action of one contracting party undermines the basis of trust existing between the two countries involved, erodes the certainty and security intended by international agreements and ultimately poses the question as to whether an international convention ... serves any purpose at all if it can be altered at will by one of the contracting parties."[451]

When a powerful and influential state like the United States is seen to treat its legal obligations as a matter of convenience or of national interest alone, other states will see this as a justification to relax or withdraw from their own commitments. If the United States wants to require another state to live up to its treaty obligations, it may find that the state has followed the U.S. example and opted out of compliance. The Chemical Weapons Convention offers an example. The United States implemented rules to exclude certain types of inspections mandated by the terms of the CWC. India adopted similar exemptions, and Russia and South Korea applied the U.S. restrictions to their inspections.[452]

Undermining the international system of treaties is likely to have particularly significant consequences in the arena of peace and security. Even though the United States is uniquely positioned as the economic and military sole superpower, unilateral decision-making and actions are insufficient to protect the security of its people. For example, since September 11, prevention of proliferation of weapons of mass destruction is an increasing priority. Cooperation is the necessary first step to successfully avoiding proliferation. As William Perry, former Secretary of Defense, has noted:

> Any actions that the United States takes to stop the spread of weapons can easily be nullified if Russia, for example, decides to sell its nuclear technology, weapons, or fissile material. Russian leaders know that it is in their interest to fight proliferation . . . The cooperation necessary to prevent proliferation is manifested through treaties already in force, such as the NPT, START and the BWC, through treaties not yet implemented, such as the CTBT, Start II, and Start III; through bilateral and multilateral agreements . . . and through cooperative programs to reduce nuclear risks and manage Cold War-era nuclear arsenals, such as the Nunn-Lugar program with Russia and other former Soviet states.[453]

The idea that a state can independently pick and choose which treaties in full or in part that it likes and which ones it rejects overlooks both the "interlocking nature of international agreements and the necessity to respect existing legal obligations and political commitments."[454] Many security treaties are interdependent. For instance, within the nuclear sphere, the stability and future of the Nuclear Nonproliferation Treaty regime depends upon entry into force of the Comprehensive Test Ban Treaty, now in doubt due in large measure to U.S. non-ratification.[455] If the nonproliferation regime breaks down and additional states acquire nuclear weapons, the United States would find the situation very difficult to manage militarily. There is much uncertainty at present about the amounts, locations, and status of nuclear weapons usable materials, and therefore about the access of states not known to have nuclear weapons as well as non-state actors to nuclear explosive devices. Consequently, the United States might increase rather than decrease the risk of a nuclear attack against it if it threatened to take unilateral military counterproliferation measures against states believed to be acquiring nuclear arms.

The question of radioactive materials demonstrates the urgency of making new security agreements in addition to complying with existing ones. As matters stand, there is no comprehensive global agreement on nuclear-weapon-usable materials that includes the materials located in the nuclear weapon states. Such an agreement is needed to better account for these materials and safeguard them. But negotiations on this issue are stuck in a familiar pattern of the powerful attempting to preserve and even enhance their own prerogatives and reduce those of others while common security issues fester. It is also imperative to create international arrangements to control radioactive materials that cannot be used to make nuclear weapons but can be used to make radioactive "dirty" bombs. National controls have been even weaker in this area than for weapons-usable materials.[456]

To take another example, the best way to detect nuclear bombs that might be hidden in cargo ships is to create cooperation between the shipping country, the countries from where ship crews are drawn, the countries where ships are registered, and the destination countries. Controls at the receiving end alone are likely to be grossly insufficient because once a ship loaded with a bomb reaches the harbor, it may already be far too late.

An even greater amount of international cooperation at every level will be needed to avoid serious climate change and its potential security implications. The reduction of greenhouse gas emissions cannot be achieved without the world's wealthy countries taking the lead even if it means some economic sacrifice. The United States is responsible for about a quarter of these emissions. A U.S. refusal to abide by common rules when it requires sacrifice will also hurt the people of the United States, because they share the world's ecosystem and climate system. And, an agreement is needed on a compliance framework for the existing ban on biological weapons, the importance of which has been highlighted by the anthrax attacks in the United States.

ENFORCEMENT

The question of enforcement of treaties is a valid concern for all countries but it is by no means a justification for non-participation. No enforcement system is perfect and indeed, generally, the issues associated with domestic law enforcement even in well-established democracies like the United States are a matter of considerable debate and continuing concern. Treaties do have enforcement mechanisms, but these mechanisms need strengthening. Instead, they are being undermined by powerful states, not least the United States.

It is generally recognized that the rule of law depends on voluntary compliance by the majority. Legal institutions, including those that enforce laws, act as a supplement to the generally expected voluntary compliance in which moral, political and judicial enforcement considerations all play a role. Enforcement in a legal system also relies on the investigative powers of the government. Without the ability to investigate, criminals cannot be brought to account in a reliable way, and innocent parties risk wrongful prosecution.

In the international sphere, enforcement similarly first of all requires machinery for deciding when there has been a violation. That in turn requires verification and transparency arrangements so that the charges may have some basis. Such arrangements also provide an incentive for compliance under ordinary circumstances. As in law enforcement within countries, which must balance privacy concerns with ensuring compliance, there also is a tension between protection of information that countries may want to keep confidential and the need for transparency and verification.

Enforcement in the case of violations can only occur when these conditions have been fulfilled. Yet for several of treaties discussed in this book, including the BWC, CWC, and CTBT, one general characteristic of the U.S. approach has been to try to exempt itself from transparency and verification arrangements. Simultaneously, it seeks greater transparancy from other states. It bespeaks a lack of good faith if the United States wants near-perfect knowledge of others' compliance so as to be able to detect all possible violations, while also wanting all too often to shield itself from scrutiny. The United States frequently claims that these treaties cannot sufficiently detect cheaters, but it is inconsistent to reject treaties because they lack the ability to be completety enforced, while at the same time undermining or rejecting the very mechanisms that will improve enforcement. Yet, the United States has done just that in resisting the creation of institutions that will improve the identification of treaty violations in two critical areas, banning nuclear testing and the biological weapons convention.

Most treaties have some internal verification requirements on which any enforcement must rest. While many treaties lack internal explicit provisions for sanctions, there are means of enforcement. Far more than is generally understood, states are very concerned to avoid formal international condemnation of their actions, whether by treaty-based agencies like the IAEA and the Organization for the Prohibition of Chemical Weapons, human rights bodies, states parties to a treaty acting collectively, or the U.N. General Assembly. A range of sanctions is also available, including withdrawal of privileges under treaty regimes, arms and commodity embargoes, travel bans, reductions in international financial assistance or loans, and freezing of state or individual leader assets. Sanctions can be applied by individual states, groups of states, states parties to treaty regimes acting collectively, or the U.N. Security Council.

Institutional mechanisms are available to reinforce compliance with treaty regimes, and the United States has been central to their creation. The two broadest arenas are the U.N. Security Council and the International Court of Justice. The United States and four other powers have a veto in the former. The latter is the forum where greater equality before the law is possible, but it depends on states submitting to the Court's jurisdiction.

When it does act concerning violations of norms or treaties, the United States has sometimes opted for the arena of the Security Council where it has veto power. Since its membership in the United Nations was and is conditioned on this veto power, this has institutionalized inequality before the law in a manner that is causing its more and more selective application. This cannot but undermine respect for international law and institutions that, for all their imperfections, were designed to diminish the prospects of war and violent conflict. Still there are at least some internal checks and balances in the Security Council. In recent years, the United States and its allies have tended to use military force without going through the Security Council, as in the case of the NATO action in Yugoslavia. This has weakened the Security Council as an instrument of international law, tending to make it more an instrument of convenience for the powerful, notably the United States. Where enforcement action regarding weapons of mass destruction involves initiating or ending severe sanctions or use of force, it should be directed by the Security Council, and the permanent members should renounce the right of veto in such cases. Legitimacy of Security Council action in these and other matters would also be greatly enhanced by Security Council reform to make it more representative of the world's states and people. In general, as Canadian Minister of Foreign Affairs Graham stated,

> But even if we recognize that coercion may in rare cases be necessary to prevent the proliferation of weapons of mass destruction and to ensure their elimination, we must require that such coercion be firmly grounded in a rules-based multilateral system. Otherwise we condemn ourselves to live in a world governed solely by power, a solution that suits our purposes today but, as history demonstrates, may not be relied upon forever.[457]

In the case of the ICJ, the United States took drastic steps that undermined its authority in the mid-1980s. In 1984, Nicaragua brought a strong case before the International Court of Justice against the United States on matters including the mining of Nicaragua's harbors, which had been widely condemned as illegal.[458] After the ICJ held it had jurisdiction over the case, the United States first boycotted the proceedings and then withdrew from the court's general jurisdiction. The ICJ ruled against the United States and required the payment of reparations to Nicaragua, which the United States refused to pay.[459]

Finally, the United States has been undermining the emergence of a new institution for enforcement. It signed the Statute of the International Criminal Court with the express intent of changing ICC procedures so that U.S. personnel would be highly unlikely to be brought before the Court. The ICJ and the ICC are venues where there is at least a chance of creating a process where the weak and the strong can appear on an equal basis, though as in all legal arenas, the rich and powerful always have far greater resources at their disposal to argue their cases in the court and in the arena of public opinion.

In sum, far from strengthening existing verification and enforcement mechanisms for treaties, the United States has been undermining them and effectively reducing their role in favor of greater room to act in an *ad hoc* fashion determined mainly by itself. The U.S. record with respect to the treaties examined in this study raises sharp and disturbing questions about the future of global security – and therefore the security of individuals by the billions around the world.

ECHOES OF MANIFEST DESTINY

It is difficult to escape the conclusion that the drift of U.S. policy is toward U.S. dominance of the international system. In a sound legal system rules apply equally to all. In a system of politics, rules need not apply to those states with the military and economic strength not only to defend themselves but also to assert themselves. The argument that "as the strongest and richest country in the world, the United States can afford to safeguard its sovereignty,"[460] assumes that the United States will not suffer consequences from opting out of the international system: "On the contrary, we have every reason to expect that other nations, eager for access to American markets and eager for other cooperative arrangements with the United States, will often adapt themselves to American preferences."[461]

In the realm of security, this school of thought puts U.S. military strength and military means above others in the pursuit of security. Alliances are second, and treaties a distant third. For instance, Senator Kyl, an opponent of both the CTBT and the ABM Treaty, and an avid critic of reliance on international agreements said:

> Honorable nations do not need treaty limits to do the right thing. Rogue states will ignore legal requirements when it suits their interests. We ignore this harsh reality at our own peril.
>
> * * *
>
> In crafting an effective national security policy for the 21st Century, I reiterate that we have to re-establish the proposition that all component strategies must be based on a foundation of strong U.S. military capability. We must be prepared for failures of treaties, for failures of diplomacy and economic sanctions, for failures of intelligence to accurately predict threats, and for failures of deterrence.[462]

Senator Kyl, whose views put the ideas of this school into sharp focus, dismissed dependence on treaties and deferred it to an unspecified future time:

> Unenforceable and unenforced treaties are worse than none at all, because they cause nations to relax defenses against tyranny in the belief that they've done something significant merely

by signing the document. Until the world community demonstrates that reliance on treaties is warranted, I believe the U.S.
Senate will prefer to rely on U.S. capabilities and strengthening
ties to allies to meet common threats, including more cooperation in enforcing nonproliferation agreements.[463]

This view rejects the notion that treaties are instruments among equals, in
which all parties give up something and get something. The assertion that
"honorable nations do not need treaties to do the right thing" begs the
question of how the right thing is to be defined, or the criteria and methods by which belonging to the group of "honorable nations" is defined and
judged. It creates a category of a country that is always moral and acts
accordingly. It also does not tell us what is to be done if a normally "honorable" country commits a manifestly dishonorable act. It ignores that
doing the right thing is sometimes made very difficult if there is no level
playing field – that is if all do not abide by the same rules. If some parties
insist on having nuclear weapons, then why should not all parties who
consider themselves honorable also exercise that same right? If some
wealthy countries can go on increasing their greenhouse gas emissions
because it is cheaper for them not to change despite mounting evidence of
climate change and treaty obligations, then it may become more costly for
other parties to try to protect the world's climate system, while at the same
time diminishing greatly their chance of success.

The argument is basically an assertion that the world must accept that the
United States is right because it is moral in some intrinsic way even
though it may transgress the bounds of morality and law upon occasion. If
the rest of the world does not accept this view, then the United States is
prepared to opt out or use military force based, in the final analysis, on the
decision of the U.S. government alone. The argument thus sets one country above the law and is reminiscent of the nineteenth century idea of
"manifest destiny." One popular view of the concept at the time was that
God had commanded the United States to "civilize the world." Military
force would be a powerful instrument in obeying this command. Finally,
"America would realize its anointed purpose as 'God's right arm in his
battle with the world's ignorance and oppression and sin.'"[464]

This American "exceptionalism" is at odds with the very notion that the
rule of law is possible in global affairs. Setting one country above others
with a license for the use of power is rather a recipe for dictatorship and
chaos. If the United States is entitled to operate out of its own claim of
morality, then any other state can claim a similar entitlement. Today there

are eight states that have nuclear weapons, and even small groups can possess the capacity to harm large numbers of people and future generations. If the rule of power rather than the rule of law becomes the norm, especially in the context of the present inequalities and injustices in the world, security is likely to be a casualty.

CONCLUSION

International security can best be achieved through coordinated local, national, regional and global actions and cooperation. Treaties, like all other tools in this toolbox, are imperfect instruments. Like a national law, a treaty may be unjust or unwise, in whole or in part. If so, it can and should be amended. But without a framework of multilateral agreements, the alternative is for states to decide for themselves when action is warranted in their own interests, and to proceed to act unilaterally against others when they feel aggrieved. This is a recipe for the powerful to be police, prosecutor, judge, jury, and executioner all rolled into one. It is a path that cannot but lead to the arbitrary application and enforcement of law.

This is an age fraught with the risk of use of nuclear weapons. It is a time when the world faces climate change whose consequences could range from severe to catastrophic. There is a global economy in which a few hundred of the world's richest people have combined wealth greater the poorest two billion, and there are vast and growing differences between haves and have-nots within and between countries. Technology makes information about these gaps easily available, as it does data about weapons of mass destruction. For the United States, a hallmark of whose history is its role as a progenitor of the rule of law, to be embarked on a path of disregard of its international legal obligations is to abandon the best that its history has to offer the world. To reject the system of treaty-based international law rather than build on its many strengths is not only unwise, it is extremely dangerous. It is urgent that the United States join with other countries in implementing existing global security treaties to meet the security challenges of the twenty-first century and to achieve the ends of peace and justice to which the United States is committed under the United Nations Charter.

APPENDIX A

RATIFICATION STATUS
OF SECURITY AND
HUMAN RIGHTS TREATIES

TABLE I: RATIFICATION STATUS OF SECURITY-RELATED TREATIES

Country	CWC	BWC	NPT	CTBT	Mine Ban	FCCC	Kyoto	ICC
Afghanistan	SI 1/14/93	3/26/75 (r)	2/4/70 (r)					
Albania	5/11/94 (r)	6/3/92 (a)	9/12/90(a)	SI 9/27 /96	2/29/00 (r)	10/3/94 (a)		SI 7/18/98
Algeria	8/14/95(r)	7/22/01 (a)	1/12/95(a)	SI 10/15/96*	10/9/01 (r)	6/9/93 (r)		SI 12/28/00
Andorra			6/7/96(a)	SI 9/24/96	6/29/98 (r)			4/30/01 (r)
Angola			10/14/96(a)	SI 9/27/96	7/5/02 (r)	5/17/00(r)		SI 10/7/98
Antigua and Barbuda			6/17/85(s)	SI 4/16/97	5/3/99 (r)	2/2/93 (r)	11/3/98(r)	6/18/01 (r)
Argentina	10/2/95 (r)	11/27/79 (r)	2/10/95(a)	12/4/98 (r)*	9/14/99 (r)	3/11/94(r)	9/28/01 (r)	2/8/01(r)
Armenia	1/27/95 (r)	6/7/94 (a)	7/15/93(a)	SI 10/1/96		5/14/93(r)		SI 10/1/99
Australia	5/6/94 (r)	10/5/77(r)	1/23/73 (r)	6/9/98 (r)*	1/14/99 (r)	12/30/92(r)	SI 4/29/98	7/1/02 (r)
Austria	8/17/95 (r)	8/10/73 (r)	6/27/69 (r)	3/13/98 (r)*	6/29/98 (r)	2/28/94(r)	5/31/02 (r)	12/28/00 (r)
Azerbaijan	2/29/00 (r)		9/22/92(a)	2/2/99 (r)		5/16/95(r)	9/28/00(a)	
Bahamas	SI 3/2/94	11/26/86 (a)	8/11/76(s)		7/31/98 (r)	3/29/94(r)	4/9/99 (a)	SI 12/29/00
Bahrain	4/28/97 (r)	10/28/88 (a)	11/3/88(a)	SI 9/24/96		12/28/94(r)		SI 12/11/00
Bangladesh	4/25/97 (r)	3/13/85 (a)	8/31/79(a)	3/8/00 (r)*	9/6/00(r)	4/15/94(r)	10/22/01(a)	SI 9/16/99
Barbados		2/16/73 (r)	2/21/80 (r)		1/26/99 (r)	3/23/94(r)	8/7/00 (a)	SI 9/8/00
Belarus	7/11/96 (r)	3/26/75(r)	7/22/93(a)	9/13/00 (r)		5/11/00(r)		
Belgium	1/27/97 (r)	3/15/79 (r)	5/02/75(r)	6/29/99 (r)*	9/4/98 (r)	1/16/96(r)	5/31/02 (r)	6/28/00 (r)
Belize		10/20/86 (a)	8/09/85(s)	SI 11/14/01	4/23/98 (r)	10/31/94(r)		6/5/00 (r)

Country	CWC	BWC	NPT	CTBT	Mine Ban	FCCC	Kyoto	ICC
Benin	5/14/98 (r)	4/25/75 (r)	10/31/72(r)	3/6/01 (r)	9/25/98 (r)	6/30/94(r)	2/25/02 (a)	1/22/02 (r)
Bhutan	SI 3/24/97	6/8/78 (a)	5/23/85(a)			8/25/95(r)		
Bolivia	8/14/98 (r)	10/30/75(r)	5/26/70 (r)	10/4/99 (r)	6/9/98 (r)	10/3/94(r)	11/30/99 (r)	6/27/02 (r)
Bosnia & Herzegovina	2/25/97 (r)	8/15/94(a)	8/15/94(s)	SI 9/24/96	9/8/98 (r)	9/7/00(r)		4/11/02 (r)
Botswana	8/31/98 (a)	2/5/92 (r)	4/28/69 (r)		3/1/00 (r)	1/27/94(r)		9/8/00 (r)
Brazil	3/13/96(r)	2/27/73 (r)	9/18/98(a)	7/24/98 (r)*	4/30/99 (r)	2/28/94(r)	SI 4/29/98	6/20/02(r)
Brunei	7/28/97(r)	1/31/91(a)	3/26/85(a)		SI 12/4/97			
Bulgaria	8/10/94(r)	2/8/72(r)	9/5/69(r)	9/29/99(r)*	9/4/98 (r)	5/12/95(r)	SI 9/18/98	4/11/02(r)
Burkina Faso	7/8/97(r)	4/17/91(a)	3/3/70(r)	4/17/02(r)	9/16/98(r)	9/2/93(r)		SI 11/30/98
Burundi	9/4/98 (r)	SI 4/10/72	3/19/71(a)	SI 9/24/96	SI 12/3/97	1/6/97(r)		SI 1/13/99
Cambodia	SI 1/15/93	3/9/83(r)	6/2/72(a)	11/10/00(r)	7/28/99(r)	12/18/95(a)	10/18/01 (a)	4/11/02 (r)
Cameroon	9/16/96 (r)		1/8/69 (r)	SI 11/16/01	SI 12/3/97	10/31/94(r)		SI 7/17/98
Canada	9/26/95(r)	9/18/72(r)	1/8/69(r)	12/18/98(r)*	12/3/97(r)	12/4/92(r)	SI 4/29/98	7/7/00(r)
Cape Verde	SI 1/15/93	10/20/77(a)	10/24/79(a)	SI 10/1/96	5/14/01(r)	3/29/95(r)		SI 12/28/00
Central African Republic	SI 1/14/93	SI 4/10/72	10/25/70(a)	SI 12/19/01		3/10/95(r)		10/3/01(r)
Chad	SI 10/11/94		3/10/71(r)	SI 10/8/96	5/6/99(r)	6/17/94(r)		SI 10/20/99
Chile	7/12/96(r)	4/22/80(r)	5/25/95(a)	7/12/00(r)*	9/10/01(r)	12/22/94(r)	SI 6/17/98	SI 9/11/98
China	4/25/97(r)	11/15/84(a)	3/9/92(a)	SI 9/24/96*		1/5/93(r)	SI 5/29/98	

Country	CWC	BWC	NPT	CTBT	Mine Ban	FCCC	Kyoto	ICC
Colombia	4/5/00(r)	12/19/83(r)	4/8/86(r)	SI 9/24/96*	9/6/00(r)	3/22/95(r)	11/30/01(a)	8/5/02(r)
Comoros	SI 1/13/93		10/4/95(a)	SI 12/12/96		10/31/94(r)		SI 9/22/00
Congo	SI 1/15/93	10/23/78(a)	10/23/78(a)	SI 2/11/97	5/4/2001(a)	10/14/96(r)		4/11/02(r)
Cook Islands	7/15/94(r)		SI 12/5/97		SI 12/3/97	4/20/93(r)	8/27/01(r)	
Costa Rica	5/31/96(r)	12/17/73(r)	3/3/70(r)	9/25/01(r)	3/17/99(r)	8/26/94(r)	SI 4/27/98	6/7/01(r)
Cote d'Ivoire	12/18/95(r)	SI 5/23/72	03/6/73(r)	SI 9/25/96	6/30/00(r)	11/29/94(r)		SI 11/30/98
Croatia	5/23/95(r)	4/28/93(a)	6/29/92(s)	3/2/01(r)	5/20/98(r)	4/8/96(r)	SI 3/11/99	5/21/01(r)
Cuba	4/29/97(r)	4/21/76(r)				1/5/94(r)	4/30/02(r)	
Cyprus	8/28/98(r)	11/6/73(r)	2/10/70(r)	SI 9/24/96	SI 12/4/97	10/15/97(r)	7/16/99(a)	3/7/02(r)
Czech Republic	3/6/96(r)	4/5/93(a)	1/1/93(s)	9/11/97(r)	10/26/99(r)	10/7/93(r)	11/15/01(Ap)	SI 4/13/98
Denmark	7/13/95(r)	3/1/73(r)	1/3/69(r)	12/21/98(r)	6/8/98(r)	12/21/93(r)	5/31/02(r)	6/21/01(r)
Djibouti	SI 9/28/93		10/16/96(a)	SI 10/21/96	5/18/98(r)	8/27/95(r)	3/12/02(a)	SI 10/7/98
Dominica	2/12/01(r)	11/8/78(a)	8/10/84(s)		3/26/99(r)	6/21/93(a)		2/12/01(a)
Dominican Republic	SI 1/13/93	2/23/73(r)	7/24/71(r)	SI 10/3/96	6/30/00(r)	10/7/98(r)	2/12/02(a)	SI 9/8/00
Ecuador	9/6/95(r)	3/21/75(r)	3/7/69(r)	11/12/01(r)	4/29/99(r)	2/23/93(r)	1/13/00(r)	2/5/02(r)
Egypt		SI 4/10/72	2/26/81(r)	SI 10/14/96*		12/5/94(r)	SI 3/15/99	SI 12/26/00
El Salvador	10/30/95(r)	12/31/91(r)	07/11/72(r)	9/11/98(r)	1/27/99(r)	12/4/95(r)	11/30/98(r)	
Equatorial Guinea	4/25/97(r)	1/16/89(a)	11/1/84(a)	SI 10/9/96	9/16/98(a)	8/16/00(a)	8/16/00(a)	

Country	CWC	BWC	NPT	CTBT	Mine Ban	FCCC	Kyoto	ICC
Eritrea	2/14/00(a)		3/3/95(a)		8/27/01(a)	4/24/95(a)		SI 10/7/98
Estonia	5/26/99(r)	6/21/93(a)	1/7/92(a)	8/13/99(r)		7/27/94(r)	SI 12/3/98	1/30/02(r)
Ethiopia	5/13/96(r)	5/26/75(r)	2/5/70(r)	SI 9/25/96	SI 12/3/97	4/5/94(r)		
European Community						12/21/93(r)	5/31/02(Ap)	
Fiji	1/20/93(r)	9/4/73(r)	7/14/72(s)	10/10/96(r)	6/10/98(r)	2/25/93(r)	9/17/98(r)	11/29/99(r)
Finland	2/7/95(r)	2/4/74(r)	2/5/69(r)	1/15/99(r)*		5/3/94(r)	5/31/02(r)	12/29/00(r)
FYR Macedonia	6/20/97(a)	12/24/96(a)	4/12/95(a)	3/14/00(r)	9/9/98(a)	1/28/98(a)		3/6/02(r)
France	3/2/95(r)	9/27/84(a)	8/3/92(a)	4/6/98(r)*	7/23/98(r)	3/25/94(r)	5/31/02(Ap)	6/9/00(r)
Gabon	9/8/00(r)	SI 4/10/72	2/19/74(a)	9/20/00(r)	9/8/00(r)	1/21/98(r)		9/20/00(r)
Gambia	5/19/98(r)	11/21/91(r)	5/12/75(r)		SI 12/4/97	6/10/94(r)	6/1/01(a)	6/28/02(r)
Georgia	11/27/95(r)	5/22/96(a)	3/7/94(a)	SI 9/24/96		7/29/94(a)	6/16/99(a)	SI 7/18/98
Germany	8/12/94(r)	11/28/72(r)	5/2/75(r)	8/20/98(r)*	7/23/98(r)	12/9/93(r)	5/31/02(r)	12/11/00(r)
Ghana	7/9/97(r)	6/6/75(r)	5/4/70(r)	SI 10/3/96	6/30/00(r)	9/6/95(r)		12/20/99(r)
Greece	12/22/94(r)	12/10/75(r)	3/11/70(r)	4/21/99(r)	SI 12/3/97	8/4/94(r)	5/31/02(r)	5/15/02(r)
Grenada	SI 4/9/97	10/22/86(a)	9/2/75(s)	8/19/98(r)	8/19/98(r)	8/11/94(r)		
Guatemala	SI 1/14/93	9/19/73(r)	9/22/70(r)	SI 9/20/99	3/26/99(r)	12/15/95(r)	10/5/99(r)	
Guinea	6/9/97(r)	8/20/76(a)	4/29/85(a)	SI 10/3/96	10/8/98(r)	5/7/93(r)	9/7/00(a)	SI 9/7/00
Guinea-Bissau	SI 1/14/93	8/20/76(a)	8/20/76(s)	SI 4/11/97	5/22/01(r)	10/27/95(r)		SI 9/12/00
Guyana	9/12/97(r)	SI 1/03/73	10/19/93(a)	3/7/01(r)	SI 12/4/97	8/29/94(r)		SI 12/28/00

Country	CWC	BWC	NPT	CTBT	Mine Ban	FCCC	Kyoto	ICC
Haiti	SI 1/14/93	SI 4/10/72	6/2/70(r)	SI 9/24/96	SI 12/3/97	9/25/96(r)		SI 2/26/99
Holy See	5/12/99(r)		2/25/71(a)	7/18/01(r)	2/17/98(r)			
Honduras	SI 1/13/93	3/14/79(r)	5/16/73(r)	SI 9/25/96	9/24/98(r)	10/19/95(r)	7/19/00(r)	7/1/02(r)
Hungary	10/31/96(r)	12/27/72(r)	5/27/69(r)	7/13/99(r)*	4/6/98(r)	2/24/94(r)		11/30/01(r)
Iceland	4/28/97(r)	2/15/73(r)	7/18/69(r)	6/26/00(r)	5/5/99(r)	6/16/93(r)	5/23/02(a)	5/25/00(r)
India	9/3/96(r)	7/15/74(r)		*		11/1/93(r)		
Indonesia	11/12/98(r)	2/19/92(r)	7/12/791(r)	SI 9/24/96*	SI 12/4/97	8/23/94(r)	SI 7/13/98	
Iran	11/3/97(r)	8/22/73(r)	2/2/70(r)	SI 9/24/96*		7/18/96(r)		SI 12/31/00
Iraq		6/19/91(r)	10/29/69(r)					
Ireland	6/24/96(r)	10/27/72(r)	7/1/68(r)	7/15/99(r)	12/3/97(r)	4/20/94(r)	5/31/02(r)	4/11/02(r)
Israel	SI 1/13/93			SI 9/25/96*		6/4/96(r)	SI 12/16/98	SI 12/31/00
Italy	12/8/95(r)	5/30/75(r)	5/2/75(r)	2/1/99(r)*	4/23/99(r)	4/15/94(r)	5/31/02(r)	7/26/99(r)
Jamaica	9/8/00(r)	8/13/75(a)	3/5/70(r)	11/13/01(r)	7/17/98(r)	1/6/95(r)	6/28/99(a)	SI 9/8/00
Japan	9/15/95(r)	6/8/82(r)	6/8/76(r)	7/8/97(r)*	9/30/98(r)	5/28/93(r)	6/4/02(At)	
Jordan	10/29/97(a)	5/30/75(r)	2/11/70(r)	8/25/98(r)	11/13/98(r)	11/12/93(r)		4/11/02(r)
Kazakhstan	3/23/00(r)		2/14/94(a)	5/14/02(r)		5/15/95(r)	SI 3/12/99	
Kenya	4/25/97(r)	1/7/76(a)	6/11/70(r)	11/30/00(r)	1/23/01(r)	8/30/94(r)		SI 8/11/99
Kiribati	9/7/00(a)		4/18/85(s)	9/7/00(r)	9/7/00(a)	2/7/95(r)	9/7/00(a)	
Korea, Dem People's Republic of		3/13/87(a)	12/12/85(a)	*		12/5/94(r)		

Country	CWC	BWC	NPT	CTBT	Mine Ban	FCCC	Kyoto	ICC
Korea, Republic of	4/28/97(r)	6/25/87(r)	4/23/75(r)	9/24/99(r)*		12/14/93(r)	SI 9/25/98	SI 3/8/00
Kuwait	5/29/97(r)	7/18/72(r)	11/17/89(r)	SI 9/24/96		12/28/94(a)		SI 9/8/00
Kyrgyzstan	SI 2/22/93		7/5/94(a)	SI 10/8/96		5/25/00(a)		SI 12/8/98
Laos	2/25/97(r)	3/20/73(r)	2/20/70(r)	10/5/00(r)		1/4/95(a)		
Latvia	7/23/96(r)	2/6/97(a)	1/31/92(a)	11/20/01(r)		3/23/95(r)	7/5/02(r)	6/28/02(r)
Lebanon		3/26/75(r)	7/15/70(r)			12/15/94(r)		
Lesotho	12/7/94(r)	9/6/77(r)	5/20/70(r)	9/14/99(r)	12/2/98(r)	2/7/95(r)	9/6/00(a)	9/6/00(r)
Liberia	SI 1/15/93	SI 4/14/72	3/5/70(r)	SI 10/1/96	12/23/99(a)			SI 7/17/98
Libya		1/19/82(a)	5/26/75(r)	SI 11/13/01		6/14/99(r)		
Liechtenstein	11/24/99(r)	6/6/91(a)	4/20/78(a)	SI 9/27/96	10/5/99(r)	6/22/94(r)	SI 6/29/98	10/2/01(r)
Lithuania	4/15/98(r)	2/10/98(a)	9/23/91(a)	2/7/00(r)	SI 2/26/99	3/24/95(r)	SI 9/21/98	SI 12/10/98
Luxembourg	4/15/97(r)	3/23/76(r)	5/2/75(r)	5/26/99(r)	6/14/99(r)	5/9/94(r)	5/31/02(r)	9/8/00(r)
Madagascar	SI 1/15/93	SI 10/13/72	10/08/70(r)	SI 10/9/96	9/16/99(r)	6/2/99(r)		SI 7/18/98
Malawi	1/11/98(r)	SI 4/10/72	2/18/86(s)	SI 10/9/96	8/13/98(r)	4/21/94(r)	10/26/01(a)	SI 3/2/99
Malaysia	4/20/00(r)	9/6/91(r)	3/5/70(r)	SI 7/23/98	4/22/99(r)	7/13/94(r)	SI 3/12/99	
Maldive Islands	5/31/94(r)	8/2/93(a)	4/7/70(r)	9/7/00(r)	9/7/00(r)	11/9/92(r)	12/30/98(r)	
Mali	4/28/97(r)	SI 4/10/72	2/10/70(r)	8/4/99(r)	6/2/98(r)	12/28/94(r)	3/28/02(r)	8/16/00(r)
Malta	4/28/97(r)	4/7/75(r)	2/6/70(r)	7/23/01(r)	5/7/01(r)	3/17/94(r)	11/11/01(r)	SI 7/17/98
Marshall Islands	SI 1/13/93		1/30/95(a)	SI 9/24/96	SI 12/4/97	10/8/92(r)	SI 3/17/98	12/7/00(r)

Country	CWC	BWC	NPT	CTBT	Mine Ban	FCCC	Kyoto	ICC
Mauritania	2/9/98(r)		10/26/93(a)	SI 9/24/96	7/21/00(r)	1/20/94(r)	5/9/01(a)	
Mauritius	2/9/93(r)	8/7/72(r)	4/8/69(r)		12/3/97(r)	9/4/92(r)	5/9/01(a)	3/5/02(r)
Mexico	8/29/94(r)	4/8/74(r)	1/21/69(r)	10/5/99(r)*	6/9/98(r)	3/11/93(r)	9/7/00(r)	SI 9/7/00
Micronesia	6/21/99(r)		4/14/95(a)	7/25/97(r)		11/18/93(r)	6/21/99(r)	
Moldova	7/8/96(r)		10/11/94(a)	SI 9/24/97	9/8/00(r)	6/9/95(r)		SI 9/8/00
Monaco	6/1/95(r)	4/30/99(a)	3/13/95(a)	12/18/98(r)	11/17/98(r)	11/24/92(r)	SI 4/29/98	SI 7/8/98
Mongolia	1/17/95(r)	9/5/72(r)	5/14/69(r)	8/8/97(r)		9/30/93(r)	12/15/99(a)	4/11/02(r)
Morocco	12/28/95(r)	SI 5/2/72	11/27/70(r)	4/17/00(r)		12/28/95(r)	1/25/02(a)	SI 9/8/00
Mozambique	8/15/00(a)		9/4/90(a)	SI 9/26/96	8/25/98(r)	8/25/95(r)		SI 12/28/00
Myanmar (Burma)	SI 1/14/93	SI 4/10/72	12/02/92(a)	SI 9/25/96		11/25/94(r)		
Namibia	11/24/95(r)		10/2/92(a)	6/29/01(r)	9/21/98(r)	5/16/95(r)		6/25/02(r)
Nauru	11/12/01(r)		6/7/82(a)	11/12/01(r)		11/11/93(r)	8/16/01(r)	11/12/01(r)
Nepal	11/18/97(r)	SI 4/10/72	1/5/70(r)	SI 10/8/96		5/2/94(r)		
Netherlands	6/30/95(r)	6/22/81(r)	5/2/75(r)	3/23/99(r)*	4/12/99(r)	12/20/93(r)	5/31/02(a)	7/17/01(r)
New Zealand	7/15/96(r)	12/13/72(r)	9/10/69(r)	3/19/99(r)	1/27/99(r)	9/16/93(r)	SI 5/22/98	9/7/00(r)
Nicaragua	11/5/99(r)	8/7/75(r)	3/6/73(r)	12/5/00(r)	11/30/98(r)	10/31/95(r)	11/18/99(r)	
Niger	4/9/97(r)	6/23/72(r)	10/9/92(a)	SI 10/3/96	3/23/99(r)	7/25/95(r)	SI 10/23/98	4/11/02(r)
Nigeria	5/20/99(r)	7/3/73(r)	9/27/68(r)	9/27/01(r)	9/27/01(a)	8/29/94(r)		9/27/01(r)
Niue				4/15/98(r)		2/28/96(a)	6/5/99(r)	

Country	CWC	BWC	NPT	CTBT	Mine Ban	FCCC	Kyoto	ICC
Norway	4/7/94(r)	8/1/73(r)	2/5/69(r)	7/15/99(r)*	7/9/98(r)	7/9/93(r)	5/30/02(r)	2/16/00(r)
Oman	2/8/95(r)	3/31/92(a)	1/23/97(a)	SI 9/23/99		2/8/95(r)		SI 12/20/00
Pakistan	10/28/97(r)	9/25/74(r)		*		6/1/94(r)		
Palau			4/12/95(a)			12/10/99(r)	12/10/99(a)	
Panama	10/7/98(r)	3/20/74(r)	1/13/77(r)	3/23/99(r)	10/7/98(r)	5/23/95(r)	3/5/99(r)	3/21/02(r)
Papua New Guinea	4/17/96(r)	10/27/80(a)	1/13/82(a)	SI 9/25/96		3/16/93(r)	3/28/02(r)	
Paraguay	12/1/94(r)	6/9/76(a)	2/4/70(r)	10/4/01(r)	11/13/98(r)	2/24/94(r)	8/27/99(r)	5/14/01(r)
Peru	7/20/95(r)	6/5/85(r)	3/3/70(r)	11/12/97(r)*	6/17/98(r)	6/7/93(r)	SI 11/13/98	11/10/01(r)
Philippines	12/11/96(r)	5/21/73(r)	10/5/72(r)	2/23/01(r)	2/15/00(r)	8/2/94(r)	SI 4/15/98	SI 12/28/00
Poland	8/23/95(r)	1/25/73(r)	6/12/69(r)	5/25/99(r)*	SI 12/4/97	7/28/94(r)	SI 7/15/98	11/12/01(r)
Portugal	9/10/96(r)	5/15/75(r)	12/15/77(a)	6/26/00(r)	2/19/99(r)	12/21/93(r)	5/31/02(Ap)	2/5/02(r)
Qatar	9/3/97(r)	4/17/75(r)	4/03/89(a)	3/3/97(r)	10/13/98(r)	4/18/96(a)		
Romania	2/15/95(r)	7/25/79(r)	2/4/70(r)	10/5/99(r)*	11/30/00(r)	6/8/94(r)	3/19/01(r)	4/11/02(r)
Russia	11/5/97(r)	3/26/75(r)	3/5/70(r)	6/30/00(r)*		12/28/94(r)	SI 3/11/99	SI 9/13/00
Rwanda	SI 5/17/93	5/20/75(r)	5/20/75(a)		6/13/00(r)	8/18/98(r)		
St. Kitts and Nevis	SI 3/16/94	4/2/91(a)	3/22/93(a)		12/2/98(r)	1/7/93(r)		
St. Lucia	4/9/97(r)	11/26/86(a)	12/28/79(s)	4/5/01(r)	4/13/99(r)	6/14/93(r)	SI 3/16/98	SI 8/27/99
St. Vincent & the Grenadines	SI 9/20/93	5/13/99(a)	11/6/84(s)		8/1/01(r)	12/2/96(a)	SI 3/19/98	

Country	CWC	BWC	NPT	CTBT	Mine Ban	FCCC	Kyoto	ICC
Samoa	SI 1/14/93		3/17/75(a)	SI 10/9/96	7/23/98(r)	11/29/94(r)	11/27/00(r)	SI 7/17/98
San Marino	12/10/99(r)	3/11/75(r)	8/10/70(r)	3/12/02(r)	3/18/98(r)	10/28/94(r)		5/13/99(r)
Sao Tome & Principe		8/24/79(a)	7/20/83(a)	SI 9/26/96	SI 4/30/98	9/29/99(r)		SI 12/28/00
Saudi Arabia	8/9/96(r)	5/24/72(r)	10/3/88(a)			12/28/94(a)		
Senegal	7/20/98(r)	3/26/75(r)	12/17/70(r)	6/9/99(r)	9/24/98(r)	10/17/94(r)	7/20/01(a)	2/2/99(r)
Seychelles	4/7/93(r)	10/11/79(a)	3/12/85(a)	SI 9/24/96	6/2/00(r)	9/22/92(r)	7/22/02(r)	SI 12/28/00
Sierra Leone	SI 1/15/93	6/29/76(r)	2/26/75(a)	9/17/01(r)	4/25/01(r)	6/22/95(r)		9/15/00(r)
Singapore	5/21/97(r)	12/2/75(r)	3/10/76(r)	11/10/01(r)		5/29/97(r)		
Slovakia	10/27/95(r)	5/17/93(a)	1/1/93(s)	3/3/98(r)*	2/25/99(AA)	8/25/94(r)	5/31/02(r)	4/11/02(r)
Slovenia	6/11/97(r)	4/7/92(a)	4/7/92(a)	8/31/99(r)	10/27/98(r)	1/12/95(r)	SI 10/21/98	12/31/01(r)
Solomon Islands		6/17/81(a)	6/17/81(s)	SI 10/3/96	1/26/99(r)	12/28/94(r)	SI 9/29/98	SI 12/3/98
Somalia		SI 7/3/72	3/5/70(r)					
South Africa	9/13/95(r)	11/3/75(r)	7/10/91(a)	3/30/99(r)*	6/26/98(r)	8/29/97(r)	7/31/02(a)	11/27/00(r)
Spain	8/3/94(r)	6/20/79(r)	11/5/87(a)	7/31/98(r)*	1/19/99(r)	12/12/93(r)	5/31/02(r)	10/24/00(r)
Sri Lanka	8/19/94(r)	11/18/86(r)	3/5/79(r)	SI 10/24/96		11/23/93(r)		
Sudan	5/24/99(a)		10/31/73(r)		SI 12/4/97	11/19/93(r)		SI 9/8/00
Suriname	4/28/97(r)	1/6/93(a)	6/30/76(s)	SI 1/14/97	5/23/02(r)	10/14/97(r)		
Swaziland	11/20/96(r)	6/18/91(a)	12/11/69(r)	SI 9/24/96	12/23/98(r)	10/7/96(r)		
Sweden	6/17/93(r)	2/5/76(r)	1/9/70(r)	12/2/98(r)*	11/30/98(r)	6/23/93(r)	5/31/02(r)	6/28/01(r)

Country	CWC	BWC	NPT	CTBT	Mine Ban	FCCC	Kyoto	ICC
Switzerland	3/10/95(r)	5/4/76(r)	3/9/77(r)	10/1/99(r)*	3/24/98(r)	12/10/93(r)	SI 3/16/98	10/12/01(r)
Syrian Arab Republic		SI 4/14/72	9/24/69(r)			4/1/96(a)		SI 11/29/00
Taiwan		2/9/73(r)	1/27/70(r)					
Tajikistan	1/11/95(r)		1/17/95(a)	6/10/98(r)	10/12/99(a)	1/7/98(a)		5/5/00(r)
Tanzania	6/25/98(r)	SI 8/16/72	5/31/91(a)		SI 12/3/97	4/17/96(r)		SI 12/29/00
Thailand	SI 1/14/93	5/28/75(r)	12/2/72(a)	SI 11/12/96	11/27/98(r)	12/29/94(r)	SI 2/2/99	SI 10/2/00
Togo	4/23/97(r)	11/10/76(r)	2/26/70(r)	SI 10/2/96	3/9/00(r)	3/8/95(r)		
Tonga		9/28/76(a)	7/7/71(s)			7/20/98(a)		
Trinidad & Tobago	6/24/97(a)		10/30/86(r)		4/27/98(r)	6/24/94(r)	1/28/99(r)	4/6/99(r)
Tunisia	4/15/97(r)	5/18/73(r)	2/26/70(r)	SI 10/16/96	7/9/99(r)	7/15/93(r)		
Turkey	5/12/97(r)	10/25/74(r)	4/17/80(r)	2/16/00(r)*				
Turkmenistan	9/29/94(r)	1/11/96(a)	9/29/94(a)	2/20/98(r)	1/19/98(r)	6/5/95(a)	1/11/00(r)	
Tuvalu			1/19/79(s)			10/26/93(r)	11/16/98(r)	
Uganda	11/30/01(r)	5/12/92(a)	10/20/82(a)	3/14/01(r)	2/25/99(r)	9/8/93(r)	3/25/02(a)	6/14/02(r)
Ukraine	10/16/98(r)	3/26/75(r)	12/05/94(a)	3/23/01*	SI 2/24/99	1/13/97(r)	SI 3/15/99	SI 1/20/00
United Arab Emirates	11/28/00(r)	SI 9/28/72	9/26/95(a)	9/18/00(r)		12/29/95(a)		SI 11/27/00
United Kingdom	5/13/96(r)	3/26/75(r)	11/27/68(r)	4/6/98(r)*	7/31/98(r)	12/8/93(r)	5/31/02(r)	10/4/01(r)
United States	4/25/97(r)	3/26/75(r)	3/5/70(r)	SI 9/24/96*		10/15/92(r)	SI 11/12/98	SI 12/31/00

Country	CWC	BWC	NPT	CTBT	Mine Ban	FCCC	Kyoto	ICC
Uruguay	10/6/94(r)	4/6/81(a)	8/31/70(r)	9/21/01(r)	6/7/01(r)	8/18/94(r)	2/5/01(r)	6/28/02(r)
Uzbekistan	7/23/96(r)	1/11/96(a)	5/2/92(r)	5/29/97(r)		6/20/93(a)	10/12/99(r)	SI 12/29/00
Vanuatu		10/12/90(a)	8/26/95(a)	SI 9/24/96	SI 12/4/97	3/25/93(r)	7/17/01(a)	
Venezuela	12/3/97(r)	10/18/78(r)	9/25/75(r)	5/13/02(r)	4/14/99(r)	12/28/94(r)		6/7/00(r)
Vietnam	9/30/98(r)	6/20/80(a)	6/14/82(a)	SI 9/24/96*		11/16/94(r)	SI 12/3/98	
Yemen	10/2/00(r)	6/1/79(a)	6/1/79(r)	SI 9/30/96	9/1/98(r)	2/21/96(r)		SI 12/28/00
Yugoslavia	4/20/00(s)	6/13/01(a)	3/4/70(r)	SI 6/8/01		9/3/97(r)		9/6/01(r)
Zaire (Dem Rep. of Congo)	SI 1/14/93	9/16/75(r)	8/4/70(r)	SI 10/4/96*	5/2/02(a)	1/9/95(r)		4/11/02(r)
Zambia	2/9/01(r)		5/15/91(a)	SI 12/3/96	2/23/01(r)	5/28/93(r)	SI 8/5/98	SI 7/17/98
Zimbabwe	4/25/97(r)	11/5/90(a)	9/26/91(a)	SI 10/13/99	6/8/98(r)	3/11/92(r)		SI 7/17/98

KEY TO TABLE I

CWC Convention on the Prohibition of the Development, Production, Stockpiling and Use of Chemical Weapons and on their Destruction. Figures as of July 2002. The source of information is the United Nations Department for Disarmament Affairs (http://disarmament.un.org). The Chart reflects date of signature if not ratified (SI), ratification (r), Accession (a) or Succession (s); those states that have signed and not ratified are also in italics.

BWC Convention on the Prohibition of the Development, Production and Stockpiling of Bacteriological (Biological) and Toxin Weapons and on their Destruction. Figures as of July 2002. The source of information is the International COmmittee of the Red Cross (www.icrc.org/ihl). The Chart reflects date of signature if not ratified (SI), ratification (r), Accession (a) or Succession (s); those states that have signed and not ratified are also in italics.

NPT Treaty on the Nonproliferation of Nuclear Weapons. Figures as of July 2002. The sources of the information are the U.S. Department of State and the Agency for the Prohibition of Nuclear Weapons in Latin America and the Caribbean (www.opanal.org). The Chart reflects date of signature if not ratified (SI), ratification (r), Accession (a) or Succession (s); those states that have signed and not ratified are also in italics.

CTBT Comprehensive Nuclear Test Ban Treaty. Figures as of July 2002. The source is the Preparatory Commission for the CTBTO. The Chart reflects date of signature if not ratified (SI), ratification (r), or Accession (a); those states that have signed and not ratified are also in italics. Also, those states marked with

asterisks are the 44 states whose ratification is required for the CTBT to enter into force.

MINE BAN 1997 Mine Ban Treaty. Figures as of July 2002. The source of information is the International Campaign to Ban Landmines (www.icbl.org). The Chart reflects date of signature if not ratified (SI), ratification (r), Accession (a); those states that have signed and not ratified are also in italics.

FCCC UN Framework Convention on Climate Change. Figures as of December 11, 2000. The source of information is the Secretariat of the UNFCCC. Figures reflect date of Ratification (r) or Accession (a); the chart does not reflect any countries that are signatories who have not ratified.

KYOTO Kyoto Protocol to the Framework Convention on Climate Change. Figures as of July 2002. The source of information is the Secretariat of the UNFCCC. The Chart reflects date of signature if not ratified (SI), ratification (r), acceptance (A+), approval (Ap) or accession (a); those states that have signed and not ratified are in italics. For an explanation of the various methods of adopting the treaty, see (http://unfccc.int/resource/kpstats.pdf).

ICC Rome Statute of the International Criminal Court. Figures as of August 2002. The source of information is the Coalition for the International Criminal Court (www.iccnow.org). The Chart reflects date of signature if not ratified (SI), ratification (r), Accession (a); those states that have signed and not ratified are also in italics.

TABLE 2: RATIFICATION STATUS OF HUMAN RIGHTS TREATIES

Country	CESCR	CCPR	CEDAW	CAT	CRC
Afghanistan	1/24/83(a)	1/24/83(a)	SI 8/14/80	4/1/87(r)	3/28/94(r)
Albania	10/4/91(a)	10/4/91(a)	5/11/94(a)	5/11/94(a)	2/27/92(r)
Algeria	9/12/1989(r)	9/12/89(r)	5/22/96(a)	9/12/89(r)	4/16/93(4)
Andorra			1/15/97(a)		1/2/96(r)
Angola	1/10/92(a)	1/10/92(a)	9/17/86(a)		12/6/90(r)
Antigua and Barbuda			8/1/89(a)	7/19/93(a)	10/5/93(r)
Argentina	8/8/86(r)	8/8/86(r)	7/15/85(r)	9/24/86(r)	12/5/90(r)
Armenia	9/13/93(a)	6/23/93(a)	9/13/93(a)	9/13/93(r)	6/23/93(a)
Australia	12/10/75(r)	8/13/80(r)	7/28/83(r)	8/8/89(r)	12/17/90(r)
Austria	9/10/78(r)	9/10/78(r)	3/31/82(r)	7/29/87(r)	8/6/92(r)
Azerbaijan	8/13/92(a)	8/13/92(a)	7/10/95(a)	8/16/96(a)	8/13/92(a)
Bahamas			10/6/93(a)		2/20/91(r)
Bahrain				3/6/98(a)	2/13/92(a)
Bangladesh	10/5/98(a)	9/7/00(a)	11/6/84(a)	10/5/98(a)	8/3/90(r)
Barbados	1/5/73(a)	1/5/73(a)	10/16/80(r)		10/9/90(r)
Belarus	11/12/73(r)	11/12/73(r)	2/4/81(r)	3/13/87(r)	2/13/92(a)
Belgium	4/21/83(r)	4/21/83(r)	7/10/85(r)	6/25/99(r)	12/16/91(r)
Belize	SI 9/6/00	6/10/96(a)	5/16/90(r)	3/17/86(a)	5/2/90(r)
Benin	3/12/92(a)	3/12/92(a)	3/12/92(r)	3/12/92(a)	8/3/90(r)
Bhutan			8/31/81(r)		8/1/90(r)
Bolivia	8/12/82(a)	8/12/82(a)	6/8/90(r)	4/12/99(r)	6/26/90(r)
Bosnia & Herzegovina	3/3/92(s)	9/1/93(s)	9/1/93(s)	9/1/93(a)	9/1/93(s)
Botswana		9/8/00(r)	8/13/96(a)	9/8/00(r)	3/14/95(a)
Brazil	1/24/92(a)	1/24/92(a)	2/1/84(r)	9/28/89(r)	9/25/90(r)
Brunei					12/27/95(a)
Bulgaria	9/21/70(r)	9/21/70(r)	2/8/82(r)	12/16/86(r)	6/3/91(r)
Burkina Faso	1/4/99(a)	1/4/99(a)	10/14/87(a)	1/4/99(a)	8/31/90(r)
Burundi	5/9/90(a)	5/9/90(a)	1/8/92(r)	2/18/93(a)	10/19/90(r)
Cambodia	5/26/92(a)	5/26/92(a)	10/15/92(a)	10/15/92(a)	10/15/92(a)

Country	CESCR	CCPR	CEDAW	CAT	CRC
Cameroon	6/27/84(a)	6/27/84(a)	8/23/94(r)	12/19/86(a)	1/11/93(r)
Canada	5/19/76(a)	5/19/76(a)	12/10/81(r)	6/24/87(r)	12/13/91(r)
Cape Verde	8/6/93(a)	8/6/93(a)	12/5/80(a)	6/4/92(a)	6/4/92(a)
Central African Republic	5/8/81(a)	5/8/81(a)	6/21/91(a)		4/23/92(r)
Chad	6/9/95(a)	6/9/95(a)	6/9/95(a)	6/9/95(a)	10/2/90(r)
Chile	2/10/72(r)	2/10/72(r)	12/7/89(r)	*SI 12/10/99*	8/13/90(r)
China	3/27/01(r)	*SI 10/5/98*	11/4/80(r)	10/4/88(r)	3/3/92(r)
Colombia	10/29/69(r)	10/29/69(r)	1/19/82(r)	12/8/87(r)	1/28/91(r)
Comoros			10/31/94(a)	*SI 9/22/00*	6/23/93(r)
Congo	10/5/83(a)	10/5/83(a)	7/26/82(r)		10/14/93(a)
Cook Islands					6/6/97(a)
Costa Rica	11/29/68(r)	11/29/68(r)	4/4/86(r)	11/11/93(r)	8/21/90(r)
Cote d'Ivoire	3/26/92(a)	3/26/92(a)	12/20/95(r)	12/18/95(a)	2/4/91(r)
Croatia	10/8/91(s)	10/12/92(s)	9/9/92(s)	10/12/92(s)	10/12/92(s)
Cuba			7/17/80(r)	5/17/95(r)	8/21/91(r)
Cyprus	4/2/69(r)	4/2/69(r)	7/23/85(a)	7/18/91(r)	2/7/91(r)
Czech Republic	1/1/93(s)	2/22/93(s)	2/22/93(s)	1/1/93(s)	2/22/93(s)
Denmark	1/6/72(r)	1/6/72(r)	4/21/83(r)	5/27/87(r)	7/19/91(r)
Djibouti			11/2/98(a)		12/6/90(r)
Dominica	6/17/93(a)	6/17/93(a)	9/15/80(r)		3/13/91(r)
Dominican Republic	1/4/78(a)	1/4/78(a)	9/2/82(r)	*SI 2/4/85*	6/11/91(r)
Ecuador	3/6/69(r)	11/9/81(r)	3/30/99(r)	3/30/88(r)	3/23/90(r)
Egypt	1/14/82(r)	1/14/82(r)	9/18/81(r)	6/25/86(a)	7/6/90(r)
El Salvador	11/30/79(r)	11/30/79(r)	8/19/81(r)	6/17/96(a)	7/10/90(r)
Equatorial Guinea	9/25/87(a)	9/25/87(a)	10/23/84(a)		6/15/92(a)
Eritrea	4/17/01(a)	1/23/02(a)	9/5/95(a)		8/3/94(r)
Estonia	10/21/91(a)	10/21/91(a)	9/4/86(r)	10/21/91(a)	10/21/91(a)
Ethiopia	6/11/93(a)	6/11/93(a)	9/10/81(r)	3/13/94(a)	5/14/91(a)
Fiji			8/28/95(r)		8/13/93(r)
Finland	8/19/75(r)	8/19/75(r)	9/4/86(r)	8/30/89(r)	6/20/91(r)

Country	CESCR	CCPR	CEDAW	CAT	CRC
FYR Macedonia	1/18/94(s)	1/18/94(s)	1/18/94(s)	12/12/94(s)	2/12/93(s)
France	11/4/80(a)	11/4/80(a)	12/14/83(r)	2/18/86(r)	8/8/90(r)
Gabon	1/21/83(a)	1/21/83(a)	1/21/83(r)	9/8/00(r)	2/9/94(r)
Gambia	12/29/78(a)	3/22/79(a)	4/16/93(r)	*SI 10/23/85*	8/8/90(r)
Georgia	5/3/94(a)	5/3/94(a)	10/26/94(a)	10/26/94(a)	6/2/94(a)
Germany	12/17/73(r)	12/17/73(r)	7/10/85(r)	10/1/90(r)	3/6/92(r)
Ghana	9/8/00(r)	9/8/00(r)	1/2/86(r)	9/8/00(r)	2/5/90(r)
Greece	5/16/85(a)	5/5/97(a)	6/7/83(r)	10/6/88(r)	5/11/93(r)
Grenada	9/6/91(a)	9/6/91(a)	8/30/90(r)		11/5/90(r)
Guatemala	5/19/88(a)	5/6/92(a)	8/12/82(r)	1/5/90(a)	6/6/90(r)
Guinea	1/24/78(r)	1/24/78(r)	8/9/82(r)	10/10/89(r)	7/13/90(a)
Guinea-Bissau	7/2/92(a)	*SI 9/12/00*	8/23/85(r)	*SI 9/12/00*	8/21/90(r)
Guyana	2/15/77(r)	2/15/77(r)	7/17/80(r)	5/19/88(r)	1/14/91(r)
Haiti		2/6/91(a)	7/20/81(r)	5/19/88(r)	1/14/91(r)
Holy See				6/26/02(a)	4/20/90(r)
Honduras	2/17/81(r)	8/25/97(r)	3/3/83(r)	12/5/96(a)	8/10/90(r)
Hungary	1/17/74(r)	1/17/74(r)	12/22/80(r)	4/15/87(r)	10/8/91(r)
Iceland	11/22/79(r)	11/22/79(r)	6/18/85(r)	10/23/96(r)	10/28/92(r)
India	4/10/79(a)	4/10/79(a)	7/9/93(r)	*SI 10/14/97*	12/11/92(a)
Indonesia			9/13/84(r)	10/28/98(r)	9/5/90(r)
Iran	6/25/71(r)	6/25/71(r)			7/13/94(r)
Iraq	1/25/71(r)	1/25/71(r)	8/13/86(a)		6/15/94(a)
Ireland	12/8/89(r)	12/8/89(r)	12/23/85(a)	4/11/02(r)	9/28/92(r)
Israel	10/3/91(r)	10/3/91(r)	10/3/91(r)	10/3/91(r)	10/3/91(r)
Italy	9/15/78(r)	9/15/78(r)	6/10/85(r)	1/12/89(r)	9/5/91(r)
Jamaica	10/3/75(r)	10/3/75(r)	10/19/94(r)		5/14/91(r)
Japan	6/21/79(r)	6/21/79(r)	6/25/85(r)	6/29/99(a)	4/22/94(r)
Jordan	5/28/75(r)	5/28/75(r)	7/1/92(r)	11/13/91(r)	5/24/91(r)
Kazakhstan			8/26/98(a)	8/26/98(a)	8/12/94(a)
Kenya	5/1/72(a)	5/1/72(a)	3/9/84(a)	2/21/97(a)	2/21/97(a)

Country	CESCR	CCPR	CEDAW	CAT	CRC
Kiribati					12/11/95(a)
Korea, Dem. People's Republic of	9/14/81(a)	9/14/81(a)	2/27/01(a)		9/21/90(r)
Korea, Republic of	4/10/90(a)	4/10/90(a)	12/27/84(r)	1/9/95(a)	11/20/91(r)
Kuwait	5/21/96(a)	5/21/96(a)	9/2/94(a)	3/8/96(a)	10/21/91(r)
Kyrgyzstan	10/7/94(a)	10/7/94(a)	2/10/97(a)	9/5/97(a)	10/7/94(a)
Laos	SI 7/12/00	SI 7/12/00	8/14/81(r)		5/8/91(a)
Latvia	4/14/92(a)	4/14/92(a)	4/14/92(a)	4/14/92(a)	4/14/92(a)
Lebanon	11/3/72(a)	11/3/72(a)	4/21/97(a)	10/5/00(a)	5/14/91(r)
Lesotho	9/9/92(a)	9/9/92(a)	8/22/95(a)	11/13/01(a)	3/10/92(r)
Liberia	SI 4/18/67	SI 4/18/67	7/17/84(r)		6/4/93(r)
Libya	5/15/70(a)	5/15/70(a)	5/16/89(a)	5/16/89(a)	4/16/93(a)
Liechtenstein	12/10/98(a)	12/10/98(a)	11/22/95(a)	11/2/90(r)	11/22/95(r)
Lithuania	11/20/91(a)	11/20/91(a)	1/18/94(a)	2/1/96(r)	1/31/92(a)
Luxembourg	8/18/83(r)	8/18/83(r)	2/2/89(r)	9/29/87(r)	3/7/94(r)
Madagascar	9/22/71(r)	7/21/71(r)	3/17/89(r)	SI 10/1/01	3/19/91(r)
Malawi	12/22/93(a)	12/22/93(a)	3/12/87(a)	6/11/96(a)	1/3/91(a)
Malaysia			7/5/95(r)		2/17/95(a)
Maldive Islands			7/1/93(a)		2/11/91(r)
Mali	7/16/74(a)	7/16/74(a)	9/10/85(r)	2/26/99(a)	9/21/90(r)
Malta	9/13/90(r)	9/13/90(a)	3/8/91(a)	9/13/90(a)	10/1/90(r)
Marshall Islands					10/5/93(r)
Mauritania			5/10/01(a)		5/16/91(r)
Mauritius	12/12/73(a)	12/12/73(a)	7/9/84(a)	12/9/92(a)	7/26/90(a)
Mexico	3/23/81(a)	3/23/81(a)	3/23/81(r)	1/23/86(r)	9/21/90(r)
Micronesia					5/5/93(a)
Moldova	1/26/93(a)	1/26/93(a)	7/1/94(a)	11/28/95(r)	1/26/93(a)
Monaco	8/28/97(r)	8/28/97(r)		12/6/91(a)	6/21/93(a)
Mongolia	11/18/74(r)	11/18/74(r)	7/20/81(r)	1/24/02(a)	7/6/90(r)

Country	CESCR	CCPR	CEDAW	CAT	CRC
Morocco	5/3/79(r)	5/3/79(r)	6/21/93(a)	6/21/93(r)	6/22/93(r)
Mozambique		7/21/93(a)	4/16/97(a)	9/14/99(a)	4/26/94(r)
Myanmar (Burma)			7/22/97(a)		7/15/91(a)
Namibia	11/28/94(a)	11/28/94(a)	11/23/92(a)	11/28/94(a)	9/30/90(r)
Nauru				*SI 11/12/01*	7/27/94(a)
Nepal	5/14/91(a)	5/14/91(a)	4/22/91(r)	5/14/91(a)	9/14/90(r)
Netherlands	12/11/78(r)	12/11/78(r)	7/23/91(r)	12/21/88(r)	2/6/95(r)
New Zealand	12/28/78(r)	12/28/78(r)	1/10/85(r)	12/10/89(r)	4/6/93(r)
Nicaragua	3/12/80(a)	3/12/80(a)	10/27/81(r)	*SI 4/15/85*	10/5/90(r)
Niger	3/7/86(a)	3/7/86(a)	10/8/99(a)	10/5/98(a)	9/30/90(r)
Nigeria	7/29/93(a)	7/29/93(a)	6/13/85(r)	6/28/01(a)	4/19/91(r)
Niue					12/20/95(r)
Norway	9/13/72(r)	9/13/72(r)	5/21/81(r)	7/9/86(r)	1/8/91(r)
Oman					12/9/96(a)
Pakistan			3/12/96(a)		11/12/90(r)
Palau					8/4/95(a)
Panama	3/8/77(a)	3/8/77(r)	10/29/81(r)	8/24/87(r)	12/12/90(r)
Papua New Guinea			1/12/95(a)		3/2/93(r)
Paraguay	6/10/92(a)	6/10/92(r)	4/6/87(a)	3/12/90(r)	9/25/90(r)
Peru	4/28/78(r)	4/28/78(r)	9/13/82(r)	7/7/88(r)	9/5/90(r)
Philippines	6/7/74(r)	10/23/86(r)	8/5/81(r)	6/18/86(a)	8/21/90(r)
Poland	3/18/77(r)	3/18/77(r)	7/30/80(r)	7/26/89(r)	6/7/91(r)
Portugal	7/31/78(r)	7/15/78(r)	7/30/80(r)	2/9/89(r)	9/21/90(r)
Qatar				1/11/00(a)	4/4/95(r)
Romania	12/9/74(r)	12/9/74(r)	1/7/82(r)	12/18/90(a)	9/28/90(r)
Russia	10/16/73(r)	10/16/73(r)	1/23/81(r)	3/3/87(r)	8/17/90(r)
Rwanda	4/16/75(a)	4/16/75(a)	3/2/81(r)		1/24/91(r)
St. Kitts and Nevis				4/25/85(a)	7/24/90(r)
St. Lucia			10/8/82(a)		6/16/93(r)
St. Vincent & the Grenadines	11/9/81(a)	11/9/81(a)	8/5/81(a)	8/1/01(a)	10/26/93(r)

Country	CESCR	CCPR	CEDAW	CAT	CRC
San Marino	10/18/85(a)	10/18/85(a)			11/25/91(a)
Sao Tome & Principe	*SI 10/31/95*	*SI 10/31/95*	*SI 10/31/95*	*SI 9/6/00*	5/14/91(a)
Saudi Arabia			9/8/00(r)	9/23/97(a)	1/26/96(a)
Senegal	2/13/78(r)	2/13/78(r)	2/5/85(r)	8/21/86(r)	8/1/90(r)
Seychelles	5/5/92(a)	5/5/92(a)	5/5/92(a)	5/5/92(a)	9/7/90(a)
Sierra Leone	8/23/96(a)	8/23/96(a)	11/11/88(r)	4/25/01(r)	6/18/90(r)
Singapore			10/5/95(a)		10/5/95(a)
Slovakia	5/28/93(s)	5/28/93(s)	5/28/93(s)	5/28/93(s)	5/28/93(s)
Slovenia	7/6/92(s)	7/6/92(s)	7/6/92(s)	7/16/93(a)	7/6/92(s)
Solomon Islands	3/17/82(s)		5/6/02(a)		4/10/95(a)
Somalia	1/24/90(a)	1/24/90(a)		1/24/90(a)	*SI 5/9/02*
South Africa	*SI 10/3/94*	12/10/98(r)	12/15/95(r)	12/10/98(r)	6/16/95(r)
Spain	4/27/77(r)	4/27/77(r)	1/5/84(r)	10/21/87(r)	12/6/90(r)
Sri Lanka	6/11/80(a)	6/11/80(a)	10/5/81(r)	1/3/94(a)	7/12/91(r)
Sudan	3/18/86(a)	3/18/76(a)		*SI 6/4/86*	8/3/90(r)
Suriname	12/28/76(a)	12/28/76(a)	3/1/93(a)		3/2/93(r)
Swaziland					9/7/95(r)
Sweden	12/6/71(r)	12/6/71(r)	7/2/80(r)	1/8/86(r)	6/29/90(r)
Switzerland	6/18/92(a)	6/18/92(a)	3/27/97(r)	12/2/86(r)	2/24/97(r)
Syrian Arab Republic	4/21/96(a)	4/21/96(a)			7/15/93(r)
Taiwan					
Tajikistan	1/4/99(a)	1/4/99(a)	10/26/93(a)	1/11/95(a)	10/26/93(a)
Tanzania	6/11/76(a)	6/11/76(a)	8/20/85(r)		6/11/91(r)
Thailand	9/5/99(a)	10/26/96(a)	8/9/85(a)		3/27/92(a)
Togo	5/24/84(a)	5/24/84(a)	9/26/83(a)	11/18/87(r)	8/1/90(r)
Tonga					11/6/95(a)
Trinidad & Tobago	12/8/78(a)	12/8/78(a)	1/12/90(r)		12/6/90(r)
Tunisia	3/18/69(r)	3/18/69(r)	9/20/85(r)	9/23/88(r)	1/31/92(r)
Turkey	*SI 8/15/00*	*SI 8/15/00*	12/20/85(a)	8/2/88(r)	4/4/95(r)
Turkmenistan	5/1/97(a)	5/1/97(a)	5/1/97(a)	6/25/99(a)	9/20/93(a)

Country	CESCR	CCPR	CEDAW	CAT	CRC
Tuvalu			10/6/99(a)		9/22/95(a)
Uganda	1/21/87(a)	6/21/95(a)	7/22/85(r)	11/3/86(a)	8/17/90(r)
Ukraine	11/12/73(r)	11/12/73(r)	3/12/81(r)	2/24/87(r)	8/28/91(r)
United Arab Emirates					1/3/97(a)
United Kingdom	5/20/76(r)	5/20/76(r)	4/7/86(r)	12/8/88(r)	12/16/91(r)
United States	*SI 10/5/77*	6/8/92(r)	*SI 7/17/80*	8/21/94(r)	*SI 2/16/95*
Uruguay	4/1/70(r)	4/1/70(r)	10/9/81(r)	10/24/86(r)	11/20/90(r)
Uzbekistan	9/28/95(a)	9/28/95(a)	7/19/95(a)	9/28/95(a)	6/29/94(a)
Vanuatu			9/8/95(r)		7/7/93(r)
Venezuela	5/10/78(r)	5/10/78(r)	5/2/83(r)	7/29/91(r)	9/14/90(r)
Vietnam	9/24/82(a)	9/24/82(a)	2/17/82(r)		2/28/90(r)
Western Samoa			9/25/92(a)		11/29/94(r)
Yemen	2/9/87(a)	2/9/87(a)	5/30/84(a)	11/5/91(a)	5/1/91(r)
Yugoslavia	3/12/01(s)	3/12/01(s)	2/26/82(r)	3/12/01(s)	1/3/91(s)
Zaire (Dem. Rep. of Congo)	11/1/76(a)	11/1/76(a)	10/17/86(r)	3/18/96(r)	9/28/90(r)
Zambia	4/10/84(a)	4/10/84(a)	6/21/85(r)	10/7/98(a)	12/6/91(r)
Zimbabwe	5/13/91(a)	5/13/91(a)	5/13/91(a)		9/11/90(r)

KEY TO TABLE 2

CESCR Convention on Economic, Social and Cultural Rights.

CCPR International Covenant on Civil and Political Rights.

CEDAW Convention on Discrimination Against Women.

CAT Convention Against Torture.

CRC Convention on the Rights of the Child.

All figures as of July 2002. The source is the Office of the United Nations High Commissioner for Human Rights (http://www.unhchr.ch/pdf/report.pdf). The chart reflects the date of the signature if not ratified (SI), ratification (r), accessions (a), or succession (s); those states that have signed and not ratified are also in italics.

APPENDIX B

CORRESPONDENCE BETWEEN
SENATOR TOM HARKIN AND
THE U.S. DEPARTMENT OF ENERGY

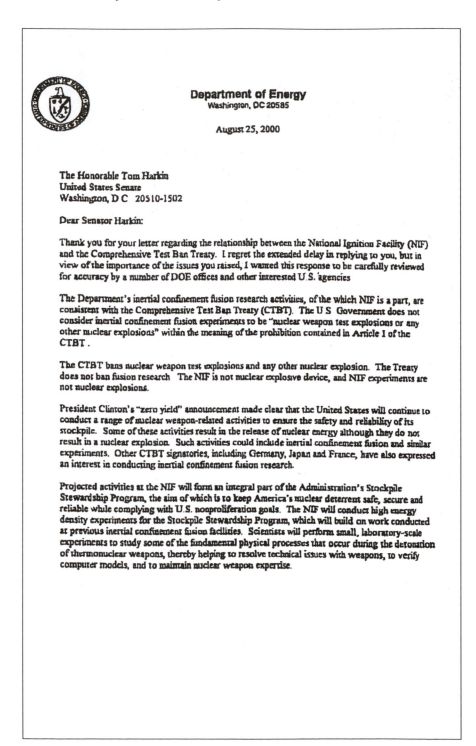

Department of Energy
Washington, DC 20585

August 25, 2000

The Honorable Tom Harkin
United States Senate
Washington, D C 20510-1502

Dear Senator Harkin:

Thank you for your letter regarding the relationship between the National Ignition Facility (NIF) and the Comprehensive Test Ban Treaty. I regret the extended delay in replying to you, but in view of the importance of the issues you raised, I wanted this response to be carefully reviewed for accuracy by a number of DOE offices and other interested U.S. agencies

The Department's inertial confinement fusion research activities, of the which NIF is a part, are consistent with the Comprehensive Test Ban Treaty (CTBT). The U S Government does not consider inertial confinement fusion experiments to be "nuclear weapon test explosions or any other nuclear explosions" within the meaning of the prohibition contained in Article I of the CTBT .

The CTBT bans nuclear weapon test explosions and any other nuclear explosion. The Treaty does not ban fusion research The NIF is not nuclear explosive device, and NIF experiments are not nuclear explosions.

President Clinton's "zero yield" announcement made clear that the United States will continue to conduct a range of nuclear weapon-related activities to ensure the safety and reliability of its stockpile. Some of these activities result in the release of nuclear energy although they do not result in a nuclear explosion. Such activities could include inertial confinement fusion and similar experiments. Other CTBT signatories, including Germany, Japan and France, have also expressed an interest in conducting inertial confinement fusion research.

Projected activities at the NIF will form an integral part of the Administration's Stockpile Stewardship Program, the aim of which is to keep America's nuclear deterrent safe, secure and reliable while complying with U.S. nonproliferation goals. The NIF will conduct high energy density experiments for the Stockpile Stewardship Program, which will build on work conducted at previous inertial confinement fusion facilities. Scientists will perform small, laboratory-scale experiments to study some of the fundamental physical processes that occur during the detonation of thermonuclear weapons, thereby helping to resolve technical issues with weapons, to verify computer models, and to maintain nuclear weapon expertise.

2

I assure you that all Stockpile Stewardship Program activities are and will remain consistent with the Comprehensive Test Ban. I trust that the enclosed answers to the specific questions you posed will be responsive to your concerns about the NIF.

If you have additional concerns or questions, please contact me at 202-586-5450

Yours sincerely,

John C. Angell
Assistant Secretary
Congressional and Intergovernmental
    Affairs

Enclosures:
Questions/Answers
The National Ignition Facility (NIF) and the
Issue of Nonproliferation" (DOE, December 1995)

Question 1.   What is the technical basis for considering a fission nuclear yield of four pounds of TNT equivalent as a violation of the CTBT, while considering a thermonuclear yield of the same magnitude as permissible? Specifically, DOE Order 452.1a defines a nuclear detonation as being "An energy release through a nuclear process, during a period of time on the order of one microsecond, in an amount equivalent to the energy released by detonating four or more pounds of trinitrotoluene (TNT)." (DOE Order 452.1a Appendix: Definitions, 7). This definition was also used during the negotiations for the CTBT to distinguish between releases of nuclear energy which were or were not banned under the treaty. However, high gain experiments at the NIF will release energy equivalent to ten pounds or more of TNT through a nuclear process and on a shorter time scale than one microsecond. Do ignition experiments at NIF fall under the definition of DOE Order 452.1a? If not, why not?

Answer 1   The definitions contained in DOE Order 452.1a are used in the context of nuclear explosive safety standards and relate to such concerns as preventing unintended nuclear detonation during the handling of nuclear explosives or nuclear weapons. The definition in question is the DOE's definition of "one point safety" of a "nuclear explosive" (also defined in the Order). NIF targets and activities are not in any way related to this Order. Nor was the definition of "nuclear detonation" contained in the DOE Order ever discussed in the Conference on Disarmament during the CTBT negotiations.

Question 2.   How does the DOE define a fusion explosion?

Answer 2.   DOE has not found it necessary to adopt a formal definition of a fusion explosion.

Question 3.   Has the DOE developed a technical definition of nuclear explosion that would enable it to determine US and foreign compliance with the CTBT? If so, would you please provide it to me. If not, what plans do you have to create such a definition?

Answer 3.   There is no DOE definition. The text governing the scope of the CTBT prohibitions is based on, and similar to, Article I of the Limited Test Ban Treaty, which has served well for over 35 years. We are confident that the distinction between nuclear explosions (including hydronuclear tests) captured by the prohibition and activities that may involve a release of nuclear energy but that are not prohibited is clear, that the distinction is clearly supported by the negotiating record, and that it is the appropriate basis on which to ensure compliance. An illustrative list of activities not prohibited by the Treaty is included in the Article-by-Article analysis forwarded to the Senate with the Treaty.

Question 4.   Official statements indicate that the DOE is using Non-Proliferation Treaty (NPT) Review Conference deliberations in its determination that NIF explosions would be legal under the CTBT. Is there a negotiating record in the CTBT process that allows NPT exemptions on nuclear explosions to be carried over to the CTBT? If so, please provide me with the documentation of that negotiating record.

Answer 4.   While the negotiating record itself is confidential, there are public documents that support this position. For example, a comparison of the Rolling Text of September 26, 1995 to the final Treaty shows that a provision that would have ruled out ICF was specifically considered and rejected during the negotiations. Moreover, President Clinton's announcement of "zero yield" on August 11, 1995 also made clear that the U.S. would continue to conduct a range of nuclear weapon-related activities to ensure the safety and reliability of its nuclear weapons stockpile. Some of these activities, while not involving a nuclear explosion, may result in the release of nuclear energy. Such activities, a number of which are planned as part of the Stockpile Stewardship Program, include the following:

computer modeling
experiments using fast burst or pulse reactors
experiments using pulse power facilities
inertial confinement fusion (ICF) and similar experiments
property research of materials, including high explosives and fissile materials
hydrodynamic experiments, including subcritical experiments involving fissile material

As is stated in the Administration's Article-by-Article analysis of the CTBT, none of these activities constitutes a nuclear explosion.

At the 1975 Non-Proliferation Treaty (NPT) Review Conference, the U.S. made the following statement on ICF:

> Certain questions have been raised by the delegation of Switzerland related to the development of a potential source of energy, and its relation to the NPT. As we understand it, the question related to research which has been reported, involving nuclear reactions initiated in millimeter-sized pellets of fissionable and/or fusionable material by lasers or by energetic beams of particles, in which energy releases, while extremely rapid, are designed to be, and will be nondestructively contained within a suitable vessel. On the basis of our present understanding of this type of energy source, which is still at an early stage of research, we have concluded that it does not constitute a nuclear explosive device within the meaning of the NPT or undertakings in IAEA safeguards agreements against diversion to any nuclear explosive device.

No NPT party at that time, nor since, has made any statement that would contradict that understanding.

Question 5.   If explosions in NIF were deemed legal under the CTBT, would there be any limitation on the yield of future experiments in this area? What are the limitations imposed on pure fusion explosions by the CTBT?

Answer 5.   The CTBT bans all nuclear weapon test explosions and any other nuclear explosion. Consistent with the U.S. statement quoted above, the NIF is not considered a nuclear explosive device and NIF experiments are not considered to be nuclear explosions. As a practical matter, the small size of inertial confinement capsules limits to small values the potential nuclear energy release; while the large size of the facilities required to achieve inertial confinement fusion rules out weaponization. In 1994 the prestigious group of independent scientists known as the JASONs concluded that "NIF technology is not a nuclear weapon [and] cannot be adapted to become a nuclear weapon."

Fusion research is not prohibited by the Treaty. The nuclear explosive testing of a pure fusion weapon device would be prohibited. In any case, it is generally acknowledged that development of a pure fusion weapon would be at the least a daunting undertaking, and may not be possible.

Question 6.   What effect would the exemption of thermonuclear laboratory explosions have on the nuclear weapons capabilities of other countries, including Russia, China, India, Germany, and Japan?

Answer 6.   The utility of ICF to a given country depends on its level of technical sophistication, the kind of weapons research (if any) it is pursuing, and its interest in peaceful application of ICF technology (a key issue for countries such as Japan and Germany). Thermonuclear laboratory experiments cannot substitute for actual nuclear tests as a means to develop weapons. For example, no ICF experiment is possible that will provide the data required to ensure that a specific boosted primary or thermonuclear secondary will indeed work as designed. For additional detail about the potential nuclear weapons value of

ICF to different countries, see pp. 4–5 and elsewhere of DOE's December, 1995 report, "The National Ignition Facility (NIF) and the Issue of Nonproliferation" (attached).

Question 7. What information was provided to parties negotiating the CTBT regarding the National Ignition Facility? Were the representatives of countries who signed the CTBT made aware that the energy release at NIF would be greater than in the hydronuclear tests they agreed to ban? Please provide me with copies of written information provided to the CTBT negotiating parties on the subject of laboratory thermonuclear explosions.

Answer 7. The nature of the NIF and its projected experiments is public. The DOE study attached was widely available during the latter part of the CTBT negotiations. NIF plans, designs and ICF experimental results to date have been published and presented at well-attended scientific conferences with broad international attendance. Countries seeking information on NIF would find it readily available.

𝔘𝔫𝔦𝔱𝔢𝔡 𝔖𝔱𝔞𝔱𝔢𝔰 𝔖𝔢𝔫𝔞𝔱𝔢

WASHINGTON, DC 20510-1502

October 28, 1999

COMMITTEES:
AGRICULTURE
APPROPRIATIONS
SMALL BUSINESS
LABOR AND HUMAN
RESOURCES

The Honorable Bill Richardson
Secretary,
The Department of Energy
1000 Independence Ave., SW
Washington, DC 20585

Dear Secretary Richardson,

It has come to my attention that questions are being raised about the legality of the thermonuclear explosions planned for National Ignition Facility (NIF), the laser fusion device being built at Lawrence Livermore National Laboratory. As I understand it, NIF is being designed to create small thermonuclear explosions in the laboratory. However, some of these explosions would go well beyond the four pounds of TNT nuclear yield equivalent that the nation renounced in August 1995 when President Clinton announced that the United States would support a "zero yield" treaty.

DOE officials have stated that thermonuclear explosions in the laboratory would be allowed under the Comprehensive Test Ban Treaty (CTBT), while nuclear fission explosions of a similar size would be banned. I would appreciate answers to a number of questions so that I can be clear in my own mind that DOE is adhering to the CTBT, while efforts continue for its ratification.

1) What is the technical basis for considering a fission nuclear yield of four pounds of TNT equivalent as a violation of the CTBT, while considering a thermonuclear yield of the same magnitude as permissible? Specifically, DOE Order 452.1a defines a nuclear detonation as being "An energy release through a nuclear process, during a period of time on the order of one microsecond, in an amount equivalent to the energy released by detonating four or more pounds of trinitrotoluene (TNT)." (DOE Order 452.1a Appendix: Definitions, 7). This definition was also used during the negotiations for the CTBT to distinguish between releases of nuclear energy which were or were not banned under the treaty. However, high gain experiments at the NIF will release energy equivalent to ten pounds or more of TNT through a nuclear process and on a shorter time scale than one microsecond. Do ignition experiments at NIF fall under the definition of DOE Order 452.1a? If not, why not?

2) How does the DOE define a fusion explosion?

3) Has the DOE developed a technical definition of nuclear explosion that would enable it determine US and foreign compliance with the CTBT? If so, would you please provide it to me. If not, what plans do you have to create such a definition?

4) Official statements indicate that the DOE is using Non-Proliferation Treaty (NPT) Review Conference deliberations in its determination that NIF explosions would be legal under the

150 FIRST AVENUE, NE
SUITE 370
CEDAR RAPIDS, IA 52407-4884
(319) 366-4504

210 WALNUT ST.
733 FEDERAL BLDG.
DES MOINES, IA 50309
(515) 284-4574

131 E. 4TH ST.
314B FEDERAL BLDG.
DAVENPORT, IA 52801
(319) 322-1338

350 WEST 6TH ST.
315 FEDERAL BLDG
DUBUQUE, IA 52001
(319) 582-2130

320 6TH ST.
110 FEDERAL BLDG.
SIOUX CITY, IA 51101
(712) 252-1550

CTBT. Is there a negotiating record in the CTBT process that allows NPT exemptions on nuclear explosions to be carried over to the CTBT? If so, please provide me with the documentation of that negotiating
record.

5) If explosions in NIF were deemed legal under the CTBT, would there be any limitation on the yield of future experiments in this area? What are the limitations imposed on pure fusion explosions by the CTBT?

6) What effect would the exemption of thermonuclear laboratory explosions have on the nuclear weapons capabilities of other countries, including Russia, China, India, Germany, and Japan?

7) What information was provided to parties negotiating the CTBT regarding the National Ignition Facility? Were the representatives of countries who signed the CTBT made aware that the energy release at NIF would be greater than in the hydronuclear tests they agreed to ban? Please provide me with copies of written information provided to the CTBT negotiating parties on the subject of laboratory thermonuclear explosions.

In view of the United States leadership role in defining and advocating a zero-yield CTBT, it is of great importance that the DOE position on laboratory thermonuclear explosions be clarified. I look forward to receiving your and your legal staff's response. Thank you for your attention to this important issue of mutual concern.

Sincerely,

Tom Harkin
United States Senator

NOTES

CHAPTER I: AN OVERVIEW OF U.S. POLICIES

1   Rogers 1999, p. 3.

2   See Restatement 1986.

3   See, *e.g.*, D'Amato 1998, p. 1.

4   See Weston 1986.

5   Foreign Relations Comm. 2001, p. 3.

6   Foreign Relations Comm. 2001, p. 6.

7   Foreign Relations Comm. 2001, pp. 8, 12.

8   Foreign Relations Comm. 2001, pp. 6-13

9   Trimble and Koff 1998.

10   Foreign Relations Comm. 2001, p. 5.

11   Foreign Relations Comm. 2001, p. 254.

12   The choice of terms to describe these two dominant trends in U.S. relations toward international law is itself a largely disputed exercise. Critics often accuse those seeking to withdraw or those who hesitate from joining treaties as "unilateralists," or "isolationists" although the proponents of the view defend that they are not unilateral, but rather "Americanists." For example, John Bolton, a proponent of what we are calling the pro-sovereignty approach stated, "[T]rying to characterize our policy as 'unilateralist' or 'multilateralist' is a futile exercise. Our policy is, quite simply, pro-American, as you would expect." Seigle 2002. But the description of this approach as "pro-American" disregards that many of those who favor engagement would also describe themselves as "pro-American," but believe that engagement serves the interests of the U.S. more than withdrawal.

13   Luck 1999, p. 3.

14   The UN Charter entered into force on October 24, 1945.

15   Edith M. Phelps, ed., Selected Articles on a League of Nations, 4th ed. (New York: H.W. Wilson Co, 1919) p. 359, cited in Luck 1999, p. 63.

16   Luck 1999, pp. 260-262.

17   Helms 1996b.

18   Luck 1999, pp. 238-9.

19   See Helms 1996b, and Luck 1999, p. 244.

20   CRLP 1999.

21   UN-USA 2001.

22   UN Charter, Article 17.2.

23   Bolton 1997.

24 Leahy 1998.

25 Boutros-Ghali 1996.

26 Associated Press 2001.

27 The Senate had passed the necessary legislation in February 2001. Eilperin 2001.

28 Dannheisser 2001.

29 Dannheisser 2001, quoting House International Relations Committee Chairman Henry Hyde.

30 King and Theofrastous 1999.

31 Jackson 1945.

32 King and Theofrastous 1999, p. 49.

33 Universal Declaration 1948.

34 See Bradley & Goldsmith 2000.

35 Bradley & Goldsmith 2000.

36 Henkin 1995, p. 348.

37 Henkin 1995, p. 349.

38 Henkin 1995, p. 348, citing the principal version of the Bricker Amendment, S.J. Res. 43, 82d Congress, 1st sess. (1953), Sec. 2.

39 Bradley & Goldsmith 2000, p. 410.

40 Henkin 1995, pp. 348-9.

41 See Roth 2000 and Henkin 1995.

42 See Roth 2000, p. 1, "The US government's approach to the ratification of international human rights treaties is unique. Once the government signs the treaty, the pact is sent to the Justice Department lawyers who comb through it looking for any requirement that in their view might be more protective of US citizens' rights than pre-existing US law. In each case, a reservation, declaration, or understanding is drafted to negate the additional rights protection. These articles are then submitted to the Senate as part of the ratification package."

43 "Why has CEDAW, the Convention of Elimination of All Forms of Discrimination Against Women, never been ratified? Because it is a bad treaty; it is a terrible treaty negotiated by radical feminists with the intent of enshrining their radical antifamily agenda into international law. I will have no part of that." Helms 2000.

44 ICJ Statute 1945, Article I.

45 Sen. Res. 1946.

46 ICJ Statute 1945, Article 36.6.

47 Meyer 2002, p. 98, citing Sen. Claude Pepper.

48 Meyer 2002, p. 98.

49 See Nicaragua v. U.S. 1984.

50 Nicaragua v. U.S. 1985.

51 Meyer 1997.

52 Senate Vote Analysis 1985.

53 For a detailed review of United States actions in the *Nicaragua v. United States* case, see Meyer 2002, pp. 130-138.

54   Under Article 25 of the UN Charter, UN member states are bound by decisions of the Security Council.

55   Luck 1999, p. 70.

56   Krauthammer 2001.

CHAPTER 2: THE NUCLEAR NONPROLIFERATION TREATY

57   G.A. Res. 1961.

58   G.A. Res. 1965.

59   Cuba, France, Guinea, Pakistan, and Romania.

60   Shaker 1980, Vol.I, pp. 274-275.

61   Ali A. Muzrui, "Numerical Strength and Nuclear Status in the Politics of the Third World," *The Journal of Politics* 29, no. 4, (Nov. 1967): 809-810, quoted in Shaker 1980, Vol. I, pp. 294-295.

62   Shaker 1980, Vol. I, p. 277.

63   Shaker 1980, Vol. I, p. 294.

64   Shaker 1980, Vol. II, p. 568.

65   Shaker 1980, Vol. II, p. 569.

66   Shaker 1980, Vol. II, pp. 496-502.

67   Bunn 1997, p. 3.

68   Shaker 1980, Vol. II, pp. 571, 573.

69   Shaker 1980, Vol. II, pp. 571, 574.

70   Shaker 1980, Vol. II, p. 572.

71   Shaker 1980, Vol. II, p. 564.

72   Shaker 1980, Vol. II, pp. 564-565.

73   ENDC/PV. 390, 15 Aug. 1968, para. 93, cited in Shaker 1980, Vol. II, p. 579.

74   Bunn 1997, p. 6.

75   Bunn 1997, p 8. The 1995 U.S. declaration provides: "The United States reaffirms that it will not use nuclear weapons against non-nuclear-weapon [NPT parties] except in the case of an invasion or any other attack on the United States, its territories, its armed forces or other troops, its allies, or on a State toward which it has a security commitment, carried out or sustained by such a non-nuclear-weapon State in association or alliance with a nuclear-weapon State."

76   Perkovich 1999b.

77   Nuclear Weapons Opinion.

78   Nuclear Weapons Opinion, para. 78.

79   Nuclear Weapons Opinion, para. 105(2)(E).

80   Comm. on Int'l Security 1997, p. 87.

81   See Burroughs 1998, esp. pp. 41-43; Moxley 2000.

82   Nuclear Weapons Opinion, para. 105(2)(F).

83   Nuclear Weapons Opinion, paras. 98-103.

84   Burroughs & Wurst 2001.

85 NPT Final Doc. 2000, pp. 13-15.

86 Burroughs 2000.

87 Burroughs 2000.

88 GA Res. 2000. The vote was 154 (including China, the United Kingdom, United States) to three (India, Israel, Pakistan), with eight abstentions (including France and Russia). See Burroughs & Epstein 2000

89 Burroughs & Epstein 2000, p. 2. Regarding a legal framework for a nuclear-weapon-free world, see Datan & Ware 1999.

90 For trenchant criticism of enforcement of the non-acquisition obligation with respect to Iraq and North Korea, as well as actions toward non-NPT nuclear-armed states Israel, India and Pakistan, see Mian 2002.

91 Wren 2002.

92 Baradei 2001a; IAEA 2002a.

93 *E.g.*, Dolley and Leventhal 2001 ("it is prudent to assume that there is a small, well-concealed nuclear weapons program in Iraq").

94 IAEA 2002b.

95 See, *e.g.*, Baradei 2001b (2000 IAEA Safeguards Implementation Report found that "for all 140 States with safeguards agreements in force, no indication was found of diversion of nuclear material or misuse of facilities or equipment that had been placed under safeguards").

96 New York Times 2002.

97 White House 2002a.

98 NRDC 2002, p. 2.

99 NRDC 2002, pp. 2-3.

100 NRDC 2002, p. 3.

101 NRDC 2002, p. 1.

102 NRDC 2002, p. 2.

103 Feith 2002, p. 7.

104 Blair 2002.

105 White House 2002b.

106 Gordon, Michael R. 2002a.

107 See Bleek 2000.

108 Pincus 2002.

109 Richter 2002; Gordon, Michael R. 2002; Nuclear Posture Review 2001.

110 Pincus 2002 reports that the NPR "would give U.S. presidents the option of conducting a preemptive strike with precision-guided conventional bombs or nuclear weapons" against "hostile countries that threaten to use weapons of mass destruction."

111 Bunn 1997, pp. 8-11.

112 George Bunn discusses this view, noting that it was the basis for the White House statement on signing the non-use protocol to the Pelindaba treaty establishing the African Nuclear Weapon Free Zone that the protocol "will not limit options available

to the United States in response to an attack by an ANFZ party using weapons of mass destruction." Bunn 1997, pp. 11-12 and note 116.

113 Nuclear Weapons Opinion, para. 78; see also Burroughs 1998, pp. 40-41.

114 Nuclear Weapons Opinion, para. 35.

115 In a March 17, 2002, *Los Angeles Times* op-ed, Sidney Drell, Raymond Jeanloz, and Bob Peurifoy write that "a 1 kiloton warhead 1/20th the yield that destroyed Hiroshima—detonated at a depth of 20 feet—would eject about 1 million cubic feet of radioactive debris from a crater about the size of ground zero at the World Trade Center," and conclude that "there is no possibility of a so-called 'clean' attack [on buried targets], free of extensive radioactive contamination spreading in the atmosphere." Drell, Jeanloz, and Peurifoy.

116 New York Times 2002.

117 Gordon, Michael R. 2002.

118 Arkin 2002.

119 NRDC 2002, p. 4.

120 New York Times 2000. See also BAS 2000.

121 Gordon, John 2002, p. 9.

122 Gordon, John 2002, p. 10.

123 For the relationship between the CTBT and expanded nuclear weapons laboratory capabilities, see Lichterman and Cabasso 2000.

124 DOE 2002, p. 5.

125 See Brookings 1998 (average was $3.64 billion in 1996 dollars).

126 Gordon, John 2002, p. 9.

127 Gordon, Michael R. 2002, p. 12.

128 Arkin 2002.

129 Mello 1997.

130 CD/1308 1995.

131 Rauf 2000, p. 43.

132 Sokolski 2002.

133 Gordon, John 2002, p. 1.

CHAPTER 3: THE COMPREHENSIVE TEST BAN TREATY

134 For texts of arms control treaties, related documents, as well as histories of the treaties see the web site of the Federation of the American Scientists (FAS) at http://www.fas.org/nuke/control/. This site includes chronologies of major events related to these treaties. Unless otherwise stated, the texts, and chronologies cited in Chapters 3 and 4 are from the FAS website. Many treaty texts can also be found at the web site of the United Nations (http://www.unog.ch/frames/disarm/distreat/warfare.htm) and of the Fletcher School of Law and Diplomacy of Tufts University (http://www.fletcher.tufts.edu/multi/warfare.html). It is interesting to note that an Internet search of the web site of the Department of State (http://www.state.gov/) and of its electronic documents repository at the University of Illinois (http://dosfan.lib.uic.edu/erc) failed to yield the text of the Comprehensive Test Ban Treaty.

135 Shapely 1993, p. 245.

136 NRDC 1994, pp. 410, 421.

137 FAS TTBT Provisions.

138 For an assessment of the health and environmental effects of testing, including underground testing, see IPPNW and IEER 1991.

139 One of clauses in the preamble to NPT reads as follows: "Recalling the determination expressed by the Parties to the 1963 Treaty … to seek to achieve the discontinuance of all test explosions of nuclear weapons for all time and to continue negotiations to this end." However, under Article V, the NPT did make an explicit exemption for "peaceful" nuclear explosions.

140 See Schrag 1992.

141 See Makhijani and Zerriffi 1998 for an analysis of the issue of defining nuclear explosions. In reference to the negotiating history regarding zero-yield, see the White House announcement on this issue of August 11, 1995.

142 Independent Commission, p.3. This is a non-governmental project of VERTIC, The Verification, Training, and Information Centre in London. The Commission included governmental as well as non-governmental experts.

143 Attachment to Angell 2000.

144 Helms 1999a.

145 The safeguards are listed on the FAS website at http://www.fas.org/nuke/control/ctbt/text/ctbtsafeguards.htm.

146 Zerriffi and Makhijani 1996 and DOE 1997.

147 Holum, *et al.* 1999.

148 Holum, *et al.* 1999.

149 Kirkpatrick 1999.

150 Perkovich 1999a.

151 Perkovich 1999b.

152 Kyl 2000.

153 Ghose 1996.

154 NRDC 2002.

155 Bunn 1999.

156 Gertz 1999.

157 Kimball 2002.

158 This section is based on Makhijani and Zerriffi 1998 unless otherwise specified. The *New York Times* published a news article on this report on July 15, 1998; see Broad 1998.

159 Makhijani and Zerriffi 1998. This report discusses both the technical issues relating the CTBT to proposed thermonuclear explosions and the potential of various devices and experiments to contribute to the development of pure fusion weapons – that is, thermonuclear weapons that do not require a fission trigger. Unless otherwise specified, this summary of the issue is taken from this report.

160 Takubo 2001.

161 Schott 2002.

162 The various U.S. arguments are discussed in Angell 2000. See also U.S. Dept. of State 1997.

163 Harkin 1999; Angell 2000.

164 Angell 2000.

CHAPTER 4: THE ANTI-BALLISTIC MISSILE TREATY

165 See the summary of the treaty on the Federation of American Scientists website at http://www.fas.org/nuke/control/abmt/text/abm2.htm. The treaty text is at the same location.

166 Helms 1999b.

167 Lawyers Alliance 2000.

168 It should also be noted in this context, that the United Nations has accepted Russia as the successor state to the Soviet Union, for instance in regard to the permanent seat on the Security Council, and that the United States has done so also, going so far as to persuade other successor states (Ukraine, Belarus, and Kazakhstan) to send back nuclear weapons on their territories to Russia.

169 Helms 1998a. Senator Helms had introduced legislation in 1996 that would have resulted in a United States withdrawal from the ABM treaty. See Helms 1996a.

170 Kyl 2001

171 Biden 2001.

172 Bush 2001b.

173 For a chronology of events related to the ABM Treaty see the web site of the Federation of American Scientists at http://www.fas.org/nuke/control/abmt/chron.htm.

174 Keller 2001.

175 For more discussion of the offense and defense arguments, see Makhijani 2000. For a list of a history of first use threats by various nuclear weapons states, including the United States and Russia, see, SDA 1998 at http://www.ieer.org/ensec/no-6/threats.html. China's liquid-fueled rockets cannot be maintained on high alert. China has a program of modernization of its nuclear arsenal, which may, in the next few years, include solid-fuel rockets which can be maintained in a state of high alert.

176 The system was deemed as unworkable. Specifically, one of the key elements of the scheme, an X-ray laser created by a nuclear explosion, was shown to be unworkable. See Broad 1992, and Fitzgerald 2000, pp. 128, 374.

177 Coyle and Rhinelander 2001.

178 National Intelligence Council 2001.

179 White House 2002.

180 Back from the Brink 2001.

181 U.S. Space Command 1997 and Rumsfeld Commission 2001, pp. 12-13. The commission that produced the latter report was chaired by Donald Rumsfeld. He was in private industry during most of the period of preparation of the report. He is now (2002) the Secretary of Defense in the Bush administration.

CHAPTER 5: THE CHEMICAL WEAPONS CONVENTION

182 The Geneva Protocol prohibits "asphyxiating, poisonous or other gases and all analogous liquids, materials or devices." Geneva Protocol 1925. The prohibitions of the Geneva Protocol are also considered customary international law, and thus are binding even on countries that are not members of the treaty.

183 In 1984, then vice-president George Bush presented a draft version to the drafting committee that "stunned the international community with its scope and intrusiveness." Smithson 2001, p. 23.

184 CWC 1993.

185 Tucker 2001.

186 CIA 2001.

187 Although Jesse Helms is retiring after this Term, other opponents of the CWC include Vice President Richard Cheney, Secretary of Defense Donald Rumsfeld, and Senator John Kyl, ranking member of the Senate Judiciary Committee.

188 See, for example, the Minority View in Executive Report 1996, p. 241.

189 Smithson 2001, p. 24.

190 Smithson 1997, p. 12.

191 In exchange for agreeing to put the Treaty to a vote, the Clinton administration agreed to restructure the State Department, submit its polices under other arms control treaties to the Senate, and consented to submitting the payment of its arrears to the U.N. to the Foreign Relations Committee. Smithson 1997, p. 23.

192 While a treaty is a legal obligation of the United States to other nations, if it requires laws to be enforced on individuals and entities within the United States, implementing legislation passed by both the Senate and the House of Representatives is required to enforce the treaty obligations within the United States.

193 CW Implementation Act 1998.

194 Facilities that work with chemicals set forth in the schedules of the CWC are subject to the declaration and inspection requirements. But the U.S. capped those declarations so that facilities working with substances containing a specified concentration of the scheduled chemicals would be subject to inspections. See Section 402 of CW Implementation Act 1998.

195 CW Implementation Act 1998.

196 CWC 1993, Verification Annex, Part VII.B.

197 Stimson 1999.

198 Stimson 2000.

199 Stimson 2000.

200 Smithson 1997, fn. 96.

201 Smithson 2001, p. 25.

202 Smithson 2001, p. 25.

203 Smithson 2001, p. 27.

204 Smithson 2001, p. 27.

205 Smithson 2001, p. 27.

206 Smithson 2001, p. 27.

207 See CIA 2001.

208 Sands & Pate 2000; see also CIA 2001.

209 ACT 2002.

210 Acronym Institute 2002; Brugger 2002a.

211 U.S. Dept. of State 2002a. See also Mahley 2002.

212 Ford 2002; Smithson 2002.

213 Ford 2002.

214 Ford 2002.

215 IHT 2002.

216 Acronym Institute 2002.

217 See Tucker 2001 and Sands & Pate 2000.

218 Mahley 2000. Ambassador Mahley also expressed assurance that the same protection would be achieved with the Biological Weapons protocol. Nevertheless, the U.S. administration cited concerns of verification and exposing secrets as the reason it would not support that convention. See Chapter 6.

CHAPTER 6: THE BIOLOGICAL WEAPONS CONVENTION

219 White House 2001.

220 The full text of the BWC can be found on the web site of the Federation of American Scientists, www.fas.org.

221 "At its peak, the former Soviet Union had the world's largest biological warfare program, with somewhere between 25,000 and 32,000 people employed in a network of 20 to 30 military and civilian laboratories and research institutions." In 1992, Russian President Boris Yeltsin reiterated Russia's commitment to the BWC and "informed Western leaders about the former Soviet biological weapons programs, and issued a decree which banned biological programmes and mandated Russia's compliance with the convention." FAS 1999. For its part, the U.S. renounced the development, production, stockpiling and use of biological warfare agents in 1969.

222 Secretary General 1995. See also http://www.fas.org/nuke/guide/iraq/bw/program.htm. Iraq was forced to ratify the BWC in 1991, after the Gulf war.

223 For a description of the history of the draft Protocol and the text of the draft Protocol, see http://www.opbw.org.

224 Tóth 2001.

225 AHG Working Paper 1998.

226 Tóth 2001.

227 During the Second BWC Review Conferences held in 1986, states parties agreed to adopt some confidence-building measures (which were enhanced during the Third BWC Review Conference) including data and information sharing on states' biodefense programs and facilities. But the confidence-building measures are voluntary.

228 For example, "under the suggested rules, if fewer than 10 facilities in any given country do meet the demanding standards for mandatory declaration, then only the largest 80 percent of them need to be declared based on measurements the country in question selects. Any facilities excluded under these restrictions will not be subject to ran-

dom visits and not necessarily even to clarification visits." Steinbruner, Gallagher & Gunther, 2001.

229 Steinbruner, Gallagher & Gunther 2001.

230 Steinbruner, Gallagher & Gunther 2001.

231 The Pharmaceutical Research and Manufacturers of America (PhRMA), which is the U.S.'s main bio-industry association, was concerned that "because medicines not on the market lack patent protection for many years . . . BWC inspections could result in the loss of proprietary business data and have significant cost implications." Stimson 2001, p. 2.

232 Steinbruner, Gallagher & Gunther 2001.

233 Stimson 2001, p. 98.

234 Rosenberg 2001.

235 Protocol Article 6(b); see also Rosenberg 2001; Rissanen 2001a.

236 Steinbruner, Gallagher and Gunther 2001 citing "Report on Two Trial Visits Based on a Transparency Visit Concept," working paper submitted by Germany, August 24, 1999, BWC/AD HOC GROUP/WP.398.

237 Stimson 2001, p. 3, n. 9; the United States conducted only two field tests to determine whether the Protocol could distinguish between facilities that complied with the BWC and those that violated it, but the results were "indeterminate."

238 See Stimson 2001, p. 99.

239 Pearson, Dando & Sims 2001, p. 6; the U.K. submitted 44 working papers, and the Russian Federation submitted 27.

240 Miller, Engelberg & Broad 2001a.

241 Mahley 2000.

242 Gordon, Michael R. & Miller 2001.

243 Gordon, Michael R. & Miller 2001.

244 Mahley 2001.

245 The text continued to be supported by the EU and other allies. On June 26, the EU and associated states "noted with concern that the United States was of the view that the costs related to the Protocol would outweigh the benefit thereof." It did not share this conclusion, or the U.S. view that "nothing could make the composite text" acceptable. The EU regretted that the United States had adopted this position after six years of joint work. "For its part, the Union wanted to preserve the fruits of that long effort." Rissanen 2001b.

246 Mahley 2001.

247 Mahley 2001.

248 Lacey 2001.

249 Lacey 2001.

250 Lacey 2001.

251 Mahley 2000.

252 Mahley 2000. Contrast this with Mahley's statement to the Ad Hoc Group that when the U.S. "examined the prospects of the most intrusive and extensive on-site activities physically possible — which we believed were likely not acceptable to most other

countries — we discovered that the results of such intrusiveness would still not provide useful, accurate, or complete information." Mahley 2001.

253 Koch 2000.

254 Mahley 2000.

255 For an overview of the Chemical Weapons Convention, see Chapter 5.

256 Mahley 2000.

257 Rosenberg 2001.

258 Pearson 2001.

259 Pearson 2001. Facilities handling toxins (including those used in the U.S. biodefense program) are covered under both treaties, and many biofacilities could be subject to challenge inspections under the CWC.

260 Pearson, Dando & Sims 2001, p. 18.

261 Mahley 2000.

262 Much of the address was focused on the issue of non-compliance, including "nam[ing] names" of alleged BWC violators. Bolton listed Iraq and North Korea as possessing biological weapons programs, Iran, he alleged "probably" has produced and weaponized biological weapons, Libya and Syria (Syria has not ratified the BWC), which the United States believes to have a biological weapons program at least in the research and development state, and the Sudan (a BWC non-party) which the U.S. believes is interested in acquiring a biological weapons program. Bolton BWC 2001.

263 White House 2001; Bolton BWC 2001.

264 Rissanen 2002.

265 Dept. for Disarmament Affairs 2001b.

266 Harris 2001. The U.S. proposal expands this system because it would also call for investigation of suspicious disease outbreaks as well as biological weapons use.

267 Harris 2001.

268 The Ad Hoc Committee, whose mandate was to exist until negotiations were complete, would continue in existence unless the conference voted for its termination. The rules of procedure for the Review Conference state that delegates should make their best efforts to achieve consensus on an issue, if they are unable to reach consensus, the vote is deferred for 48 hours. If after that time consensus is not reached, a vote will be taken of 2/3 majority of states parties present.

269 Rissanen 2002.

270 The Final Declaration is the report setting forth the agreements made during the conference, and is "politically binding — a non-legally binding document." Dept. for Disarmament Affairs 2001a, quoting Ambassador Tóth.

271 At the time the conference was disbanded, many measures to strengthen the BWC had been agreed to: "these included calling on BWC states to support the World Health Organization's disease surveillance and control, criminalize BWC violations with national legislation, institute a code of conduct for scientists working with pathogenic microorganisms, and contribute to an international team that would provide assistance with disease outbreaks." Brugger 2002. These proposals were part of what the U.S. had proposed at the beginning of the conference, but they were not intended by the other states parties as a substitute for a legally binding multi-lateral agreement.

272 Miller, Engelberg & Broad 2001a; Miller, Engelberg & Broad 2001b.

273 Miller, Engelberg & Broad 2001a, p. 298.

274 Borger 2001.

275 Wright 2002.

276 Shane 2001.

277 Prophylactic and protective purpose would include making vaccines, creating masks, and devising programs responsive to an attack

278 Miller, Engelberg & Broad 2001a, p. 295.

279 Miller, Engelberg & Broad 2001a, p. 296.

280 Miller, Engelberg & Broad 2001b.

CHAPTER 7: TREATY BANNING ANTIPERSONNEL MINES

281 U.S. Dept. of State 1998, the quantities of landmines (and landmine injuries) are rough estimates because of the difficulties in obtaining accurate statistics, particularly in countries in the midst of conflict and in developing countries.

282 ICBL Fact Sheet 2001.

283 ICBL Fact Sheet 1999.

284 Hambric & Schneck 1996, pp. 3-11.

285 HRW & VVAF 1997.

286 Hambric & Schneck 1996, pp. 3-28, 3-33. The authors note that unexploded ordnances (UXOs) are included in this total. UXOs are weapons that were designed to detonate on impact, but failed to. Examples are mortar shells or bombs which did not explode on impact.

287 ICBL Landmine Monitor 2001, "United States of America."

288 The ten-year period for destruction may be extended.

289 CCW Protocol II 1996.

290 White House 1996.

291 GA Res. 1996a.

292 Walkling 1997.

293 Clinton 1997

294 White House 1997.

295 Presidential Decision Directive (PDD) 64 issued June 23, 1998. PDD 64 is classified, but military and civilian officials have used details from it in many public forums and publications; see for example Dresen 1999.

296 HRW 2001b.

297 CNN 1997.

298 HRW 1993, p. 64. This book contains a chart on U.S. mine exports since 1969. The information is primarily drawn from U.S. Army, Armament, Munitions, and Chemical Command (USAMCCOM), Letter to Human Rights Watch, August 25, 1993, and attached statistical tables, provided under the Freedom of Information Act.

299 Patierno & Franceschi 2000, p. 21. Both authors are officials with the U.S. Department of State's landmine policy office.

300 According to a Korean Defense Ministry Report to the National Assembly, over one million mines, antipersonnel mines and antitank mines have already been laid "around the civilian control line and the demilitarized zone." Yonhap 1999. All of these emplaced mines are under the jurisdiction and control of South Korea.

301 ICBL Letter 1998.

302 ICBL Letter 1998.

303 See General Hollingsworth's Foreword to Demilitarization for Democracy 1997, p. ii. He also said, "To be blunt, if we are relying on these weapons to defend the Korean peninsula, we are in big trouble. . . North Korea's mechanized assault can be destroyed well north of Seoul without the use of U.S. APLs. I never counted on our APLs to make much of a difference." p. i.

304 HRW 2001a.

305 HRW 2001a.

306 HRW 2001a.

307 White House 1996.

308 Berger Letter 1998; see also Leklem 1998.

309 Clinton Certification 1999.

310 For an explanation of the alternatives, see HRW 2000, Alternatives to Antipersonnel Mines.

311 Strohm 2001.

312 ICBL Landmine Monitor 2001, "United States of America."

313 ICBL Landmine Monitor 2001, "United States of America."

314 ICBL Landmine Monitor 1999, "Banning Antipersonnel Mines."

CHAPTER 8: THE UNITED NATIONS FRAMEWORK CONVENTION ON CLIMATE CHANGE AND THE KYOTO PROTOCOL

315 UNFCCC 1992; Kyoto Protocol 1997. Our reasons for considering these two treaties within the framework of a report on security treaties have been discussed in the preface. Text of UNFCCC can be found on the Web at: http://unfccc.int/. Text of the Kyoto Protocol can be found on the Web at: http://unfccc.int/resource/docs/convkp/kpeng.html.

316 See Makhijani and Gurney 1995, Chapters 1 and 2 for a survey of the causes and consequences of ozone layer depletion.

317 Different greenhouse gases have differing properties; specifically they differ in their ability to trap and re-radiate infra-red radiation, which is the primary mechanism by which global warming occurs. Natural greenhouse gases, notably carbon dioxide and water vapor, maintain the Earth at temperatures at which life can flourish. Without this natural greenhouse gas effects, the Earth would be a frigid place, inhospitable to life. Anthropogenic greenhouse gases add to the natural levels. These additions affect climate in a variety of complex ways.

318 The text of the Kyoto Protocol is available on the web at http://unfccc.int/resource/docs/convkp/kpeng.html.

319 Sen. Res. 1997.

320 Helms 1998a.

321 For summary and legislative history of Senate bill S.882, 106th Congress, "Energy and Climate Policy Act of 1999," search at: http://thomas.loc.gov/.

322 Senator Frank Murkowski as quoted in UMWA 1999.

323 As quoted in Carlisle 2001.

324 Whitman 2001.

325 See for example Jehl & Revkin 2001.

326 NAS-NRC 2001, p. 1.

327 See Bush Energy Plan 2001 and Makhijani 2001, p. 16, Figure 7: Projections for total annual carbon emissions 2000-2004.

328 Climate Action Report 2002, a communication made pursuant to the reporting requirements of the UNFCCC (articles 4 and 12).

329 Climate Action Report 2002, chapter 6, p. 82.

330 NW Energy Coalition 2001.

331 COP-7 Report 2001.

332 Australian Greenhouse Office 2001.

333 Climate Network Europe 2002. In September 2002, Russia announced that it would ratify the Kyoto Protocol, which essentially ensures that the treaty shall enter into force. Swarns 2002.

334 IPCC 2001, p. 10.

335 BBC 2002. The removal of Dr. Watson was controversial because ExxonMobil, the world's largest oil company, had passed on a memo to the Bush administration that contained the suggestion that it would be desirable to replace Watson. The company denies that it had a position on the issue of IPCC chairmanship. BBC 2002a. Dr. Watson is recognized as one of the world's foremost scientific authorities on ozone layer and on global climate change. He is an advocate of strong action, both private sector and governmental, to reduce or avert the risk of human-induced build up of greenhouse gases.

336 IPCC website at http://www.ipcc.ch/about/about.htm, viewed on 23 May 2002.

337 Climate Action Report 2002, chapter 6, citing NAS-NRC 2001.

338 Streets, *et al.* 2001.

339 EIA 2001, p. vii.

340 European Environment Agency 2001, p. 5.

341 For examples, see the website of the Pew Center on Global Climate Change at http://www.pewclimate.org/projects/ghg_targets_belc.cfm.

342 This possibility has been raised due to the injection of freshwater into the oceans as a result of melting of Arctic ice. It is considered unlikely, but evidence shows that it has occurred due to natural factors in the past, and that there is some risk of it occurring due to anthropogenic emissions of greenhouse gases. See for instance, NASA 2001, which describes a study done by the National Aeronautics and Space Administration. Huge releases of methane in the geologic past have affected global climate, according to recent research, and there is the possibility that that might happen again, though there is considerable debate as to the magnitude of the risk. See also Kanipe 1999.

343 NAS-NRC 2002, p.1.

344 There is a vast official and non-governmental literature on this subject. See the web site of the American Council for an Energy Efficient Economy (http://www.aceee.org), for instance. See also Makhijani 2001. For official information, see the U.S. Energy Information Administration publications. For instance, one of these estimates that "Universal replacement of lamps and fixtures by more efficient equivalents, together with lighting controls, could save as much as 72 percent of current commercial lighting energy use" in commercial buildings. EIA 1992, p. ix.

CHAPTER 9: THE ROME STATUTE OF THE INTERNATIONAL CRIMINAL COURT

345 Rome Statute 1998, Preamble.

346 Article 126 of the Rome Statute requires 60 ratifications for entry into force. On April 11, 2002, the UN Treaty Office hosted a special ratification event where the remaining ratifications necessary for entry into force were officially completed. Bosnia-Herzegovina, Bulgaria, Cambodia, the Democratic Republic of Congo, Ireland, Jordan, Mongolia, Niger, Romania and Slovakia took part in the historic ceremony. The Statute entered into force on July 1, 2002, at which time the Court's jurisdiction took effect. The Statute was adopted by 120 countries with 21 abstentions and 7 no-votes from China, Iraq, Israel, Libya, Qatar, United States and Yemen. For discussion of the voting dynamics, see Benedetti & Washburn 1999, p 27.

347 European IMT 1951; Far East IMT 1946.

348 ICTFY 1993; ICTR 1994.

349 See for example the dissent of Justice Pal on grounds of "victor's justice" in the judgement of the International Military Tribunal for the Far East, Pal 1953. See also Annan 1998. The Secretary-General stated:

> Even when they were judged -- as happily some of the worst criminals were in 1945 -- they could claim that this is happening only because others have proved more powerful, and so are able to sit in judgement over them. Verdicts intended to uphold the rights of the weak and helpless can be impugned as "victors' justice". Such accusations can also be made, however unjustly, when courts are set up only ad hoc, like the Tribunals in The Hague and in Arusha, to deal with crimes committed in specific conflicts or by specific regimes. Such procedures seem to imply that the same crimes, committed by different people, or at different times and places, will go unpunished.

350 GA Res. 1948.

351 Genocide Convention 1948.

352 GA Res. 1989. See also Benedetti & Washburn 1999.

353 GA Res. 1996b.

354 Rome Statute 1998, Arts. 5-8.

355 Rome Statute 1998, Art. 5.

356 Rome Statute 1998, Art. 27.

357 See for example, Women's Caucus 1998; Amnesty International 1997; HRW 1998.

358 Brownlie 1990.

359 Geneva Convention I, Art. 49; Geneva Convention II, Art. 50; Geneva Convention III, Art. 129; Geneva Convention IV, Art. 146.

360 See Geneva Convention I, Art. 50; Geneva Convention II, Art. 51; Geneva Convention III, Art. 130; Geneva Convention IV Art. 147.

361 Rome Statute 1998, Art. 12.

362 Rome Statute 1998, Art. 12 and Art. 13. Article 13 sets out three ways a case can come before the Court: (1) By referral by a State Party to the Rome Statute; (2) by referral from the UN Security Council acting under Chapter VII of the UN Charter; or (3) when the Prosecutor has initiated an investigation.

363 Rome Statute 1998, Art. 7(1)g & h, Art. 8(2)(b)(xxii) and (2)(e)(vi). Compare Art. 46 of the Hague Convention (1907) referring to protections of "family honour," which was intended to encompass rape, and Art. 27 of Geneva Convention IV providing that women should be "protected against any attack on their honour, in particular against rape, enforced prostitution, or any form of indecent assault."

364 Rome Statute, Art. 7. The list of crimes against humanity includes enslavement, defined as "the exercise of any or all of the powers attaching to the right of ownership over a person and includes the exercise of such power in the course of trafficking in persons, in particular women and children" and "persecution against any identifiable group or collectivity on…gender or other grounds…" The Statute also contains groundbreaking provisions relating to the participation and protection of victims and witnesses, women and experts on violence against women on the Court and among staff at all levels. See Rome Statute, Arts. 68, 36, and 42-44.

365 Rome Statute 1998, Art. 8(2)(b)(xvii) and (xviii).

366 See, *e.g.*, Rome Statute 1998, Art. 8(2)(b)(iv) and 8(2)(b)(xx). See also Burroughs & Cabasso 1999, pp. 471-472.

367 Rome Statute preamble and Art. 2.

368 See Secretary General 1993; Security Council Res. 1994, respectively.

369 European IMT 1951; Far East IMT 19561946.

370 Rome Statute 1998, Art. 112.

371 See Resolution F 1998.

372 Helms 1998b.

373 Benedetti & Washburn 1999.

374 Benedetti & Washburn 1999.

375 See for example, Clinton 2000.

376 See Scharf 1999. The author, who at one time was the State Department official assigned to the ICC negotiations, states: "The Rome Diplomatic Conference represented a tension between the United States, which sought a Security Council-controlled Court, and most of the other countries of the world which felt no country's citizens who are accused of war crimes or genocide should be exempt from the jurisdiction of a permanent international criminal court."

377 Scharf 1999. The author states: "Unlike a permanent international criminal court, there was no risk of American personnel being prosecuted before the ad hoc tribunals since their subject matter, territorial and temporal jurisdiction were determined by the Security Council, which the United States could control with its veto."

378 Scharf 1999.

379 Scharf 1999.

380 See Benedetti & Washburn 1999.

381 Rome Statute 1998, Art. 15.

382 Rome Statute 1998, Art. 16.

383 See LaFave & Scott 1986, sec. 2.9(a).

384 Status of Forces Agreements (a/k/a SOFAs) are agreements governing the placement and conduct of military contingents in foreign territories.

385 See Scharf 1999: "Had the U.S. amendment been adopted, the United States could have declined to sign the Rome Statute, thereby ensuring its immunity from the second track of the court's jurisdiction, but at the same time permitting the United States to take advantage of the first track of the Court's jurisdiction (Security Council referrals) when it was in America's interest to do so."

386 See for example ABA Resolution 2001. See also NACDL Resolution 2002.

387 ABA Resolution 2001, p. 8 of its associated *Report*.

388 Helms 1998b.

389 Kissinger 2001.

390 Rome Statute 1998, Art. 17.

391 Rome Statute 1998, Art. 12.

392 Rome Statute 1998, Art. 13.

393 Scharf 1999.

394 Scharf 1999.

395 Benedetti & Washburn 1999.

396 See US Proposal 1998. See also, A/CONF.183/C.1/L.70, July 14, 1998.

397 Benedetti & Washburn 1999.

398 Benedetti & Washburn 1999.

399 Benedetti & Washburn 1999.

400 The Preparatory Commission for the International Criminal Court was established by Resolution F adopted at the Diplomatic Conference to carry on the follow-up work of further negotiations of supplemental texts and preparations for the eventual Assembly of States Parties.

401 Resolution F 1998, provided in paragraph 2 that States which signed the Final Act of the Rome Conference and those invited to participate in the Conference would constitute the Preparatory Commission on the International Criminal Court. The United States signed the Final Act of the Rome Conference.

402 For more background into the substance of the U.S. proposals in the post-Rome negotiations, see Pace & Schense 2001.

403 Pace & Schense 2001.

404 Stanley 1998.

405 Stanley 1998.

406 Letter of US Secretary of State Madeleine Albright to foreign ministers around the world, 17 April 2000. (On file). For more background into this strategy and full text of the letter, see Pace & Schense 2001, p. 727.

407 See Statement of David Scheffer, Ambassador-at-Large for War Crimes Issues and Head of the U.S. Delegation to the UN Diplomatic Conference on the Establishment of an International Criminal Court wherein he states, "No other country has shown as much support for the International Criminal Tribunals for the former Yugoslavia and Rwanda as the United States of America.... We have been hoping, as a potential state party of an international criminal court, that the full weight of the United States could be used to support its critical investigations and prosecutions in the future." Scheffer 1998.

408 Vienna Convention 1969, Art. 18.

409 Clinton 2000.

410 Clinton 2000.

411 Helms 2000a.

412 WICC 2001a.

413 See Bolton 2002. See also official notation of the UN depository on the web at http://untreaty.un.org/ENGLISH/bible/englishinternetbible/partI/chapterXVIII/treaty10.asp.

414 See Vienna Convention 1969, Art. 18.

415 Sen. Helms foretold of this strategy shortly after the adoption of the Rome Statute: "The US has thousands of soldiers stationed in Germany. Will the German government now consider those forces under the jurisdiction of the International Criminal Court? ... Indeed, the Clinton administration will now have to renegotiate the status of our forces agreements not only with Germany, but with every other signatory state where American soldiers are stationed. And we must make clear to these governments that their refusal to do so will force us to reconsider our ability to station forces on their territory, participate in peacekeeping operations and meet our Article Five commitments under the NATO charter." Helms 1998b.

416 See Foreign Relations Comm. 1999.

417 Romania, Israel, Tajikistan and East Timor are among the most recent states to have signed such agreements. U.S. Dept. of State 2002b.

418 Article 98 of the Rome Statute provides:

1. The Court may not proceed with a request for surrender or assistance which would require the requested State to act inconsistently with its obligations under international law with respect to the State or diplomatic immunity of a person or property of a third State, unless the Court can first obtain the cooperation of that third State for the waiver of the immunity.

2. The Court may not proceed with a request for surrender which would require the requested State to act inconsistently with its obligations under international agreements pursuant to which the consent of a sending State is required to surrender a person of that State to the Court, unless the Court can first obtain the cooperation of the sending State for the giving of consent for the surrender.

419 See, for example, Amnesty International 2002b.

420 Lynch 2002; Sengupta 2002.

421 Sengupta 2002.

422 Schmemann 2002.

423 See, for example, government statements made at the Open Debate of the Security Council addressing the US proposal on UN Peacekeeping and the ICC, July 10, 2002. Available at www.iccnow.org.

424 Security Council Res. 2002a. The Bosnian mission was renewed in a separate resolution, Security Council Res. 2002b.

425 Security Council Res. 2002a.

426 Rome Statute 1998, Art. 16: "No investigation or prosecution may be commenced or proceeded with under this Statute for a period of 12 months after the Security Council, in a resolution adopted under Chapter VII of the Charter of the United Nations, has requested the Court to that effect; that request may be renewed by the Council under the same conditions."

427 See Yee 1999, HRW 2002, Amnesty International 2002a.

428 For analyses of the resolution, including the impropriety of the resolution's invocation of Chapter VII, see CICC 2002 and Amnesty International 2002.

429 See, for example, CICC 2002 and Amnesty International 2002.

430 ASPA 2002.

431 ASPA 2002.

432 Milder versions of the legislation have existed since last year. See Hyde Amendment 2001, sec. 2101, which provides that none of the Defense Department funds authorized in the act can be used to provide support or other assistance to the International Criminal Court or in any criminal investigation or related activity of the Court. See also Craig Amendment 2001, Sec. 624, providing the same with respect to funds authorized in the Commerce, Justice, State and the Judiciary Appropriations Bill.

433 Fischer 2001. Fischer's letter went on to state: "The future International Criminal Court will provide us with an opportunity to fight with judicial means crimes such as the mass murder perpetrated by terrorists in New York and Washington on 11 September 2001."

434 Michel 2001.

435 Terrorist Bombings Convention 1998; Financing Terrorism Convention 1999.

436 Ridgeway 2001.

437 See USA Patriot Act 2001. See also President Bush's Military Order of November 13, 2001. For analyses of incompatibility of the USA Patriot Act with the Constitution, see Chang 2002. For an analysis of the constitutional problems with the plan for military commissions, see Fitzpatrick 2001.

438 Though "terrorism" was not explicitly included as a named crime in the Rome Statute, the attacks against the World Trade Center and the Pentagon are widely viewed as constituting crimes against humanity. Similar acts which occur after entry into force of the Rome Statute could thus be subject to the jurisdiction of the ICC. See, for example, CICC 2001; Kiergis 2001; Women's Caucus 2001.

439 See Fitzpatrick 2001.

440 See Lewis 2002. See also Becker 2002.

CHAPTER 10: TREATIES AND GLOBAL SECURITY

441 Dhanapala 2002.

442 Currie 2001, p. 1.

443 Dhanapala 2002.

444 Graham 2002, p. 3

445 Kyl 2000.

446 Spiro 2000.

447 Bolton 2000, p. 1.

448 Bolton 2000, p. 4.

449 Bolton 2000, p. 4.

450 Bolton 2000, p. 10.

451 Vagts 2001, p. 320, citing Memorandum from the [EEC] Group of Six on Certain Treaty Override Issues (July 15, 1987).

452 See Chapter 5.

453 Perry 2001, p. 33.

454 Currie 2001, p. 2.

455 See above. The 1995 and the 2000 review conferences of the NPT mentioned conclusion and entry into force, respectively, of the CTBT as a condition of indefinite extension (1995) and as one of the next steps to which states parties committed themselves (2000).

456 See, for instance, Warrick 2002, which describes poor control of and records about radioactive thermoelectric generators containing huge amounts of radioactive strontium-90. Radioactive weapons made with the materials from just one of these devices could have a severe radiological and economic impact. A modest U.S.-Russian cooperative program is being implemented, but the need is global since a variety of devices using large amounts of radioactivity are widely dispersed throughout the world.

457 Graham 2002, pp. 3-4.

458 For instance, a U.S. Senate resolution condemned the mining by a vote of 84 to 12. See Issues 2000 website at http://www.issues2000.org/Celeb/Ronald_Reagan_Foreign_Policy.htm.

459 Smith, no date, provides a summary of the case with links to more detailed materials.

460 Spiro 2000, quoting Jeremy Rabkin.

461 Spiro 2000, quoting Jeremy Rabkin.

462 Kyl 2000.

463 Kyl 2000.

464 Stephanson 1995, p. 80. Stephanson has used a quote from a very popular nineteenth century book, *Our Country*, by Reverend Josiah Strong (first printing 1885) to illustrate his point. Stephanson traces the history of the concept of Manifest Destiny from 1690 to 1990.

REFERENCES

ABA Resolution 2001   American Bar Association. Resolution in Support of U.S.
                         Accession to the Rome Statute of the International Criminal
                         Court. February 20, 2001. Accompanied by an explanatory
                         Report.

Acronym Institute 2002   Acronym Institute. "US Diplomatic Offensive Removes
                         OPCW Director General." *Disarmament Diplomacy* Issue
                         No. 64 (May-June 2002).   On the Web at
                         http://www.acronym.org.uk/dd/dd64/64nr01.htm.

ACT 2002   "Expounding Bush's Approach to U.S. Nuclear Security, An
                         Interview With John R. Bolton." *Arms Control Today* 32,
                         no. 2 (March 2002). On the Web at http://www.armscontrol.
                         org/act/2002_03/boltonmarch02.asp.

AHG 1998   Ad Hoc Group of the States Parties to the Convention on the
                         Prohibition of the Development, Production and Stockpiling
                         of Bacteriological (Biological) and Toxin Weapons and on
                         Their Destruction. *Working Paper Submitted by Argentina,
                         Australia, Austria, Belgium, Bulgaria, Canada, Czech
                         Republic, Denmark, Finland, France, Germany, Greece,
                         Ireland, Italy, Japan, Netherlands, New Zealand, Norway,
                         Poland, Portugal, Republic of Korea, Romania, Slovakia,
                         Spain, Sweden, Switzerland, Turkey, United Kingdom of
                         Great Britain and United States of America.* 11th Session,
                         Geneva, 22 June - 10 July. BWC/Ad Hoc Group/WP.296.
                         July 10, 1998. On the Web at http://www.opbw.org.

Amnesty International 1997 Amnesty International. "The International Criminal Court:
                         Making the Right Choices, Part 1." IOR 40/001/1997.
                         January 1, 1997. On the Web at: http://web.amnesty.org/
                         ai.nsf/index/ior400011997?OPenDocument&of=THEMES/
                         INTERNATIONAL+JUSTICE.

Amnesty International   Amnesty International. "International Criminal Court:
2002a   Immunity for Peace-Keepers is a Set Back for International
                         Justice." Public Statement. July 15, 2002. On the Web at
                         http://www.iccnow.org/html/AmnestyStatement15
                         July02.pdf.

Amnesty International   Amnesty International. "International Criminal Court: US
2002b   Efforts to Obtain Impunity for Genocide, Crimes Against
                         Humanity and War Crimes." August 2002. On the Web at
                         http://www.iccnow.org/html/aiusimpunity200208.pdf.

190   *Rule of Power or Rule of Law?*

Angell 2000 — John C. Angell (U.S. Department of Energy). Letter to Senator Tom Harkin, August 25, 2000. With an attachment containing Senator Harkin's questions and the Department of Energy's answers to them. Reproduced in Appendix B of this book.

Annan 1998 — Kofi Annan. "Statement of UN Secretary-General Kofi Annan on the Occasion of the Adoption of the Rome Statute of the International Criminal Court at the Diplomatic Conference of Plenipotentiaries." 17 July 1998.

Arkin 2002 — William M. Arkin. "Secret Plan Outlines the Unthinkable." *Los Angeles Times*, March 10, 2002. On the Web at http://www.latimes.com/news/opinion/la-op-arkinmar10.story.

Arms Control Assn. 2002 — "Moving Beyond 'MAD'? A Briefing on Nuclear Arms Control and the Bush-Putin Summit." Arms Control Association Press Conference with John Holum, Karl Inderfurth, James Goodby, and Daryl Kimball, May 15, 2002. On the Web at http://www.armscontrol.org/aca/bpsumconmay02.asp.

ASPA 2001 — American Servicemembers' Protection Act of 2001 (H.R. 1794). May 10, 2001.

ASPA 2002 — American Servicemembers' Protection Act of 2002. PL 107-206 signed into law August 2, 2002.

Associated Press 2001 — "US to Make Second Dues Payment to UN." *Associated Press*, October 6, 2001.

Australian Greenhouse Office 2001 — Australian Greenhouse Office. *A Message from Marrakesh - What Were the Outcomes of COP-7?* On the Web at http://www.greenhouse.gov.au/international/marrakesh.html.

Back from the Brink 2001 — Back from the Brink Campaign and Project for Participatory Democracy. *Short Fuse to Catastrophe: The Case for Taking Nuclear Weapons Off Hair-trigger Alert.* Facing Reality series. Washington, DC: BfB, February 2001.

Baradei 2001a — Mohamed El Baradei (IAEA Director General). "Statement to the Fifty-Sixth Regular Session of the UN General Assembly." October 22, 2001. On the Web at http://www.iaea.org/worldatom/Press/Statements/2001/ebsp2001n010.shtml.

Baradei 2001b — Mohamed El Baradei. "Excerpts from the Introductory Statement by IAEA Director General Dr. Mohamed ElBaradei." [re: 2000 IAEA Safeguards Implementation Report] Vienna: IAEA Board of Governors, June 11, 2001. On the Web at http://www.iaea.org/worldatom/Press/Statements/2001/ebsp2001n006.shtml.

BAS 2000

Bulletin of the Atomic Scientists. "ABM Treaty 'Talking Points.'" May/June 2000 web edition of *The Bulletin of Atomic Scientists.* On the Web at http://www.thebulletin.org/issues/2000/mj00/treaty_doc.html.

BBC 2002

BBC News. "Climate Scientist Ousted." April 19, 2002. On the Web at http://news.bbc.co.uk/hi/english/sci/tech/newsid_1940000/1940117.stm.

BBC 2002a

BBC News. "ExxonMobil Hits Back In Memo Row." 5 April 2002. On the Web at http://news.bbc.co.uk/hi/english/world/americas/newsid_1913000/1913640.stm.

Becker 2002

Elizabeth Becker. "U.S. Ties Military Aid to Peacekeepers' Immunity." *New York Times*, August 10, 2002.

Benedetti & Washburn 1999

Fanny Benedetti and John L. Washburn. "Drafting the International Criminal Court Treaty: Two Years to Rome and an Afterward on the Rome Diplomatic Conference." *Global Governance* 5, no. 1 (Jan-Mar.1999).

Berger Letter 1998

Samuel Berger (U.S. National Security Advisor). Letter to Senator Patrick Leahy, 15 May 1998.

Biden 2001

Joseph Biden. "Defeating and Preventing Terrorism Takes More than Missile Defense." December 12, 2001." On the Web at http://foreign.senate.gov/press/statements/statements_011212.html.

Blair 2002

Bruce Blair. "U.S. Nuclear Posture and Alert Status Post Sept. 11." January 28, 2002. On the Web at http://www.cdi.org/nuclear/post911.cfm.

Bleek 2000

Philip C. Bleek. "Russia Adopts New Security Concept; Appears to Lower Nuclear Threshold." *Arms Control Today* 30, no.1 (January/February 2000). On the Web at http://www.armscontrol.org/act/2000_01-02/rujf00.asp.

Bolton 1997

John Bolton. "U.S. Isn't Legally Obligated to Pay the U.N." *Wall Street Journal*, Nov. 17, 1997, *cited in* Luck 1999, pp. 241-242.

Bolton 2000

John Bolton. "Is there Really 'Law' in International Affairs." *Transnational Law and Contemporary Problems* 10 (Spring 2000).

Bolton 2002

John R. Bolton. Letter of John R. Bolton (Under Secretary of State for Arms Control and International Security) to United Nations Secretary General Kofi Annan, May 6, 2002. On the Web at http://www.state.gov/r/pa/prs/ps/2002/9968.htm.

Bolton BWC 2001 | John R. Bolton. Remarks to the 5th Biological Weapons Convention RevCon Meeting, Geneva, Switzerland, November 19, 2001." On the Web at http://www. state.gov/t/us/rm/janjuly/6231.htm.

Borger 2001 | Julian Borger. Pentagon Approves Super Strain. *Guardian Unlimited*, October 24, 2001.

Boutros-Ghali 1996 | Boutros Boutros-Ghali. "The US Must Pay Its Dues." *New York Times*, April 8, 1996.

Bradley & Goldsmith 2000 | Curtis A. Bradley and Jack L. Goldsmith. "Treaties, Human Rights, and Conditional Consent." *Pennsylvania Law Review* 149 (May 2000): 399.

Broad 1992 | William J. Broad. *Teller's War: The Top-Secret Story Behind the Star Wars Deception.* New York: Simon & Schuster, 1992.

Broad 1998 | William J. Broad. "Fusion-Research Effort Draws Fire." *New York Times*, July 15, 1998.

Brookings 1998 | U.S. Nuclear Weapons Cost Study Project. *Expenditures for U.S. Nuclear Weapons Research, Development, Testing, and Production, 1948-1998.* Washington, DC: Brookings Institution, 1998. On the Web at http://www.brook.edu/dyb docroot/fp/projects/nucwcost/rd&t.HTM.

Brownlie 1990 | Ian Brownlie. *Principles of Public International Law.* 4th ed. Oxford: Oxford University Press, 1990.

Brugger 2002 | Seth Brugger. "BWC Conference Suspended After Controversial End." *Arms Control Today* 32, no. 1 (January/February 2002).

Brugger 2002a | Seth Brugger. "Chemical Weapons Convention Chief Removed at U.S. Initiative." *Arms Control Today* 32, no. 4 (May 2002).

Bunn 1997 | George Bunn. "The Legal Status of U.S. Negative Security Assurances to Non-Nuclear Weapon States." *The Nonproliferation Review*, Spring-Summer 1997.

Bunn 1999 | George Bunn. "The Status of Norms Against Nuclear Testing." *The Nonproliferation Review*, Winter 1999.

Burroughs 1998 | John Burroughs. *The Legality of Threat or Use of Nuclear Weapons: A Guide to the Historic Opinion of the International Court of Justice.* Münster: Lit Verlag, 1997; Piscataway, NJ: Transaction Publishers, 1998.

Burroughs 2000 | John Burroughs. "More Promises to Keep: 2000 NPT Review Conference." *Bombs Away!,* Fall 2001. On the Web at http://www.lcnp.org/pubs/Bombsaway!%20fall00/arti cle4.htm.

Burroughs & Cabasso 1999   John Burroughs and Jacqueline Cabasso. "Confronting The Nuclear-Armed States in International Negotiating Forums: Lessons For NGOs." *International Negotiation* 4, no. 3 (1999): 457-480.

Burroughs & Epstein 2000   John Burroughs and William Epstein. "Hopes for Revival of Nuclear Disarmament Efforts?" *Nuclear Disarmament Commentary* 2, no. 5 (December 2000). On the Web at http://www.lcnp.org/pubs/index.htm.

Burroughs & Wurst 2001   John R. Burroughs and Jim Wurst. "A New Agenda for Nuclear Disarmament: The Pivotal Role of Mid-Size States." September 2, 2001 Panel, 2001 Annual Meeting of the American Political Science Association, San Francisco. On the Web at http://pro.harvard.edu/papers/019/019014 BurroughsJ.pdf.

Bush 2001a   George W. Bush. "President's Statement on The 'Departments of Commerce, Justice, State, Judiciary, and Related Agencies Appropriations Act, 2002.'" November 28, 2001. Running title: Bush Statement on Signing of HR 2500. On the Web at http://www.usnewswire.com/topnews/Current_Releases/112 8-148.html.

Bush 2001b   George W. Bush. "Remarks by the President on National Missile Defense." In "Bush Announces U.S. Withdrawal From ABM Treaty," issued by U.S. Department of State's Office of International Information, December 13, 2001. On the Web at http://www.fas.org/nuke/control/abmt/ news/bushabm121301.htm or http://usinfo.state.gov/topi- cal/pol/arms/stories/01121302.htm.

Bush Energy Plan 2001   National Energy Policy Development Group. *Reliable, Affordable, and Environmentally Sound Energy for America's Future*. Washington, DC: U.S. Govt. Print. Off., May 2001. Cover title: *National Energy Policy*. Also known as the Cheney Plan.

BWC 1972   Convention on the Prohibition of the Development, Production, and Stockpiling of Bacteriological (Biological) and Toxin Weapons and on Their Destruction. Opened for signature, April 10, 1972.

Carlisle 2001   John Carlisle. "President Bush Must Kill Kyoto Global Warming Treaty and Oppose Efforts to Regulate Carbon Dioxide." *National Policy Analysis*, no. 328. (February 2001). A publication of the National Center for Public Policy Research. On the Web at http://www.nationalcen ter.org/NPA328.html.

CCW Protocol II 1996

Protocol II to the Convention on Prohibitions or Restrictions on the Use of Certain Conventional Weapons Which May Be Deemed to Be Excessively Injurious or to Have Indiscriminate Effects, as amended on May 3, 1996.

CD/1308 1995

Conference on Disarmament. CD/1308. 6 April 1995. [A declaration by France, Russia, the United Kingdom and the United States made at the Conference on Disarmament. The statement was later issued as a document of the 1995 Review and Extension Conference (NPT/CONF.1995/20)]. On the Web at http://www.un.org/Depts/ddar/npt-conf/2102.htm.

Chang 2002

Nancy Chang. *Silencing Political Dissent: How Post-September 11 Anti-Terrorism Measures Threaten Our Civil Liberties.* New York: Seven Stories, 2002. On the Web at www.sevenstories.com.

CICC 2001

Coalition for the International Criminal Court. "U.S. Tragedy Must Be Addressed Through Systems of Justice." Statement of the Coalition for the International Criminal Court. September 2001.

CIA 2001

U.S. Central Intelligence Agency. *Unclassified Report to Congress on the Acquisition of Technology Relating to Weapons of Mass Destruction and Advanced Conventional Munitions, July 1 Through 31 December 2000.* Washington, DC, September 2001. On the Web at http://www.cia.gov/cia/publications/bian/bian_jan_2002.htm.

Climate Action Report 2002

United States. Department of State. *U.S. Climate Action Report -- 2002: Third National Communication of the United States of America Under the United Nations Framework Convention on Climate Change.* Washington, DC, May 2002. On the Web at http://www.epa.gov/global-warming/publications/car/index.html.

Climate Network Europe 2002

Climate Network Europe. Ratification of the Kyoto Protocol. On the Web at http://www.climnet.org/EUenergy/ratification.htm.

Clinton 1997

William Clinton. Remarks on Landmines. September 17, 1997. On the Web at http://usinfo.state.gov/topical/pol/arms/mines/minearch.htm.

Clinton 2000

William Clinton. "Remarks on Signature of ICC Treaty." December 31, 2000. On the Web at http://www.wfa.org/issues/wicc/prestext.html.

Clinton Certification 1999	William Clinton. "Notice on Amended Protocol on Prohibitions or Restrictions on the Use of Mines, Booby-Traps and Other Devices, Together with its Technical Annex—Message From The President—PM 32." *Congressional Record -- Senate* (May 24, 1999): S5827.
CNN 1997	CNN. "U.S. Says Its Land Mines Aren't the Problem." October 10, 1997. On the Web at http://www.cnn.com/US/9710/10/landmine.treaty/.
Comm. on Int'l Security 1997	National Academy of Sciences. Committee on International Security and Arms Control. *The Future of U.S. Nuclear Weapons Policy.* Washington: National Academy Press, 1997.
COP-7 report 2001	*Report of the Conference of the Parties on Its Seventh Session, Held at Marrakesh from 29 October to 10 November 2001.* United Nations Framework Convention on Climate Change. FCCC/CP/13/Add.1. January 21, 2002. On the Web at http://unfccc.int/resource/docs/cop7/13.pdf.
Coyle and Rhinelander 2001	Philip E. Coyle and John B. Rhinelander. National Missile Defense and the ABM Treaty: No Need to Wreck the Accord. *World Policy Journal,* Fall 2001. Summary on the Web at http://worldpolicy.org/journal/wpj01-3.html.
Craig Amendment 2001	The Commerce, Justice, State and the Judiciary Appropriations Bill, H.R. 2500. EAS1S. September 10, 2001.
CRLP 1999	Janet Benshoof. "United Nations Dues Paid, But Not Without A Price." Center for Reproductive Law & Policy. November 19, 1999. On the Web at http://www.crlp.org/pr_99_1115undues.html.
CTBT 1996	Comprehensive Nuclear-Test-Ban Treaty. Opened for signature, September 24, 1996.
Currie 2001	Duncan Currie. *United States Unilateralism and the Kyoto Protocol, CTBT and ABM Treaties: The Implications Under International Law.* Greenpeace, June 9, 2001. On the Web at http://www.stopstarwars.org/html/docslegalsum.html.
CWC 1993	The Convention on the Prohibition of the Development, Production, Stockpiling, and Use of Chemical Weapons and on Their Destruction. Opened for signature January 13, 1993.
CW Implementation Act 1998	Chemical Weapons Convention Implementation Act of 1998, Public Law 105-277.
D'Amato 1998	Anthony D'Amato. "Customary International Law: A Reformulation." *International Legal Theory* 4(1): 1-5 (1998). On the Web at http://law.ubalt.edu/cicl/ilt/4_1_1998.pdf.

Dannheisser 2001

Ralph Dannheisser. "House Approves $582 Million Back Dues Payment to U.N." Washington: U.S. Department of State, Office of International Information Programs, September 25, 2001. On the Web at http://usinfo.state.gov/topical/pol/terror/01092508.htm.

Datan and Ware 1999

Merav Datan and Alyn Ware. *Security and Survival: The Case for a Nuclear Weapons Convention.* Cambridge, MA: IPPNW, 1999.

Dee 2002

Joseph Dee. "Expert: Anthrax Suspect ID'd." *Trenton Times,* February 19, 2002.

Demilitarization for Democracy 1997

Demilitarization for Democracy. *Exploding the Landmine Myth in Korea.* Washington, DC, August 1997.

Dept. for Disarmament Affairs 2001a

UN Department for Disarmament Affairs. "Highlights of Press Conference Held On Developments in the Fifth Review Conference of States Parties to the Biological Weapons Convention on 27 November 2001 at the Palais des Nations." November 27, 2002. On the Web at http://www.unog.ch/news/documents/newsen/pc011127.html.

Dept. for Disamament Affairs 2001b

UN Department for Disarmament Affairs. "Highlights of Press Conference Held On Developments in the Fifth Review Conference of States Parties to the Biological Weapons Convention on 30 November 2001 at the Palais des Nations." November 30, 2001. On the Web at http://www.unog.ch/news/documents/newsen/pc011130.html.

Dept. of Defense 1999

U.S. Department of Defense. "Landmines Information Paper." March 3, 1999.

Dhanapala 2001

Jayantha Dhanapala. "Multilateralism and the Future of the Global Nuclear Nonproliferation Regime." *The Nonproliferation Review,* Fall 2001. On the Web at http://www.un.org/Depts/dda/speech/nprvwfall01.pdf.

Dhanapala 2002

Jayantha Dhanapala. "International Law, Security, and Weapons of Mass Destruction." 2002 Spring Meeting of the Section of International Law and Practice, American Bar Association, New York City, May 9, 2002. On the Web at http://www.un.org/depts/dda/speech/statements.htm.

DOE 1997

United States. Department of Energy. Office of Defense Programs. *Stockpile Stewardship and Management Plan: First Annual Update.* (Deleted Version). [Washington, DC] October 1997. Also known as the Green Book.

DOE 2002   United States. Department of Energy. National Nuclear Security Administration. "Weapons Activities, Executive Summary." *FY 2003 Congressional Budget Request.* On the Web at http://www.cfo.doe.gov/budget/03budget/content/weapons/weapons.pdf.

Dolley and Leventhal 2001   Steve Dolley and Paul Leventhal. "Overview of IAEA Nuclear Inspections in Iraq." NCI Reports. Washington, DC: Nuclear Control Institute, June 14, 2001. On the Web at http://www.nci.org/new/iraq-ib.htm.

Drell, Jeanloz, and Peurifoy 2002   Sidney Drell, Raymond Jeanloz, and Bob Peurifoy. "Commentary: Bunkers, Bombs, Radiation." *Los Angeles Times*, March 17, 2002.

Dresen 1999   Thomas Dresen. "Anti-Personnel Landmine Alternatives (APL-A)." A briefing delivered by Colonel Thomas Dresen, Project Manager for Mines, Countermine, and Demolitions to the National Defense Industrial Association's Forty-third Annual Fuze Conference, April 7, 1999. On the Web at http://www.dtic.mil/ndia/fuze/dresen.pdf.

EIA 1992   United States. Department of Energy. Energy Information Administration. Office of Energy Markets and End Use. *Lighting in Commercial Buildings.* Energy Consumption Series. Washington, DC, March 1992. On the Internet at ftp://tonto.eia.doe.gov/consumption/0555921.pdf.

EIA 2001   United States. Department of Energy. Energy Information Administration. Office of Integrated Analysis and Forecasting. *Emissions of Greenhouse Gases in the United States 2000.* DOE/EIA-0573(2000). [Washington, DC] November 2001. On the Internet at ftp://ftp.eia.doe.gov/pub/oiaf/1605/cdrom/pdf/ggrpt/057300.pdf.

Eilperin 2001   Juliet Eilperin. "House Approves UN Payment." *Washington Post*, September 25, 2001.

European Environment Agency 2001   European Environment Agency. *Annual European Community Greenhouse Gas Inventory 1990-1999: Submission to the Secretariat of the UNFCCC.* Prepared by Manfred Ritter and Bernd Gugele. Copenhagen, April 11, 2001. On the Web at http://reports.eea.eu.int/Technical_report_No_60/en/tech60.pdf.

European IMT 1951   Agreement for the Prosecution and Punishment of Major War Criminals of the European Axis, and Establishing the Charter of the International Military Tribunal (IMT), annex. 1951.

Executive Report 1996   Senate Executive Report of the Chemical Weapons Convention. Ex. Rep 104-33. September 11, 1996.

Far East IMT 1946   International Military Tribunal for the Far East, 1946-48. Charter of the International Military Tribunal for the Far East, 19 January 1946 (General Orders no. 1), Tokyo, as amended. General Orders no. 20, 26 April 1946. T.I.A.S no. 1589.

FAS 1999   Federation of American Scientists. *WMD Around the World*, Russia, June 1999. On the Web at http://www.fas.org/nuke/guide/russia/cbw/.

FAS TTBT Provisions   Federation of American Scientists. *Threshold Test Ban Treaty [Provisions]*. Washington, DC [no date]. On the Web at http://fas.org/nuke/control/ttbt/intro.htm.

Feith 2002   Douglas J. Feith. "Statement of Douglas J. Feith, Undersecretary of Defense for Policy, Senate Armed Services Hearing on the Nuclear Posture Review." February 14, 2002. On the Web at http://www.senate.gov/~armed_services/statemnt/2002/Feith.pdf.

Financing Terrorism Convention 1999   International Convention for the Suppression of the Financing of Terrorism. UN Res. 54/109/1999. Treaty Document 106-49.

Fischer 2001   Joschka Fischer. Letter to Secretary of State Colin Powell. October 30, 2001. On file with the Women's Caucus for Gender Justice.

Fitzpatrick 2001   Joan Fitzpatrick. "The Constitutional and International Invalidity of Military Commissions Under the November 13, 2001 'Military Order.'" [undated]. On the Web at http://www.impunity.org/MilitaryCommissions.htm.

Fitzgerald 2000   Frances Fitzgerald. *Way Out There in the Blue: Reagan, Star Wars, and the End of the Cold War*. New York: Simon & Schuster, 2000.

Ford 2002   Peter Ford. "US Diplomatic Might Irks Nations." *Christian Science Monitor*, April 24, 2002.

Foreign Relations Comm. 1999   Senate Foreign Relations Committee Hearing, Regarding Extradition Treaty with South Korea. October 20, 1999.

Foreign Relations Comm. 2001   *Treaties and Other International Agreements: The Role of the United States Senate. A Study*. Prepared for the Committee on Foreign Relations, United States Senate. S. Print 106-71. Washington, DC: US Govt. Print. Off., 2001.

GA Res. 1948   United Nations. General Assembly. Resolution 260. 9 December 1948.

GA Res. 1961	United Nations. General Assembly. Resolution 1665 [XVI]. 4 December 1961. Also known as The Irish Resolution.
GA Res. 1965	United Nations. General Assembly. Resolution 2028 (XX). 19 November 1965. Also known as The Five Principles.
GA Res. 1989	United Nations. General Assembly. Resolution 44/39. 4 December 1989.
GA Res. 1996a	United Nations. General Assembly. Resolution 51/45S of 10 December 1996.
GA Res. 1996b	United Nations. General Assembly. Resolution 51/207 of 17 December 1996.
GA Res. 1998	United Nations. General Assembly. Resolution A/RES/53/77Y. "Towards a Nuclear-Weapon-Free World: the Need for a New Agenda." 4 December 1998.
GA Res. 1999	United Nations. General Assembly. Resolution A/54/54G. "Towards a Nuclear-Weapon-Free World: the Need for a New Agenda." 1 December 1999.
GA Res. 2000	United Nations. General Assembly. Resolution A/55/33C. 20 November 2000.
Geneva Protocol 1925	The Protocol for the Prohibition of the Use in War of Asphyxiating, Poisonous or Other Gases, and of Bacteriological Methods of Warfare. Opened for signature on June 17, 1925.
Geneva Conventions 1949	Geneva Convention for the Amelioration of the Condition of the Wounded and Sick in Armed Forces in the Field (I); Geneva Convention for the Amelioration of the Condition of Wounded, Sick and Shipwrecked Members of Armed Forces at Sea (II); Geneva Convention Relative to the Treatment of Prisoners of War (III); Geneva Convention Relative to the Protection of Civilian Persons in Time of War (IV). August 12, 1949.
Genocide Convention 1948	Convention on the Prevention and Punishment of the Crime of Genocide. Approved and opened for signature, ratification and accession by United Nations General Assembly resolution 260 (III) on 9 December 1948.
Gertz 1999	Bill Gertz. "Albright Says U.S. Bound by CTBT." *Washington Times*, November 2, 1999.
Ghose 1996	Arundhati Ghose. *Statement in Explanation of Vote by Ms. Arundhati Ghose, Ambassador/Permanent Representative of India to the UN Offices at Geneva, on Item 65: CTBT at the 50th Session of the UN General Assembly at New York on September 10, 1996*. On the Web at http://www.indianem bassy.org/policy/CTBT/ctbt_UN_september_10_96.htm.

Gordon, John 2002

John A. Gordon. "Statement of John A. Gordon, Under Secretary for Nuclear Security and Administrator, National Nuclear Security Administration, U.S. Department of Energy, before the Senate Armed Services Committee." February 14, 2002. On the Web at http://www.senate.gov/~armed_services/statemnt/2002/Gordon.pdf.

Gordon, Michael R. 2002

Michael R. Gordon. "U.S. Nuclear Plan Sees New Targets and New Weapons." *New York Times*, March 10, 2002.

Gordon, Michael R. 2002a

Michael R. Gordon. "Treaty Offers Pentagon New Flexibility for New Set of Nuclear Priorities," *New York Times*, May 13, 2002.

Gordon, Michael R. & Miller 2001

Michael R. Gordon and Judith Miller. "U.S. Germ Warfare Review Faults Plan on Enforcement." *New York Times*, May 20, 2001.

Graham 2002

Bill Graham. "Notes For An Address By The Honourable Bill Graham, Minister of Foreign Affairs, To The Conference On Disarmament, Geneva, Switzerland." March 19, 2002.

Hambric & Schneck 1996

Harry Hambric and William Schneck. "The Antipersonnel Mine Threat." Presented to the Technology and the Mine Problem Symposium, Monterey, California, November 18-21, 1996.

Harkin 1999

Tom Harkin (United States Senate). Letter to Bill Richardson (Secretary, Department of Energy). October 28, 1999. Reproduced in Appendix B of this book.

Harris 2001

Elisa Harris. "The BWC After the Protocol: Previewing the Review Conference." *Arms Control Today* 31, no. 10 (December 2001).

Helms 1996a

Jesse Helms. "Need for National Ballistic Defense System, Senator Jesse Helms (R-NC) Senate Foreign Relations Committee, Tuesday, September 24, 1996." On the Web at http://www.fas.org/spp/starwars/congress/1996_h/s960924h.htm.

Helms 1996b

Jesse Helms. "Saving the UN: A Challenge to the Next Secretary-General." *Foreign Affairs* 75, no. 6 (September-October 1996), *cited in* Luck 1999, p. 70.

Helms 1998a

Jesse Helms (United States Senate, Committee on Foreign Relations). Letter to President Clinton. January 21, 1998. On the Web at http://www.clw.org/pub/clw/coalition/helm0121.htm.

Helms 1998b

Jesse Helms. Letter. *Financial Times*, 31 July 1998.

Helms 1999a

Jesse Helms. "Statement by Senator Jesse Helms Prepared for the Senate Foreign Committee Hearing on the CTBT." October 7, 1999. On the Web at http://www. fas.org/nuke/control/ctbt/text/100799helms.htm.

Helms 1999b

Jesse Helms. "Amend the ABM Treaty? No, Scrap It?" *Wall Street Journal*, January 22, 1999. On the Web at http://www.clw.org/pub/clw/coalition/helm0199.htm.

Helms 2000

Jesse Helms. "The Radical Agenda of CEDAW." Statement to the Congress, March 8, 2000. On the Web at http://www.senate.gov/~helms/Speeches/CEDAW/cedaw.ht ml. Also published in the *Congressional Record — Senate* (March 8, 2000): S1276.

Helms 2000a

Jesse Helms. "Helms Press Release on Clinton Signature December 31, 2000." Statement of Sen. Helms, reprinted by WICC. Washington: Washington Working Group on the International Criminal Court. On the Web at http://www. wfa.org/issues/wicc/helmsrel.html.

Henkin 1995

Louis Henkin. "U.S. Ratification of Human Rights Conventions: The Ghost of Senator Bricker." *American Journal of International Law* 89 (April 1995): 341.

Holum, *et al.* 1999

John Holum, Ted Warner, Ernie Moniz, and Bob Bell. "Excerpts of Remarks by Under Secretary of State for Arms Control John Holum, Assistant Secretary of Defense for Strategy and Requirements Ted Warner, Under Secretary of Energy Ernie Moniz, and Former NSC Senior Director for Defense and Arms Policy Bob Bell on the Comprehensive Test Ban Treaty." White House Press Briefing Transcript. October 5, 1999. On the Web at http://www.fas.org/nuke/ control/ctbt/text/1000599holum.htm.

HRW 1993

Human Rights Watch and Physicians for Human Rights. *Landmines: A Deadly Legacy.* New York: HRW, October 1993.

HRW 1998

Human Rights Watch. *Justice in the Balance: Recommendations for an Independent and Effective International Criminal Court.* New York, June 1998.

HRW 2000

Clintons Landmine Legacy. Human Rights Watch, vol. 12, no. 3 (G). June 2000. On the Web at http://www.hrw.org/ reports/2000/uslm/.

HRW 2001a

Human Rights Watch. *Landmines: Almost Half of Korea Mines in U.S.* New York, December 3, 2001. On the Web at http://www.hrw.org/press/2001/12/koreamines1203.htm.

HRW 2001b

Human Rights Watch. *U.S. Pentagon Mine Policy Rollback.* New York, December 21, 2001. On the Web at http://www.hrw.org/press/2001/11/usmines121.htm.

HRW 2002   Human Rights Watch. Letter to the Security Council, 9 July
                            2002. Subject: Extension of the United Nations Mission to
                            Bosnia-Herzegovina and U.S. Proposals. On the Web at
                            http://www.iccnow.org/html/hrw20020709.pdf.

HRW & VVAF 1997   Human Rights Watch and Vietnam Veterans of America
                            Foundation. "Retired Generals Call for Total Antipersonnel
                            Mine Ban, Pentagon Documents Reveal Devastating Effect
                            of U.S. Landmines in Korea and Vietnam." Press Release.
                            Washington, D.C., July 29, 1997.

Hyde Amendment 2001   H.R. 3338. 107th Cong. 1st Sess. November 29, 2001.

IAEA 2002a   L. Wedekind. "IAEA Team Concludes Inspections in Iraq."
                            Worldatom Front Page News. January 31, 2002. On the Web
                            at http://www.iaea.org/worldatom/Press/News/31012002_
                            news01.shtml.

IAEA 2002b   International Atomic Energy Agency. "IAEA Team to Visit
                            North Korean Nuclear Facilities." IAEA press release.
                            Vienna, January 10, 2002. On the Web at http://www.
                            aea.org/worldatom/Press/P_release/2002/prn0201.shtml.

ICBL Fact Sheet 1999   International Campaign to Ban Landmines. "The Problem."
                            Updated August 16, 1999. On the Web at http://www.
                            icbl.org, under Resources, The Problem.

ICBL Fact Sheet 2001   International   Campaign   to   Ban   Landmines.
                            "Landmine/UXO Casualties and Survivor Assistance."
                            Landmine Monitor Fact Sheet. New York: Human Rights
                            Watch, September 2001. On the Web at http://www.icbl.
                            org/lm/factsheets/va_sep_2001.html.

ICBL Landmine Monitor   International Campaign to Ban Landmines. *Landmine
1999   Monitor Report 1999*. New York: Human Rights Watch,
                            1999. On the Web at http://www.icbl.org/lm/1999/.

ICBL Landmine Monitor   International Campaign to Ban Landmines. *Landmine
2001   Monitor Report 2001*. New York: Human Rights Watch,
                            August 2001. On the Web at http://www.icbl.org/lm/2001.

ICBL Letter 1998   International Campaign to Ban Landmines. Letter to
                            President William Jefferson Clinton. August 7, 1998.
                            Signed by 60 nongovernmental organizations.

ICJ Statute 1945   Statute of the International Court of Justice. June 26, 1945.
                            On the Web at http://www.un.org/Overview/Statute/con
                            tents.html.

ICTFY 1993   Statute of the International Criminal Tribunal for the Former
                            Yugoslavia. UN Doc. S/RES/827, annex. 1993.

ICTR 1994

Statute of the International Criminal Tribunal for Rwanda. UN Doc. S/RES/955, annex. 1994.

IHT 2002

"Chemical Arms Foe Pressured to Resign." *International Herald Tribune*, April 22, 2002.

Independent Commission 2000

Independent Commission on the Verifiability of the CTBT. *Final Report of the Independent Commission on the Verifiability of the CTBT.* London: Verification, Training, and Information Centre (VERTIC), November 7, 2000. On the Web at http://www.ctbtcommission.org/FinalReport.pdf.

IPCC 2001

Intergovernmental Panel on Climate Change. *Climate Change 2001: The Scientific Basis.* Edited by J.T. Houghton, Y.Ding, D.J. Griggs, M. Noguer, P.J. van der Linden, X. Dai, K. Maskell, and C.A. Johnson. Contribution of Working Group I to the Third Assessment Report of the Intergovernmental Panel on Climate Change. Cambridge: Cambridge University Press, 2001.

IPPNW and IEER 1991

International Physicians for the Prevention of Nuclear War and Institute for Energy and Environmental Research. *Radioactive Heaven and Earth: The Health and Environmental Effects of Nuclear Weapons Testing In, On, and Above the Earth.* A report of the IPPNW International Commission to Investigate the Health and Environmental Effects of Nuclear Weapons Production and the Institute for Energy and Environmental Research. New York: Apex Press, 1991.

Jackson 1945

Robert H. Jackson. "Report to the President on Atrocities and War Crimes." June 7, 1945. On the Web at http://www.yale.edu/lawweb/avalon/imt/jack01.htm.

Jehl & Revkin 2001

Douglas Jehl with Andrew C. Revkin. "Bush, in Reversal, Won't Seek Cut In Emissions of Carbon Dioxide." *New York Times,* March 14, 2001.

Kanipe 1999

Jeff Kanipe. "Methane Gas Research Could Help Scientists Understand Global Warming." Special to *space.com.* October 29, 1999. On the Web at http://www.space.com/sci enceastronomy/planetearth/climate_globalwarm ing_991029.html.

Keller 2001

Bill Keller. "Missile Defense: The Untold Story." *New York Times,* December 29, 2001.

Kiergis 2001

Frederic L. Kiergis. "Terrorist Attacks on World Trade Center and the Pentagon." *American Society of International Law Insights*, September 2001.

Kimball 2002

Daryl Kimball. "Maintaining U.S. Support for the CTBT Verification System." Presentation for VERTIC Seminar, CTBT Verification: Achievements and Opportunities, March 18, 2002, Vienna. On the Web at http://www.arm scontrol.org/aca/ctbtver.asp.

King and Theofrastous
1999

Henry T. King and Theodore C. Theofrastous. "From Nuremberg to Rome: A Step Backward for U.S. Foreign Policy." *Case Western Reserve Journal of International Law*, 31 (1999): 47.

Kirkpatrick 1999

Jeane Kirkpatrick. "Statement by Jeane Kirkpatrick, Professor of Government, Georgetown University, and Senior Fellow, American Enterprise Institute." Prepared for the Senate Foreign Relations Committee Hearing on the CTBT. October 7, 1999. On the Web at http://www.fas.org/ nuke/control/ctbt/text/100799kirkpatrick.htm.

Kissinger 2001

Henry A. Kissinger. "The Pitfalls of Universal Jurisdiction." *Foreign Affairs*, July/August 2001.

Koch 2000

Dr. Susan Koch (Deputy Assistant Secretary of Defense for Threat Reduction Policy, Office of the Secretary of Defense). "The Biological Weapons Convention: Status and Implications." Before the House Government Reform Committee, Subcommittee on National Security, Veterans Affairs and International Relations. September 13, 2000.

Korb & Tiersky 2001

Lawrence J. Korb and Alex Tiersky. "End of Unilateralism? Arms Control After September 11." *Arms Control Today* 31, no. 8 (October 2001).

Krauthammer 2001

Charles Krauthammer. "The Real New World Order." *The Weekly Standard*, November 12, 2001. "Commended" by John Kyl and printed into the *Congressional Record -- Senate* (November 15, 2001): S11936-11938.

Kyl 2000

John Kyl. "Why the Senate Rejected the CTBT and the Implications of Its Demise." Remarks of Senator Jon Kyl, given at the Carnegie Endowment for International Peace. June 5, 2000.

Kyl 2001

Jon Kyl. "Kyl: ABM Withdrawal 'Removes Straitjacket From Our National Security.'" Press Release. *Jon Kyl, U.S. Senator for Arizona, News*. December 12, 2001. On the Web at http://www.senate.gov/~kyl/p121201.htm.

Kyoto Protocol

Kyoto Protocol to the United Nations Framework Convention on Climate Change. On the Web at http://unfc cc.int/resource/docs/convkp/kpeng.html.

Lacey 2001

Edward Lacey. "Testimony before the House Government Reform Committee, Subcommittee on National Security, Veterans Affairs And International Relations. July 10, 2001." On the Web at http://www.fas.org/bwc/news/laceytest.htm.

LaFave & Scott 1986

Wayne R. LaFave & Austin W. Scott. *Criminal Law*. 2d ed. St. Paul, MN: West Publishing Co., 1986.

Lawyers Alliance 2000

"State Succession and the Legal Status of the ABM Treaty." *Lawyers Alliance for World Security/Committee for National Security Occasional Paper* (May 9, 2000): 1-2.

Leahy 1998

Patrick Leahy. [Statement] *Congressional Record — Senate* 144, no. 35 (March 25, 1998): S2552. 105th Congress, 2d Sess., *cited in* Luck 1999, pp. 242.

Leklem 1998

Erik J. Leklem. "U.S. Pledges to Sign APL Ban; Lists Conditions to Be Met First." *Arms Control Today* 28, no. 4 (May 1998).

Lewis 2002

Neil A. Lewis. "U.S. Rejects All Support for New Court on Atrocities." *New York Times*, May 7, 2002.

Lichterman and Cabasso 2000

Andrew Lichterman and Jacqueline Cabasso. *Faustian Bargain 2000: Why 'Stockpile Stewardship' Is Fundamentally Incompatible With the Process of Nuclear Disarmament*. Revised and updated. Oakland, CA: Western States Legal Foundation, May 2000. On the Web at http://wslfweb.org/docs/fb2000.pdf.

Luck 1999

Edward C. Luck. *Mixed Messages, American Politics and International Organization 1919-1999*. Washington, DC: Brookings Institution Press, 1999.

Luck and Doyle 2002

Edward C. Luck and Michael W. Doyle (eds.). *International Law and Organization: Closing the Compliance Gap* (forthcoming).

Lynch 2002

Colum Lynch. "U.S. Seeks Court Immunity for E. Timor Peacekeepers." *Washington Post*, May 16, 2002.

Mahley 2000

Donald Mahley. "The Biological Weapons Convention: Status and Implications." Testimony before the House Government Reform Committee, Subcommittee on National Security, Veterans Affairs and International Relations. September 12, 2000. On the Web at http://www.fas.org/bwc/news.htm#TESTIMONY.

Mahley 2001

Donald Mahley. Statement by the US to the Ad Hoc Group of Biological Weapons Convention States Parties." July 25, 2001. On the Web at http://www.fas.org/bwc/bio.htm.

Mahley 2002

Donald A. Mahley. "Statement by Ambassador Donald A. Mahley, U.S. Representative to the OPCW." April 21, 2002. On the Web at http://www.acronym.org.uk/docs/0204/doc06.htm.

Makhijani 2000

Arjun Makhijani. "Nuclear Defense and Offense: An Analysis of US Policy." *Science for Democratic Action* 8, no. 2 (February 2000). On the Web at http://www.ieer.org/sdafiles/vol_8/8-2/defoff.html.

Makhijani 2001

Arjun Makhijani. *Securing the Energy Future of the United States: Oil, Nuclear, and Electricity Vulnerabilities and a Post-September 11, 2001 Roadmap for Action.* Takoma Park, MD: Institute for Energy and Environmental Research, November 2001. A preliminary report of IEER's energy assessment project. On the Web at http://www.ieer.org/reports/energy/bushtoc.html.

Makhijani and Gurney 1995

Arjun Makhijani and Kevin R. Gurney. *Mending the Ozone Hole: Science, Technology and Policy.* Cambridge: MIT Press, 1995.

Makhijani and Zerriffi 1998

Arjun Makhijani and Hisham Zerriffi. *Dangerous Thermonuclear Quest: The Potential of Explosive Fusion Research for the Development of Pure Fusion Weapons.* Takoma Park, MD: Institute for Energy and Environmental Research, July 1998. On the Web at http://www.ieer.org/reports/fusion/fusn-toc.html.

Mello 1997

Greg Mello. "New bomb, no mission." *Bulletin of the Atomic Scientists*, May/June 1997. pp. 28-32.

Meyer 1997

Howard N. Meyer. "When the Pope Rebuked the U.S. at the World Court." *American Society of International Law* Issue 15 (August 1997).

Meyer 2002

Howard N. Meyer. *The World Court In Action: Judging Among Nations.* Lanham, MD: Rowan & Littlefield, 2002.

Mian 2002

Zia Mian. "Elementary Aspects of Noncompliance in the World of Arms Control and Nonproliferation." Forthcoming in *International Law and Organization: Closing the Compliance Gap.* See Luck and Doyle 2002.

Michel 2001

Louis Michel. Letter of Belgian Foreign Minister Louis Michel on behalf of the European Union to Senator Tom Daschle and Secretary of State Colin Powell. October 30, 2001.

Miller, Engelberg & Broad 2001a	Judith Miller, Stephen Engelberg, and William Broad. *Germs: Biological Weapons and America's Secret War*. New York: Simon & Schuster, 2001.
Miller, Engelberg & Broad 2001b	Judith Miller, Stephen Engelberg, and William Broad. "U.S. Germ Warfare Research Pushes Treaty Limits." *New York Times*, September 4, 2001.
Montreal Protocol	Protocol on Substances that Deplete the Ozone Layer (Montreal, 16 September 1987) (Montreal Protocol). On the Web at http://sedac.ciesin.org/pidb/texts/montreal.proto-col.ozone.1987.html. Adjustments and amendments on the Web at http://sedac.ciesin.org/pidb/texts/montreal.proto col.ozone.amend.1992.html.
Moxley 2000	Charles J. Moxley, Jr. *Nuclear Weapons and International Law in the Post Cold War World*. Lanham, MD: Austin & Winfield, 2000.
NACDL Resolution 2002	National Association of Criminal Defense Lawyers. "Resolution Calling for United States Ratification of and Participation in the International Criminal Court and for Creation of Independent Defense Function Therein." Washington, DC, February 23, 2002. On the Web at http://www.nacdl.org/public.nsf/resolutions/2002_02a?open document.
NAS-NRC 2001	National Research Council. Division on Earth and Life Studies. Committee on the Science of Climate Change. *Climate Change Science: An Analysis of Some Key Questions*. Washington, DC: National Academy Press, 2001. On the Web at http://www.nap.edu/catalog/10139.html.
NAS-NRC 2002	National Research Council. Division on Earth and Life Studies. Committee Abrupt Climate Change. *Abrupt Climate Change: Inevitable Surprises*. Committee on Abrupt Climate Change, Ocean Studies Board, Polar Research Board, Board on Atmospheric Sciences and Climate, Division on Earth and Life Studies, National Research Council. Washington DC: National Academy Press, 2002.
NASA 2001	US. National Aeronautics and Space Administration. Goddard Space Flight Center. *Ocean Circulation Shut Down by Melting Glaciers After Last Ice Age*. On the Web at http://www.gsfc.nasa.gov/topstory/20011116meltwater.html. November 19, 2001 - (date of web publication).

National Intelligence Council 2001 — National Intelligence Council. "Foreign Missile Developments and the Ballistic Missile Threat Through 2015." December 2001. On the Web at http://www.fas.org/irp/nic/bmthreat-2015.htm.

New Agenda Declaration 1998 — Towards a Nuclear-Weapons-Free World: The Need for a New Agenda. Joint Declaration by the Ministers for Foreign Affairs of Brazil, Egypt, Ireland, Mexico, New Zealand, Slovenia, South Africa and Sweden. [UN document number: A/53/138]. 9 June 1998. A copy on the Web at http://www.irlgov.ie/iveagh/policy/nuclearfreeworld.htm.

New Agenda Working Paper 2000 — New Agenda Coalition (NAC) Working Paper. The 2000 NPT Review Conference, 14 April - 19 May 2000, New York. [24 April 2000]. On the Web at http://www.basicint.org/nuclear/NPT/2000revcon/wp_nac.htm.

New York Times 2000 — "Proposal on ABM: 'Ready to Work with Russia.'" *New York Times*, April 28, 2000. p. A10.

New York Times 2002 — "America as Nuclear Rogue." Editorial. *New York Times*, March 12, 2002. p. A26.

Nicaragua v. U.S. 1984 — International Court of Justice. 10 May 1984. Case Concerning Military and Paramilitary Activities in and Against Nicaragua (*Nicaragua v. United States of America*). Request for the Indication of Provisional Measures.

Nicaragua v. U.S. 1985 — U.S. Withdrawal from the Proceedings Initiated by Nicaragua in the International Court of Justice (January 1985). On the Web at http://www.gwu.edu/~jaysmith/nicuswd.html.

NPT Final Doc. 2000 — 2000 Review Conference of the Parties to the Treaty on the Non-Proliferation of Nuclear Weapons. *Final Document*. Vol. I. NPT/CONF.2000/28 (parts I and II). 2000. On the Web at http://disarmament.un.org/wmd/npt/2000FD.pdf.

NRDC 1994 — Robert S. Norris, Andrew S. Burrows, and Richard W. Fieldhouse. *British, French, and Chinese Nuclear Weapons*. A book by the Natural Resources Defense Council, Inc. Nuclear Weapons Databook, vol. V. Boulder: Westview Press, 1994.

NRDC 2002 — Natural Resources Defense Council. "Faking Nuclear Restraint: The Bush Administration's Secret Plan For Strengthening U.S. Nuclear Forces." Press Release. Washington DC, February 13, 2002. On the Web at http://www.nrdc.org/media/pressreleases/020213a.asp.

Nuclear Posture Review
2001

"Nuclear Posture Review [Excerpts] Submitted to Congress on 31 December 2001. 8 January 2002, Nuclear Posture Review Report." (Brackets in original.) On the Web at http://www.globalsecurity.org/wmd/library/policy/dod/npr.htm.

Nuclear Weapons Opinion

International Court of Justice. *Legality of the Threat or Use of Nuclear Weapons, Advisory Opinion.* ICJ Reports. The Hague, July 8, 1996. Summary on the Web at http://www.icj-cij.org/icjwww/idecisions/isummaries/iunanaummary960708.htm.

NW Energy Coalition
2001

Marc Sullivan. "Bonn Deal Inked by 178 Nations, But Not U.S." *NW Energy Coalition Report* 20, no.8 (August 2001): 5. On the Web at http://www.nwenergy.org/publications/report/01_aug/rp_0108_5.html.

Pace & Schense 2001

William R. Pace and Jennifer Schense. "Coalition for the International Criminal Court at the Preparatory Commission." In *The International Criminal Court: Elements of Crimes and Rules of Procedure and Evidence*, Roy S. Lee, editor. Ardsley, NY: Transnational Publishers, 2001.

Pal 1953

Justice Pal (India). Dissent of Justice Pal on grounds of 'victor's justice' in the judgment of the International Military Tribunal for the Far East, later published under the title *International Military Tribunal for the Far East; Dissentient Judgement*. Calcutta, 1953.

Patierno & Franceschi
2000

Donald F. "Pat" Patierno and Natasha Franceschi. "The Convention on Conventional Weapons and Ottawa: Working Collectively to Eliminate the Landmine Threat." *American Foreign Policy Interests* 22, no. 6 (December 2000).

PDD 64 1998

Presidential Decision Directive (PDD) 64. June 23, 1998.

Pearson 2001

Graham S. Pearson. "The Biological Weapons Convention: Status and Implications." Written Testimony to the House Government Reform Committee, Subcommittee on National Security, Veterans Affairs and International Relations. July 10, 2001.

Pearson, Dando, & Sims
2001

Graham S. Pearson, Malcolm R. Dando and Nicholas Sims. *The US Rejection of the Composite Protocol: A Huge Mistake Based on Illogical Assessment.* Evaluation Paper No. 22. Bradford, West Yorkshire, UK: University of Bradford, Department of Peace Studies, August 2001.

Perkovich 1999a

George Perkovich. "…The Next President Will Pay the Price." *Washington Post*, October 7, 1999. p. A35. (Ellipses in original title).

Perkovich 1999b	George Perkovich. *India's Nuclear Bomb: The Impact on Global Proliferation*. Berkeley: University of California Press, 1999.
Perry 2001	William J. Perry. "Preparing for the Next Attack." *Foreign Affairs*, 80, no. 6 (November/December 2001).
Pincus 2002	Walter Pincus. "U.S. Nuclear Arms Stance Modified by Policy Study." *Washington Post*, March 23, 2002.
Rauf 2000	Tariq Rauf. *Towards NPT 2005: An Action Plan for the "13-Steps" Toward Nuclear Disarmament Agreed At NPT 2000*. Prepared for the Middle Powers Initiative. Monterey, CA: Monterey Institute of International Studies, Center for Nonproliferation Studies, 2000. On the Web at http://cns.miis.edu/pubs/reports/npt2005.htm.
Resolution F 1998	Resolution F of the Rome Conference, adopted on 17 July 1998 by the United Nations Diplomatic Conference of Plenipotentiaries on the Establishment of an International Criminal Court.
Restatement 1986	Restatement (Third) of Foreign Relations Law of the United States §702 (1986).
Richter 2002	Paul Richter. "U.S. Works Up Plan for Using Nuclear Arms." *Los Angeles Times*, March 9, 2002.
Ridgeway 2001	James Ridgeway. "Manhattan's Milosevic: How You Can Arrest Henry Kissinger for War Crimes." *Village Voice*, August 15-21, 2001.
Rissanen 2001a	Jenni Rissanen. "Hurdles Cleared, Obstacles Remaining: the Ad Hoc Group Prepares for the Final Challenge." *Disarmament Diplomacy* Issue No. 56 (April 2001). On the Web at http://www.acronym.org.uk/bwc/index.htm.
Rissanen 2001b	Jenni Rissanen. "Turning Point to Nowhere: BWC In Trouble as US Turns Its Back on Verification Protocol." *Disarmament Diplomacy* Issue No. 59 (July-August 2001). On the Web at http://www.acronym.org.uk/bwc/index.htm.
Rissanen 2002	Jenni Rissanen. "Left in Limbo: Review Conference Suspended on Edge of Collapse." *Disarmament Diplomacy* Issue No. 62 (January-February 2002). On the Web at http://www.acronym.org.uk/bwc/index.htm.
Rogers 1999	John M. Rogers. *International Law and United States Law*. Brookfield, VT: Ashgate, 1999.
Rome Statute 1998	Rome Statute of the International Criminal Court. U.N. Doc. A/CONF.183/9. 17 July 1998. With corrections, on the Web at http://www.un.org/law/icc/statute/romefra.htm.

Rosenberg 2001   Barbara Hatch Rosenberg. "Allergic Reaction: Washington's Response to the BWC Protocol." *Arms Control Today* 32, no. 6 (July/August 2001).

Roth 2000   Kenneth Roth. "The Charade of US Ratification of International Human Rights Treaties" *Chicago Journal of International Law* 1 (2000): 347.

Rumsfeld Commission 2001 Commission to Assess United States National Security Space Management and Organization. *Report of the Commission to Assess United States National Security Space Management and Organization, Executive Summary.* Chair, Donald Rumsfeld. Washington, DC, January 11, 2001. On the Web at http://www.defenselink.mil/pubs/space20010111.html.

Sands & Pate 2000   Amy Sands and Jason Pate. "Chemical Weapons Convention Compliance Issues." In *The Chemical Weapons Convention, Implementation Challenges and Solutions,* Jonathan B. Tucker, editor. Washington, DC: Center for Nonproliferation Studies, Monterey Institute of International Studies, April 2001. On the Web at http://cns.miis.edu/pubs/reports/tuck cwc.htm.

Scharf 1999   Michael Scharf. "The Politics Behind the U.S. Opposition to the International Criminal Court." *New England International and Comparative Law Annual* 5 (1999). Based on the author's remarks at the ABA Standing Committee on Law and National Security's Symposium, "The Rome Treaty: Is the International Criminal Court Viable?" Washington D.C., November 13, 1998.

Scheffer 1998   Scheffer (U.S. Ambassador at Large for War Crimes Issues and Head of the U.S. Delegation to the U.N. Diplomatic Conference on the Establishment of an International Criminal Court). Statement by David Scheffer. July 15, 1998. Statement made at the Rome Diplomatic Conference. On the Web at http://www.lchr.org/icc/rome/scheffer.htm.

Schmemann 2002   Serge Schmemann. "US Vetoes Bosnia Mission, Then Allows 3-Day Reprieve." *New York Times*, July 1, 2002.

Schott 2002   Schott Glass Technologies Inc. "Laser Glass for High Technology," Press release. Duryea, PA, February 2, 2002. On the Web at http://www.us.schott.com/sgt/english/news/press.html?NID=42.

Schrag 1992   Philip G. Schrag. *Global Action: Nuclear Test Ban Diplomacy at the End of the Cold War.* Boulder, CO: Westview Press, 1992.

SDA 1998

"A Chronology of Nuclear Threats." *Science for Democratic Action*, v. 6, no. 4 & v. 7, no.1 (October 1998). Also *Energy & Security* nos. 6 & 7. On the Web at http://www.ieer.org/ ensec/no-6/threats.html.

Secretary General 1993

Report of the Secretary-General Pursuant to Paragraph 2 of Security Council Resolution 808 (1993). (S/25704). Presented 3 May 1993. On the Web at http://www.un.org/ icty/basic/statut/S25704 con.htm.

Secretary General 1995

Report of the Secretary-General on the Status of the Implementation of the Special Commission's Plan for the Ongoing Monitoring and Verification of Iraq's Compliance with Relevant Parts of Section C of Security Council Resolution 687 (1991). UN Doc S/1995/864. October 11, 1995.

Security Council Res. 1994

United Nations. "Resolution 955 (1994)." Adopted by the Security Council at its 345rd meeting on 8 November 1994. S/RES/955 (1994). On the Web at http://www.un.org/ Docs/scres/1994/9443748e.htm.

Security Council Res. 2002a

United Nations. "Resolution 1422 (2002)." Adopted by the Security Council at its 4572nd meeting on, 12 July 2002. S/RES/1422 (2002). On the Web at http://www.un.org/ Docs/scres/2002/sc2002.htm.

Security Council Res. 2002b

United Nations. "Resolution 1423 (2002)." Adopted by the Security Council at its 4573nd meeting on, 12 July 2002. S/RES/1423 (2002). On the Web at http://www.un.org/ Docs/scres/2002/sc2002.htm.

Seigle 2002

Greg Seigle. "Disarmament: Official Defends U.S. Approach at Geneva Talks." *UN Wire*, Jan. 24, 2002.

Sen. Res. 1946

Senate Resolution 196, 79th Congress. "Acceptance of Compulsory Jurisdiction of the International Court of Justice." August 2, 1946. On the Web at http://www. yale.edu/lawweb/avalon/decade/decad030.htm.

Sen. Res. 1997

Senate Resolution 98, First Session, 105th Congress. "A Resolution To Express the Sense of the Senate on Necessary Conditions for Any Treaty That It May Consider to Reduce 'Greenhouse' Gas Emissions . . ." July 25, 1997. One version on Web at http://www.senate.gov/~rpc/rva/1051/ 1051205.htm. Final complete text on Web by searching at http://thomas.loc.gov.

Senate Vote Analysis 1985

Senate Record Vote Analysis, 99th Congress, First Session, Vote No. 249, October 24, 1985.

Sengupta 2002   Somini Sengupta. "U.S. Fails in U.N. to Exempt Peacekeepers from New Court." *New York Times*, 18 May 2002.

Shaker 1980   Mohamed I. Shaker. *The Nuclear Non-Proliferation Treaty: Origin and Implementation, 1959-1979.* 3 vols. London: Oceana Publications, 1980.

Shane 2001   Scott Shane. "Military Laboratory in Utah Says Powder is All Accounted for." *Baltimore Sun*, December 13, 2001.

Shanker 1999   Thom Shanker. "Sexual Violence." In *Crimes of War: What the Public Should Know,* Roy Gutman and David Rieff, editors. New York: W.W. Norton, 1999.

Shapely 1993   Deborah Shapely. *Promise and Power: The Life and Times of Robert McNamara.* Boston: Little, Brown, 1993.

Slevin 2002   "U.S. Drops Bid to Strengthen Germ Warfare Accord." *Washington Post*, September 19, 2002.

Smith no date   James McCall Smith. "Nicaragua v. the United States of America: Military and Paramilitary Activities In and Against Nicaragua: International Court of Justice, 1984-1986." Notes by James McCall Smith. http://www.gwu.edu/~jay smith/Nicaragua.html.

Smithson 1997   Amy E. Smithson. "Bungling a No-Brainer: How Washington Barely Ratified the Chemical Weapons Convention." In *The Battle to Obtain U.S. Ratification of the Chemical Weapons Convention,* by Michael Krepon, Amy E. Smithson, John Parachini, pp. 7-33. Occasional Paper 35. Washington, DC: Henry L. Stimson Center, July 1997. On the Web at http://www.stimson.org/pubs.cfm?ID=33.

Smithson 2001   Amy E. Smithson. "U.S. Implementation of the Chemical Weapons Convention." In *The Chemical Weapons Convention, Implementation Challenges and Solutions,* Jonathan B. Tucker, editor, pp. 23-29. Washington, DC: Center for Nonproliferation Studies, Monterey Institute of International Studies, April 2001. On the Web at http://cns.miis.edu/pubs/reports/tuckcwc.htm.

Smithson 2002   Amy E. Smithson. "The Failing Inspector." *New York Times*, April 8, 2002.

Sokolski 2002   Henry Sokolski. "Post-9/11 Non-Proliferation." *E-Notes.* Philadelphia: Foreign Policy Research Institute, January 25, 2002. On the Web at http://www.fpri.org/enotes/ameri cawar.20020125.sokolski.post911nonproliferation.html.

Spencer 1995   Metta Spencer. "'Political' Scientists." *Bulletin of the Atomic Scientists* 51, no.4 (July-August 1995): 62-68. On the Web at http://www.pugwash.org/reports/pim/pim1.htm.

Spiro 2000   Peter J. Spiro. "The New Sovereigntists; American Exceptionalism and Its False Prophets." *Foreign Affairs* 79, no. 6 (November/December 2000): 9-15.

Stanley 1998   Alessandra Stanley. "US Presses Allies to Rein in Proposed War Crimes Court." *New York Times*, July 15, 1998.

Statement of Permanent 5   Statement by the Delegations of France, the People's Republic of China, the Russian Federation, the United Kingdom of Great Britain and Northern Ireland and the United States of America. The 2000 NPT Review Conference (RevCon), 14 April - 19 May 2000, New York. [May 1, 2000]. On the Web at http://www.basicint. org/nuclear/NPT/2000revcon/p5statement.htm.

Steinbruner, Gallagher   John Steinbruner, Nancy Gallagher, and Stacy Gunther. "A
& Gunther 2001   Tough Call." *Arms Control Today* 31, no. 4 (May 2001).

Stephanson 1995   Anders Stephanson. *Manifest Destiny: American Expansion and the Empire of Right.* New York: Hill and Wang, 1995.

Stimson 1999   Henry L. Stimson Center. "Chemical Treaty Being Implemented Unevenly." *CBW Chronicle* 2, issue 6 (August 1999). On the Web at http://www.stimson.org/cbw/ ?sn=cb20020113262.

Stimson 2000   Henry L. Stimson Center. "CWC Industry Inspections Underway at US Facilities." *CBW Chronicle* 3, issue 2 (December 2000). On the Web at http://www.stimson.org/ cbw/?sn=cb20020113252.

Stimson 2001   Henry L. Stimson Center. *House of Cards: the Pivotal Importance of a Technically Sound BWC Monitoring Protocol.* Stimson Center Report no. 37. Washington, DC, May 2001. On the Web at http://www.stimson.org/ pubs.cfm?ID=13.

Streets, *et al.* 2001   David G. Streets, Kejun Jiang, Xiulian Hu, Jonathan E. Sinton, Xiao-Quan Zhang, Deying Xu, Mark Z. Jacobson, and James E. Hansen. "Recent Reductions in China's Greenhouse Gas Emissions." *Science* 294, no.5548 (November 30, 2001): 1835-1837. Summary On the Web at http://www.sciencemag.org/cgi/content/summa ry/294/5548/1835.

Strohm 2001   Chris Strohm. "Army Decision to Kill Alternative Land Mine Program Draws Criticism." *Inside the Army* 13, no. 47 (November 26, 2001).

Swarns 2002

Rachel L. Swarns. "Broad Accord Reached at Global Environment Meeting." *New York Times*, September 4, 2002.

Takubo 2001

Masa Takubo. "Japanese Optical Glass Giant Involved in U.S. Nuclear Weapons Development." *Nuke Info Tokyo*, no. 86 (Nov./Dec. 2001): 7. On the Web at http://www.gen-suikin.org/english/index.html.

Terrorist Bombings Convention 1998

International Convention for the Suppression of Terrorist Bombings. UN Res. 52/164/1998. Treaty Document 106-6.

Tóth 200

Tibor Tóth. Testimony to the Subcommittee on National Security, Veterans Affairs, and International Relations of the Committee on Government Reform, U.S. House of Representatives. July 10, 2001.

Trimble & Koff 1998

Phillip R. Trimble and Alexander W. Koff. "All Fall Down: The Treaty Power in the Clinton Administration." *Berkeley Journal of International Law* 16 (1998): 55-70.

Tucker 2001

Jonathan B. Tucker. "The Chemical Weapons Convention: Has It Enhanced U.S. Security?" *Arms Control Today* 31, no. 3 (April 2001).

UMWA 1999

"UMWA Supports 'Energy and Climate Policy Act of 1999.'" *United Mine Workers Journal* 110, no. 3 (May-June 1999). On the Web at http://www.umwa.org/journal/VOL110NO3/globwm.shtml.

UNFCCC

United Nations Framework Convention on Climate Change. On the Web at http://unfccc.int/resource/conv/conv.html.

UN-USA 2001

"U.N. Arrears Update: Payment Threatened by Linkage to Passage Of American Servicemembers' Protection Act." *UN-USA Washington Report,* August 20, 2001. On the Web at http://www.unausa.org/newindex.asp?place=http://www.unausa.org/programs.

Universal Declaration 1948

Universal Declaration of Human Rights. U.N. G.A. Res. 217 (1948). December 10, 1948.

U.S. Dept. of State 1997

U.S. Department of State. "Article-By-Article Analysis Of The Comprehensive Nuclear Test-Ban Treaty." On the Web at http://www.state.gov/www/global/arms/ctbtpage/treaty/artbyart.html. This was included with the Letter of Transmittal of the CTBT from President Clinton to the Senate on September 22, 1997. On the Web at http://www.state.gov/www/global/arms/ctbtpage/treaty/ltr_tran.html.

U.S. Dept. of State 1998

U.S. Department of State. Bureau of Political-Military Affairs. Office of Humanitarian Demining Programs. *Hidden Killers 1998: The Global Landmine Crisis.* Washington, DC, September 1998.

U.S. Dept. of State 2002a

Richard Boucher (Spokesman). Daily Press Briefing. U.S. Department of State, March 19, 2002. On the Web at http://www.state.gov/r/pa/prs/dpb/2002/8845.htm.

U.S. Dept of State 2002b

Richard Boucher (Spokesman). Daily Press Briefing. U.S. Department of State, August 27, 2002. On the Web at http://www.state.gov/r/pa/prs/dpb/2002/13102.htm.

US Proposal 1998

Proposal Submitted by the United States of America to Rome Conference. A/CONF.183/C.1/L.90. 16 July 1998.

U.S. Space Command 1997

U.S. Space Command. *Vision for 2020.* Peterson AFB, CO: US Space Command, Director of Plans, 1997. On the Web at http://www.peterson.af.mil/usspacecom/visbook.pdf.

USA Patriot Act 2001

Uniting and Strengthening America by Providing Appropriate Tools Required to Intercept and Obstruct Terrorism Act of 2001. Pub. L. No. 107-56.

Vagts 2001

Detlev F. Vagts. "The United States and its Treaties: Observance and Breach." *American Journal of International Law* 95, no. 2 (April 2001): 313-334.

Vienna Convention 1969

Vienna Convention on the Law of Treaties. UN Doc. A/CONF. 39/27 (1969). Opened for signature on May 23, 1969.

Walkling 1997

Sarah Walkling. "U.S. Favors CD Negotiations To Achieve Ban on Landmines." *Arms Control Today* 26, no. 10 (January/February 1997): 20. On the Web at http://www.armscontrol.org/act/1997_01-02/mines.asp.

Warrick 2002

Joby Warrick. "Makings of a 'Dirty Bomb' Radioactive Devices Left by Soviets Could Attract Terrorists." *Washington Post,* March 18, 2002. p. A1.

Watson 2000

Robert Watson. *Transcript: Dr. Robert Watson, Chair, UN Intergovernmental Panel on Climate Change, EMS Conference Call.* Washington, DC: Environmental Media Services, November 21, 2000. On the Web at http://www.ems.org/climate/bob_watson_statement.html.

Weston 1986

Burns Weston. "Treaty Power." In *Encyclopedia of the American Constitution*, Leonard W. Levy, editor-in-chief; Kenneth L. Karst, associate editor; Dennis J. Mahoney, assistant editor. Vol. 4, pp. 1910-1911. New York: Macmillan Library Reference USA, 1986.

White House 1995 — The White House. Office of the Press Secretary. Statement by the President. August 11, 1995. On the Web at http://www.chinfo.navy.mil/navpalib/policy/nuclear/clin0811.txt.

White House 1996 — The White House. Office of the Press Secretary. "Fact Sheet: U.S. Announces Anti-Personnel Landmine Policy." May 16, 1996.

White House 1997 — The White House. Office of the Press Secretary. "Fact Sheet: Anti-Tank Munitions." September 17, 1997.

White House 2001 — The White House. "Strengthening the International Regime against Biological Weapons." Statement by the President. November 1, 2001.

White House 2002 — The White House. Office of the Press Secretary. "President Signs Defense Appropriations Bill." Press Release. January 10, 2002. On the Web at http://www.whitehouse.gov/news/releases/2002/01/20020110-5.html.

White House 2002a — The White House. Office of the Press Secretary. "Text of the Strategic Offensive Reductions Treaty." May 24, 2002. Known as the Moscow Treaty. On the Web at http://www.whitehouse.gov/news/releases/2002/05/20020524-3.html.

White House 2002b — The White House. Office of the Press Secretary. "Text of Joint Declaration." May 24, 2002. On the Web at http://www.whitehouse.gov/news/releases/2002/05/20020524-2.html.

Whitman 2001 — Christine Todd Whitman. Talking Points for Governor Christine Todd Whitman, Administrator, United States Environmental Protection Agency at the G8 Environmental Ministerial Meeting Working Session on Climate Change, Trieste, Italy. March 3, 2001. On the Web at http://yosemite.epa.gov/administrator/speeches.nsf/b1ab9f485b098972852562e7004dc686/36bca0e3a69a0d8b85256a41005d2e63?OpenDocument.

WICC 2001a — "Status of U.S. ICC Legislation and Policy Review." Washington, DC: Washington Working Group on the International Criminal Court. On the Web at http://www.iccnow.org/html/presswicc2001short.pdf.

WICC 2001b — "ASPA Removed from Defense Appropriations Bill (Dec. 20, 2001)." Washington, DC: Washington Working Group of the International Criminal Court. On the Web at http://www.wfa.org/issues/wicc/aspadefeat.html.

WICC 2002

"High Level Policy Review of ICC Under Way in Bush Administration (March 18, 2002)" Washington, DC: Washington Working Group. On the Web at http://www.wfa.org/issues/wicc/wicc.html.

Women's Caucus 1998

Women's Caucus for Gender Justice. Position papers. "Gender Justice and the ICC." Submitted to the United Nations Diplomatic Conference of Plenipotentiaries on the Establishment of an International Criminal Court, June 15-July 17, 1998, Rome, Italy.

Women's Caucus 2001

Women's Caucus for Gender Justice. "Statement on Terrorist Attacks in the U.S." September 2001. On the Web at http://www.cwgl.rutgers.edu/911/caucus.htm.

Wren 2002

Christopher S. Wren. "U.N. Inspector Tells Council Work in Iraq Could Be Fast." *New York Times*, March 22, 2002.

Wright 2002

Susan Wright. "U.S. Vetoes Verification." *Bulletin of Atomic Scientists*, March/April 2002.

Yee 1999

Lionel Yee. "The International Criminal Court and the Security Council: Articles 13(b) and 16." In *The International Criminal Court: The Making of the Rome Statute*, Roy Lee, ed. The Hague, Boston: Kluwer Law International, 1999.

Yonhap 1999

"Over 1.12 Million Landmines Laid Throughout ROK." Yonhap News Agency, Seoul, Korea, September 28, 1999.

York 1970

Herbert F. York. *Race to Oblivion: A Participant's View of the Arms Race*. New York: Simon and Schuster, 1970. On the web at http://www.learnworld.com/ZNW/LWText.York.RaceToOblivion.html.

Zerriffi and Makhijani 1996

Hisham Zerriffi and Arjun Makhijani. *The Nuclear Safety Smokescreen: Warhead Safety and Reliability and the Science Based Stockpile Stewardship Program*. Takoma Park, MD: Institute for Energy and Environmental Research, May 1996.

Note: All web sites last viewed in July 2002.

INDEX

CONTRIBUTORS

JOHN BURROUGHS, J.D., Ph.D., is executive director of the Lawyers' Committee on Nuclear Policy (www.lcnp.org). He is author of *The Legality of Threat or Use of Nuclear Weapons: A Guide to the Historic Opinion of the International Court of Justice* (Transaction Publishers, 1998), and has published articles on nuclear weapons issues in *The Bulletin of the Atomic Scientists* and the *World Policy Journal*. He is the principal author of the chapter on the Nuclear Nonproliferation Treaty, contributed to the introductory and concluding chapters, and is an editor of this book.

MERAV DATAN, J.D., is presently director of the United Nations Office of the Women's International League for Peace and Freedom. At the time she worked on the report that became this book, she was director of the UN Office of the International Physicians for the Prevention of Nuclear War and Physicians for Social Responsibility. Previously she was research director for the Lawyers' Committee on Nuclear Policy. She is co-author of *Security and Survival: The Case for A Nuclear Weapons Convention* (IPPNW, 1999). During 1985-90 she worked as news analyst and translator at the Ethiopian Consulate in Jerusalem. She contributed to the concluding chapter.

S. NICOLE DELLER, J.D., is an attorney with experience in commercial litigation and public international law, including advocacy of human rights and women's rights. She is a researcher and consultant for IEER and LCNP. She authored the chapters on the Chemical Weapons Convention and the Biological Weapons Convention, and is the principal author of the introductory and concluding chapters and the principal editor of this book.

MARK HIZNAY is senior researcher at Human Rights Watch specializing in landmines and other indiscriminate weapons. He was a researcher and member of the final editing team for the *Landmine Monitor Report 2001*. Human Rights Watch is a founding member of the International Campaign to Ban Landmines (ICBL), and serves on its thirteen member Coordinating Committee and as the main contact point and editor for the ICBL's Landmine Monitor initiative. He authored the chapter on the Mine Ban Treaty.

ARJUN MAKHIJANI, Ph.D., is president of the Institute for Energy and Environmental Research (www.ieer.org). He is author or co-author of numerous books, reports, and articles on nuclear-related security, environment, and energy issues. He is principal editor of *Nuclear Wastelands* (MIT Press, 1995 and 2000), which was nominated for a Pulitzer Prize. He authored the chapters on the Comprehensive Test Ban Treaty, the Anti-Ballistic Missile Treaty, the UN Framework Convention on Climate Change and the Kyoto Protocol, contributed to the concluding chapter, and is an editor of this book.

ELIZABETH SHAFER, J.D., is an attorney, artist, and member of the board of directors of LCNP. She contributed to the chapter on the Nuclear Nonproliferation Treaty.

PAM SPEES, J.D., is program director of the Women's Caucus for Gender Justice, a global network of individuals and organizations that formed in 1997 to advocate for gender mainstreaming in the process of establishing the International Criminal Court. She has been involved in the ICC process since 1997, and has also worked with campaigns in the U.S. for the recognition of economic and social rights as well as on issues of consumer protection and housing rights. She authored the chapter on the Statute of the International Criminal Court.

This book is an updated version of a joint report released in April 2002 by:

INSTITUTE FOR ENERGY AND ENVIRONMENTAL RESEARCH
6935 LAUREL AVENUE, SUITE 204
TAKOMA PARK, MARYLAND 20912
301-270-5500
www.ieer.org

LAWYERS' COMMITTEE ON NUCLEAR POLICY
211 EAST 43RD STREET, SUITE 1204
NEW YORK, NEW YORK 10017
212-818-1861
www.lcnp.org